# The Prisoner

## A Televisionary Masterpiece

by Alain Carrazé and Hélène Oswald

Including an interview with Patrick McGoohan

*With contributions from*

Roland Topor, Roger Langley, Jacques Sternberg, Isaac Asimov, Christian Durante, François Rivière, Jacques Baudou, Jean-Michel Philibert

*and with help from*

Jean-Marc Lofficier

Translated from the French by Christine Donougher
English edition textual verification by Roger Langley

BARNES
&NOBLE
BOOKS
NEW YORK

ACKNOWLEDGEMENTS

With my grateful thanks:
– to my parents, who scrupulously taped for me the sound track of all the episodes I missed in 1968 without realising what they were exposing me to;
– to my friend Daniel, without whom I would not have had the will, among other things, to make this book;
– to Patrick, who overcame his fear of flying to help me so efficiently in my London research;
– to my close friends, from Laurent to Alexandrine, whose presence often liberated me from *The Prisoner* and thereby prevented me from becoming just a number.

*Dedicated to D.A.*

Alain Carrazé

With thanks from both of us:
– to ITC, and especially to Mrs James, whose kindness made this project possible, to Frank Ratcliffe, whose help and willingness were invaluable, and to Valérie Delcourt, Jim Marrinan, Peter Harrington, Edward Gilbert and Claudette Rinaudo;
– to Philippe Ferrar, Roland Pourquery and Xavier Bouquet of Agence Ciné-Star;
– to Bernard Bidoret, Jean-Pierre Chevalier, Yves Di Mano, David Fakrikian, Jean-Pierre Jordanidès, Xavier Perret;
– to Six of One, appreciation society for *The Prisoner*, whose remarkable research work was of great help to us.

Photographs:
– Daniel Gelli (*Interview with Patrick McGoohan*)
– Bruno Poiret (*The Real Village: Portmeirion* and *Six of One*)

Design:
– P J Oswald

Material from the TV series *The Prisoner* © Incorporated Television Company Ltd 1967
Extract from *Hitch Your Wagon To A Rock* © Triangle Publications and Isaac Asimov 1968
Text © Alain Carrazé and Hélène Oswald 1989
French edition © Editions Huitième Art 1989

Typeset by Phoenix Photosetting, Chatham, Kent
Printed and bound in Spain by Artes Graficas Toledo, S.A.
This edition Published by Barnes & Noble, Inc. by arrangement with Virgin Publishing Ltd. 1995 Barnes & Noble Books.

ISBN: 1-56619-819-4

10 9 8 7 6 5 4 3 2 1

# Contents

# A Televisionary Masterpiece

In that mythical year of 1967, the year of love-ins and incipient revolution, one event, and not the least important, passed almost unnoticed: the screening of a work of art produced for television.

*Almost* unnoticed: for *The Prisoner* created a scandal in its day. The scandal arose from a misunderstanding. Many viewers who were expecting passively to consume a new variation on *James Bond* were outraged when their screen reflected back at them, like a boomerang, a reality they could not accept: they were expected to react as individuals, capable of thought and understanding.

Yet this enigmatic and extraordinary work has, with the passage of time, become the object of a cult and has captivated several generations of demanding viewers. Whilst on one level the series tells an unusual spy story, its seventeen episodes are so rich in meaning on every other level that there has been endless debate about their true significance, fuelling a considerable number of articles, conferences, and even academic theses. The list of allusions seems to go on for ever: Kafka, Orwell, Lewis Carroll, Chesterton are the most often cited, but also, on account of the dream-like beauty of the images, surrealist painters such as Magritte.

An ode to liberty, total nonsense, a defence of the individual threatened by a totalitarian society, a psychedelic trip, a voyage of initiation, a metaphysical parable or religious allegory, *The Prisoner* – and herein lies its profound originality – gives rise to as many interpretations as there are individual viewers, the oldest of whom recognise that their own vision of the series has changed with successive screenings.

Whilst being the result of remarkable teamwork, the episodes as a whole should nonetheless be considered the work of a single artist, an inspired creator and visionary, the actor-director Patrick McGoohan, who also played the title role. Moreover, he did not escape Swift's prediction: *When a true genius appears in the world, you may know him by this sign, that the dunces are all in confederacy against him.* The outcry that followed the first screening forced him to leave England.

After so much controversy we thought it necessary to allow his work to speak for itself; and it seemed logical to us to devote to this first masterpiece of the eighth art, that of television, an art book of a new kind.

A collective work, this book falls into three very distinct parts, preceded by an interview with Patrick McGoohan. In the first part, writers and journalists offer their own vision of the series, each from a different angle. In the second part, the story is allowed to speak for itself through a summary of each of the seventeen episodes, with extracts from the scripts and, most importantly, a great many photographic illustrations.

After these two parts which offer a subjective reading of the work – given its very nature, it seemed impossible to us to imagine any other – we set ourselves the task of taking an objective look at the series in the third, also highly illustrated, section. We tried to demonstrate the programme's unique nature in articles devoted to its forerunner, *Danger Man*, to the magical place where it was produced and to its actors and to the enthusiastic appreciation society to which it has given rise. And through a detailed account of its filming, rich in incident, we have tried in particular to show how it departed from established norms from its very conception.

The aim of any art book is to let the work it presents have centre stage. We now hope that ours will turn those readers as yet unfamiliar with the series into dazzled admirers of *The Prisoner*.

AC/HO

# Interview with Patrick McGoohan

On the eighteenth of September, only a few days before the first French edition of this book was due at the printers, Daniel Gelli and I arrived in a sunny, hot Los Angeles to meet Patrick McGoohan, who wanted to contribute to the writing of this book. The discussion that follows is not the result of a short, impromptu interview; it is a constructed text, written and edited by Patrick McGoohan and myself. While Daniel took the accompanying photographs, the interview developed over the course of three meetings, during which, accompanied by the illustrator and animator Jacques Muller, our friend and host in the city, Patrick McGoohan and ourselves came to know each other, to share ideas, opinions ... and some wonderful gastronomic experiences.

Alain Carrazé

*After twenty years of debate and speculating about what you are supposed to have said in* The Prisoner, *do you think the time has come to say what you really said?*

I don't particularly enjoy talking about it. I finished with the series after editing it and delivering the last episode and would just as soon leave it alone. The work, if it can be called that, is done, and should stand or fall on its merits or otherwise. Explanation lessens what the piece was supposed to be: an allegorical conundrum for people to interpret for themselves. If one gives answers to a conundrum, it is no longer a conundrum. If, however, you are more confused after talking to me than you were before, then the conundrum continues. Besides, you and your colleagues are doing this splendid book in the spirit of the series, and I'm most grateful.

*Do you regard the place where the Prisoner was confined, the Village, as an external thing, or something we carry around with us all the time?*

The Village is symbolic – we are all prisoners of this or that, many things – each in his own 'Village'. On the most basic level we are prisoners of food and sleep – without either we die.

*But surely you were concerned with more than that. Shall we say the political and the sociological?*

The series was conceived to make it *appear* that our hero was striving to be 'completely free', 'utterly himself'. Too much of that and society would be overrun by rampant extremists and there would be anarchy. The intention was satirical. Be as free as possible within our situation, but the war is with Number One.

*Number One represented the evil side of our nature?*

To continue the allegory, Number One tries to run the Village his way if we let him. We have to challenge the so-and-so. When Hitler was an infant someone for sure crooned over him 'What a lovely baby!' But he grew up to let Number One take over the show. Naughty boy.

*Did you know at the beginning that you were going to finish it the way that you did?*

Given the premise, there was no other way to finish it, but even my colleagues were not sure until I wrote the last script. When that final episode screened in England, a sizeable audience watched to see who Number One would be. The majority expected a James Bond-type ultimate evil villain and when they got Number 6's alter ego they were none too happy. They, the majority, felt cheated. The TV station was jammed with complaints. There was considerable genuine resentment, and I had to take to the hills until the dust settled.

*You are quoted as saying you hoped there would be anger, disagreement, fights.*

Blood? No, I don't attach that much importance to any of it. I think the quote was exaggerated. Some lively debate is appreciated. It means the series achieved its objective. Not to everyone's taste. It was never intended to be. I wasn't making Coca-Cola.

*How was it possible in the climate of television to get such a thing made at all?*

I knew a man who backed hunches, and his decisions were his alone. Lew Grade, now Lord Grade, is such a man. He was behind my previous series (called *Danger Man* in England, *Secret Agent* in the United States). It was to him I took *The Prisoner*. He didn't like reading scripts, but preferred to *hear* the idea, to see it in his mind's eye. After listening to the bizarre concept, he took a few puffs on his cigar, walked around the office a couple of times and said 'It's so crazy it might work. Let's do it. Shake.' And we did. He gave me *carte blanche*. I was very fortunate.

*Again, you are quoted as saying you never wanted to hear the word* television *while you were filming. Is that true?*

Yes. Too often in the making of TV shows there is such a desperate scramble for scripts and making air dates that skimping is the order of the day. We were well-prepared and had a superb production team. The result looked expensive. But each episode cost only £56,000. They were spending more than that on a one-minute commercial in the United States at the time.

*What significance did you attach to the, shall we say, gimmicks, the logo and so on?*

Returning to your earlier political and sociological reference – the gimmicks, as you called them, were symbolic comments on aspects of society. For instance, the ancient bicycle represented progress: one has only to be in a traffic jam for hours on the highway with a few thousand other automobiles to know what that meant. In the traffic jam, in the immobile cars, one is a statistic, a number, futile, a prisoner – you'd get home quicker on the bicycle. The balloon represented the greatest fear of all – the Unknown. Or the invasion of privacy. Or hidden bureaucracy. Or interviews. Or death. Or taxes. Or whatever.

*It's interesting that in most of the confrontations in the series, there was little violence, almost a gentle dialogue, cat and mouse.*

It's all a joke. But there comes a time when rebellion is necessary. The last episode, 'Fall Out', was by no means gentle. There were machine guns, people died. Revolution time. Set against a background of the Beatles singing 'All You Need Is Love'.

*In a general sense, how do you see the present and future of theatre, motion pictures and television?*

The people who buy the tickets and switch the channels decide that. It's called 'show business' for a reason. If $40,000,000 of special effects sells $200,000,000 of tickets, you'll get more of the same. But when an $8,000,000 movie about a black man chauffeuring an eccentric old lady, with no sex or violence (*Driving Miss Daisy*) grosses over $100,000,000 domestic, it's considered a long shot freak success. There'll be no sequel. But I'd sure like for someone to make *My Right Foot*. Let's hope there will always be a place for the experimental which advances the medium, whether theatre, motion pictures or television. Good work can be buried without the funds to support the publicity hype which can be as big a production as the piece itself. A TV show in prime time can be seen in the States by *only* ten million viewers and considered a failure. Which does not imply that every smash hit lacks quality.

*That being so, and since you broke all the rules with* The Prisoner, *don't you think if you had made a more conventional but still original series of another kind which might have been a big commercial success, it would have given you more opportunities for the future?*

I had the chance to do something as nutty as I did. A chance that might come only once in a lifetime. If I was an idiot, so be it.

*Each episode of* The Prisoner *had a theme or statement on education, politics, whatever. Wouldn't it have been interesting to have made more to cover further themes?*

No. On the contrary. I think seven episodes would have been the ideal number. Less would have been more. More enigmatic. There are seven I consider completely true to the concept. The others on occasion were stretching it a bit.

*Number 6 was often attacked by his fellow Villagers because he was an individualist. You, personally, were criticised by a lot of baffled viewers. Do you think it was worthwhile doing something so controversial?*

Always.

*As the years go by, more and more people are discovering* The Prisoner *the way you intended. This book is proof of that. In the end, you succeeded. The series is now a cult. People are discussing and debating it. Fans of the series are legion. Are you happy with that?*

Cults can be a bother. Otherwise I'm not complaining.

*But are* you *a prisoner?*

Of course, but on parole. And, as they say, be seeing you.

*Patrick McGoohan*

# About *The Prisoner*

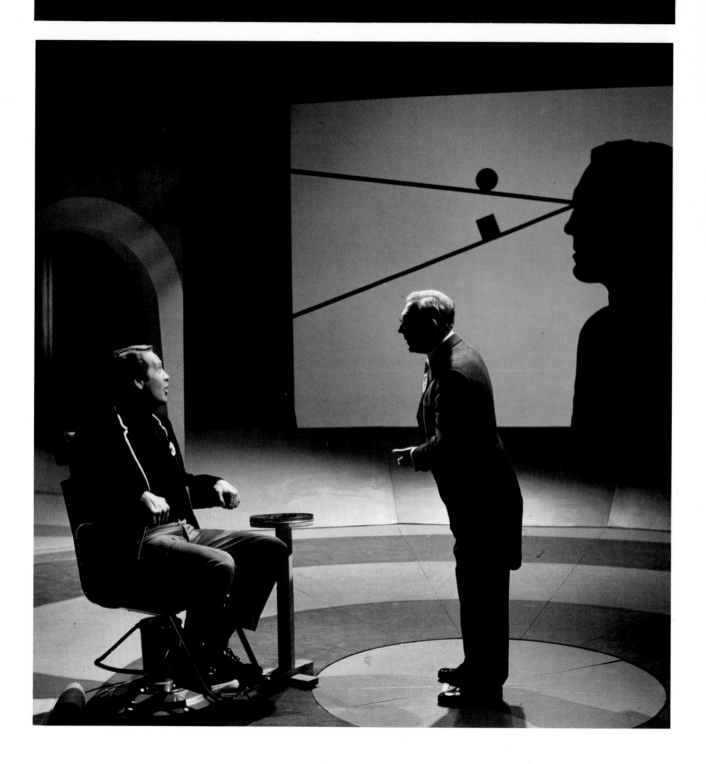

# The Greatest Science Fiction Film of All Time

## ROLAND TOPOR

Number 6 meets Number 2. They exchange a few polite words about the weather. Number 2 invites Number 6 in for a cup of tea. He readily accepts.

For anyone who knows how to decode the real, this apparent uneventfulness is transformed into a breathlessly dramatic situation.

The questions the viewer familiar with *The Prisoner* asks himself are:
 – is Number 6 really Number 6?
 – If he is indeed Number 6, has he been drugged, hypnotised or is he suffering a momentary bout of amnesia?
 – Is Number 6 pretending to accept the invitation because he has worked out a new escape plan, which in any case we know will fail?
 – Is Number 2 really Number 2?
 – Might not Number 2 be Number 1?

The situation is all the more explosive for appearing quiet. The originality of this series resides in its ability to create suspense from exactly those situations where it is noticeable by its absence.

Not to worry: we know our hero Number 6 well enough to feel confident that he will bring the drama out into the open. Being by nature a free man, refusing both his number and integration into the Village, he is able to escape the widespread schizopohrenia. If he torpedoes the comforting rituals of everyday life, if he persists in tearing away the shrouds of banality, it is because he is constantly on the defensive.

His paranoia is the sole guarantee of his identity.

We know he is right. We are ashamed not to follow his example.

The Village is simply the most contemporary version of the realm of Circe. Those who allow themselves to be seduced by her vulgar charms will be turned into animals: in this case, asses and sheep. Number 6 is another Ulysses.

Peace, luxury and sensual delight?

Crime, oppression and brain-washing, the paranoid Prisoner replies.

Order conceals a greater violence than disorder. It embraces the additional violence of untruth.

Number 6 struggles in a world of sham, in which those who wield power – a mysterious and indisputably arbitary power – have decided in their own self-interest upon a moral order that denies the individual, an order without conflict and with no minorities. Woe to the rebels who cling to their revolt, to their immaturity. They will be labotomised so that, as in Huxley's best of all possible worlds, everything should be sweetness and light.

Huxley's world, but also that of Orwell, Kafka, Lewis Carroll, Ambler and many others. Without them, the maverick members of our cultural family, we would be mere puppets, creatures with no minds of our own, at the mercy of the perversity of appearance.

But the matchless strength of *The Prisoner*, that which makes it the best science fiction film of all time, is that it does not end with each episode. It continues well beyond the final credits. It carries on into subsequent programmes on our television screens.

The soothing ambiance of the Village is there in the female announcer's smile, in the twee décor and in the *dramatis personœ* of political and cultural debates. In the pleasant faces of the presenters of variety shows. In the brazen jokes of the hosts of idiotic game shows. In those who feature in the wonderful world of advertising.

In the end the Prisoner will manage to escape. But the Village Authorities will have won anyway.

The Village was too small, not big enough for them.

They have conquered our world.

We are all numbers.

Be seeing you.

Signed: 1 38 01 75 110 104
(alias Roland Topor)

# Prisoner of *The Prisoner*

## ROGER LANGLEY

Why has a television series – *The Prisoner* – played a big part in my life of over 20 years? I still do not know! In 1967, when I first watched the series on British television, I recorded episodes on sound tape. After the final episode, 'Fall Out', early in 1968, I still wanted to see the series again and again – but it had gone. I listened to my sound tapes, especially to the theme music. I bought from a shop a model Village taxi, made by the British company Dinky Toys. On its box was a small picture of a *Prisoner* scene. These souvenirs, and my memories, were all I had.

In later years the programme was repeated on British television several times; I watched it again and finally I was able to have video tapes. At last I could watch the episodes without having to wait for television repeats. I began to collect every article I could find about *The Prisoner*. After many years, I am still buying magazines with *Prisoner* articles, plus any other souvenirs I can find. Why such an obsession?

For me, *The Prisoner* was – and still is – the best television programme I have ever seen. I must therefore explain why this is so. This is difficult for me now, as I have watched the episodes many times. I have seen them in French and in German. I have also watched some episodes which have been dubbed in Japanese! I feel a closeness with the programme as it was as important to me in the Sixties as it is today. Each year when I visit Portmeirion, where the series was filmed, it seems like the stories in *The Prisoner* come back to life, for real. I have written books about *The Prisoner* and even my own novels from the series. And yet, I have not got *The Prisoner* out of my blood – it continues to have its effect on me. Many other people have shared my feelings, but many more people have disagreed and think that *The Prisoner* made no sense. If you are reading this new book, you must already be interested in *The Prisoner*! So, what do we share? Is it the acting of Patrick McGoohan, the beauty of Portmeirion, the excitement of the episodes or the strange atmosphere of the series as a whole? Is it the issues raised by the stories, the strange happenings in the Village, the unusual music or the striking costumes? These things, and many more, are all vital ingredients of *The Prisoner*, providing many reasons for its appeal.

*The Prisoner* has been hailed as the first television classic. It has been described as the thinking person's television. It always provokes reactions from the viewers when it is repeated around the world. For many, McGoohan portrays the safeguarding of freedom and individuality. It is as though the character of Number 6 represents the never-ending challenge to our struggles in life from the establishment. McGoohan himself stands against the erosion of free thought and free choice. His character, Number 6, is frequently applauded as a role-model – a man who is confident, resourceful and honourable. The Village, in which he is trapped, shows us the comfortable lives of its citizens, who are brainwashed and subjected to constant surveillance. The rebellion by one man influences and dares us to find answers to the many questions. Fortunately, for we viewers, the progamme was made with a high budget and with the greatest attention to detail. For example, the pennyfarthing bicycle emblem itself appears throughout the episodes and causes us to wonder about its significance. McGoohan has said that he dislikes attempts to categorise the series. Whether it is science fiction, fantasy, allegory, political drama or plain adventure, depends upon the imagination of the viewer. I like to think that the episodes provide half of the jigsaw puzzle and that the viewers themselves provide the other half!

The editing of scenes in the episode is fast. McGoohan wanted it that way. One of the most important scenes, when Number 6 meets Number 1 in 'Fall Out', lasts only for a few seconds. McGoohan wants his audience to think about what they are watching; he does not provide them with much time or any ready answers. This way, there is much space for one's own interpretation. If you have inside you the elements which make up the character of Number 6, you will be able to fight off the temptation to arrive at simple or superficial conclusions. Instead, there is a positive delight in meeting the challenge of *The Prisoner* head-on. McGoohan never required us to think one way or the other – everything is left to the individual.

I have read many interpretations of the programme. Many attempts have been made to answer questions which emerge from the series. There are obvious questions, such as the background of Number 6, the identity of Number 2, the force or power in control of The Village and whether Number 6 really escaped at the end of the series. There are also much deeper questions, such as whether science should be used to control people, whether rules and regulations should be blindly accepted, whether the opinion or will of the majority should be inflicted upon the minority and whether the private thoughts and dreams of any person should be interfered with or controlled. McGoohan's own hatred of bureaucracy is, without doubt, a major influence within the series. However, there were so many other writers who brought their own ideas and fresh approaches to the

series, that the final result was a very varied collection of stories which did not depend upon each other for integrity. *The Prisoner* series, I have said before, is the sum of its parts and in my opinion it is impossible to choose certain episodes or plots to consider in isolation. Like a painting, *The Prisoner* – if it is a work of television art – must be appreciated by reference to its creator, its history, its production and its meaning. A painting can be discussed for many years and I think that *The Prisoner* will continue to demand scrutiny and provoke argument and debate. Unlike other television series, *The Prisoner* will always defy classification. I hope that it will continue to be appreciated for its high standards of creativity, original ideas, direction, acting, scripts, music and camera work.

*The Prisoner* series for me is a television epic. It is colourful, defiant and challenging. McGoohan said that the stories were all about one man's unflinching battle for survival as an individual. He also said that the worst enemy of many is surely himself – the evil in him is the worst thing on earth. I find these statements contradictory, but I know what McGoohan meant. His efforts continue to compel us to think about everything which is going on in the world around us. *The Prisoner* presents on one side a doctrine of responsibility and conscience. On the other side, it represents unrest and unanswered questions. At the beginning of every episode, Number 6 asks 'Whose side are you on?' Well, as the viewer, do *you* know? Millions of people have watched *The Prisoner* and many of them have rejected it as a waste of time. Like McGoohan, I see *The Prisoner* as an abstract impression of the world we are living in. The episode 'Fall Out', with the powerful rocket, suggests that we might be in danger of destroying our planet – or our ideals. The statement 'Be Seeing You' can also be spoken as a question – 'Be Seeing You?'.

Will we survive, will there always be a Number 6 to challenge those in power, or will the whole world become the Village? For over 20 years *The Prisoner* has concentrated our minds upon questions, whilst allowing us to enjoy the very best that television can offer. It is hardly surprising that the series eventually spawned its own appreciation society. The name of the society, 'Six of One', comes from a catchphrase in the series. I and my wife Karen have together helped run the society for a collective total between us of twenty-seven years. That is a long time to be imprisoned by a television programme!

# The Prisoner, Pioneer Without Heirs

## JACQUES STERNBERG

Being wary of thinkers and analysts, I have never had a vocation to be a scholar; still less a critic. This is why, even though I was amazed to discover, in 1968, *The Prisoner*, which contrasted strongly with the overwhelming mediocrity of television output, I have never felt a need to go any more deeply into the work in question, to examine it more closely or to spawn a thesis on the extremely unexpected explosion of Kafkaesque surrealism on our television screens.

The proof? In my personal dictionary of creative writers who have fascinated me (apart from those who feature in all the various published encyclopaedias), the only ones I can remember from my years as a television viewer (and I had a television as early as 1952) are those responsible for an amazing British serial, *The Prisoner*. Only Don Chaffey and George Markstein are credited, with no mention of Patrick McGoohan, quite simply because I did not know that he was the mastermind behind this serial which I would discreetly recommend to all and sundry without, it must be said, encountering much agreement.

This is my way of saying that I am not to be taken very seriously as an expert, never having been greatly tempted by the quicksands such knowledge represents. On the other hand, like Jules Renard who prided himself on it, I have always been very sure of my dislikes – which generally extend to the point of allergy. And in 1968 television not only brought me out in spots but also caused me overdose sickness, since from 1963 to 1964 I had to watch it as part of my job. Walter Lewino had come up with the amusing idea of giving me a cranky column as a television viewer for the cultural pages of the *Observateur*, a position from which I was of course ousted with the arrival of the thoughtful Jean Daniel. This did not send me into a nervous breakdown: for one thing, I was earning a good enough living as literary director of the Planète anthologies; for another, watching television had become a chore for me.

In 1968 matters worsened; not only was I watching practically no television any more, I was not even tempted to switch it on because I was very rarely at home. So it was purely by chance that one evening I happened to watch the first episode of *The Prisoner*. It so surprised me, so fascinated me that not for anything would I have missed the second episode the following week, some day, same time. And no other engagement ever made me miss a single episode. I, who regretted the distressing lack of imagination, absurdity, black humour and the unusual in films in general and – alas! – in fantasy films in particular, could hardly believe my eyes! And what was even more amazing was that these ingredients were there for all to see not in a film but in a series conceived for the Sacred Telly, that conduit for the dissemination of endless banality evening after evening. As for dissecting everything *The Prisoner* liberated, appropriated, stirred, salvaged and invented, I leave that to other exegetists. I shall find nothing they do not detect. But I doubt there are many people who watched these visual fireworks with such great naivety as I did, with such amazement, and above all such curiosity to follow a story, hoping that the end would never come, yet having 'dreamed' of it so often.

A final word: I have always loathed filmed debates, game shows, variety shows, telefilms – that sub-cinema – but on my scale of pet hates serials have always had the edge for the irritated indifference they inspire in me. There is only one brilliant exception to the general rule.

I shall add a postscript, a purely personal opinion. Like many avowedly revolutionary works, by rejecting the conventional, *The Prisoner* seems to have inspired no other work of the same kind. It has not changed the television serial, which, on the contrary, has wallowed for at least fifteen years in a tireless repetition of the same humdrum rubbish. Being ahead of one's time does not always lead to being taken up later or caught up with. More often than not it leads to being suppressed.

# Theodore Prisoner

## ISAAC ASIMOV

In the first program, our Hero (he was called 'The Prisoner', I noted, which is an odd name; it would sound better if they used his full name and called him Theodore Prisoner, I think) resigned from the British secret service. I wasn't worried; he was going to be a double agent.

Then he got captured, but I wasn't worried. He would escape. I kept looking at my watch and chuckling. In 10 minutes he would escape; now in only five minutes, four minutes, three minutes. I was overwhelmed at the ingenuity of the writers, for he had only one minute left and there was no sign of an escape yet.

He didn't escape. You won't believe me, but he didn't. I was thunderstruck!

Could it be a two-parter? Surely he would escape next week.

He didn't escape. The Bad Guys had these huge spheres that – oh, well, he didn't escape.

The next week he didn't escape either. Week after week he didn't escape. To be sure, he won some minor skirmishes. For instance, he never told them why he left the secret service.

But we, the audience, never found out either. We never found out anything. We never found out where the place was where Theodore Prisoner was being held prisoner, or who ran it, or why it was run, or who everybody else was, or why they wanted to know why he resigned, or *anything*.

Failure, failure, failure! Theodore P. failed. He never got out. We failed. We never understood.

I took the matter up with my young daughter, who is 13 and highly regarded throughout her junior high school for her keen perception. 'How do you explain it?' I asked.

'Well,' she said, thoughtfully, 'I think that Mr. McGoohan is trying to portray the plight of modern man trapped in a conventional society that he is incapable of altering and yet from which he cannot escape. The Number 2 villain changes each week, as do many of his fellow prisoners, to show that although society superficially alters as different men come to power, it remains always a prison for individuality, as is indicated by the fact that the protagonist does not even have a name but is known only as The Prisoner. It means –'

But I sighed and walked away. Poor child! She is bright for her age but she lacks the necessary sophistication to grasp the deeper meanings. She, too, had failed –

And I believe it was then that I grasped the point. *Failure*! That was the key!

What is so noble about success? How many people can be successful? To be successful, you must work and slave and even then you may not make it. How few are successful; how many aren't!

To preach a drive for success is to preach human inequality and that is undemocratic!

In a blinding flash, the words of a tender and touching ballad came to me:

*It takes a million dollars to be a millionaire,*
*But a pauper can be poor without a cent!*

That was it. We can't all succeed, but we can all fail; and in this common, universal failure we can find the brotherhood of man we all seek, the true equality at last.

This is a new age we live in. The old shibboleths are gone. Let us, all of us together, with Patrick McGoohan showing us the way, backtrack to failure. Let us shamble along the leaden road to obscurity, head sunk low. Let us all of us together, aspire to the depths, grasp for the ground, hitch our wagon to a rock, and look the other way when opportunity knocks.

Is it any wonder that *The Prisoner* proved a tremendously popular programme? Surely you wouldn't have thought so. Can you think of a single confusing, obscure novel that has become famous? Or a single piece of poetry of this type? A single play? Artistic production?

Well, then, *The Prisoner* can't have become popular because it was obscure and confusing. It must be popular because it cracks the old undemocratic folly of success for the few; because it points the way to comfortable attainment of failure for everybody.

My young daughter, when I enthusiastically explained this to her, pointed out that if I were to write this thesis in the form of an article and sell it, I would be cutting myself off from humanity by being successful.

I had to smile faintly at her naivete. Poor dear! She was obviously too young to see that I had passed on to the next stage: I was even failing to achieve failure, and that was the ultimate failure of all.

*Taken from an article titled 'Hitch Your Wagon to a Rock' which appeared in* TV Guide *in August 1968. It was sent to us by Jean-Mark Lofficier.*

# We Are Living in the Village

## CHRISTIAN DURANTE

One of these days we are going to have to admit it: we are living in the Village. And we are numbers – from our social security number to one of our credit card numbers. And while we are about it, we might as well own up to the fact that there are not many Number 6s – sorry, Patrick McGoohan – amongst us. One of the earliest dialogues in the first episode of *The Prisoner*, one that takes place between Number 6 and a maid, strikes an all too familiar chord:

*NUMBER 6: Who runs this place?*
*MAID: I don't know. I really don't know.*
*NUMBER 6: Have you never wondered? Have you never tried to find out?*

Do many of us today try to find out, to react, to live, to speak for ourselves? Or do we idly rely on someone else, on other people, whether known to us or not, because we don't want to have to form a personal opinion? 'We live in secondhand civilizations', as the Austrian philosopher Karl Popper put it some twenty years ago. Time has since borne out the accuracy of his brilliant remark. Without leaving his armchair, everyone has climbed Annapurna, visited Tierra del Fuego, seen whales trapped in the ice, lived on Wall Street and taken part in the war in Beirut. Schizophrenia? Did you say schizophrenia?

Each age has its Cassandra. It is not impossible that McGoohan is ours – if the legend about Priam's daughter with the gift of prophecy is agreeable to him, that is. For *The Prisoner* is above all a global work that acts on the viewer like a gigantic mirror. Throughout the seventeen episodes, McGoohan exhorts us to 'recognise who you are and choose which side you are on.' But what question do we ask ourselves?

If television had existed in Ancient Greece, no doubt some McGoohan would have already made this series. And all that one can hope is that in several thousand years' time, another McGoohan might make it again, unless he is already long since 'filed, stamped, indexed, briefed, debriefed or numbered'.

Everyone is familiar with the critical part played by imprisonment in all its forms in totalitarian states, which make up the majority of the world's governments. But reticence, even terror, prevents us from speaking about our own supposedly liberal societies which are rapidly 'socialising' and gradually becoming treacherous, grey societies that will soon join the large battalions of totalitarian states referred to above. Faced with this false and truly crazy Manicheism, Patrick McGoohan conceived *The Prisoner*. He says: 'I have always been obsessed by idea of imprisonment in a liberal society.' And he shows us that the notion is imprisonment, of enslavement, is inside our heads. It is the consequence of a choice we make for ourselves.

In 'The Chimes of Big Ben' he shouts at his superior in the hierarchy of the British Secret Service: 'I risked my life and hers to come back here, home, because I thought it was different . . . it is, isn't it? Isn't it different?'

What mode of expression other than a complete work of art could allow this ontological question to be worked over, dwelt upon, voiced? So McGoohan shows a computer exploding, incapable of answering the basic question: 'Why?' Anticipating 'cocooning', now the subject of pseudo-sociological articles in large-circulation newspapers, he sets this series within the confines of a village. And not just any village, but the life's work of Sir Clough Williams-Ellis, a Welsh architect who created a jigsaw puzzle whose pieces were brought together from all over the world, so that the place makes one feel as if one is everywhere and nowhere. The inhabitants may have something to do with this impression, being completely unbalanced; sheeplike, they grovel to whatever authority is in power. The will of a supposed majority prevails. Hence, this spicy dialogue from 'Dance of the Dead', where Number 6 is asked to come to a carnival:

*NUMBER 2: . . . You'll come?*
*NUMBER 6: I have a choice?*
*NUMBER 2: You do as you want.*
*NUMBER 6: As long as it's what you want.*
*NUMBER 2: As long as it's what the majority wants. We're democratic. In some ways.*

Note the violence of Number's protest, his determination to let nothing past that might inadvertently get him caught up in something fatal. This insistent 'invitation' reveals the superficially playful side, in the mould of other well-known holiday camps, of the Village. We know nothing about the food there. All we see, on one occasion, are some tins in the cupboards in Number 6's kitchen; the inhabitants never seem to eat. There is no sign of any restaurant or grocery. Epicurism, a dangerous form of intellectual escapism, is certainly frowned upon in this place. Only tea and coffee, two drinks that are easy to drug, are recommended. But festivities and even elections are organized. And these are all the more popular for not changing anything; confrontation remains within the bounds of good taste, with the hope that after psychiatric treatment 'for their own good' the few rebels will rejoin the bleating herd of the police-citizens of the Village, thought, after the fashion of the ancients, to be the centre

of the universe. Hence this conversation between Number 2 and Number 6 in 'The Chimes of Big Ben':

*NUMBER 2: What in fact has been created? An International Community. A perfect blueprint for World Order. When the sides facing each other suddenly realize that they're looking into a mirror, they'll see that this is the pattern for the future.*
*NUMBER 6: The whole earth as the Village?*
*NUMBER 2: That is my hope. What's yours?*
*NUMBER 6: I'd like to be the first man on the moon.*

For of course – and our present democracies actively demonstrate this – the search for a consensus, whether political or otherwise, is an open door to the most thoroughgoing totalitarianism. And Patrick McGoohan tackles this head on: democracy is not a panacea, nor a lesser evil. It is also an evil. Quite simply, this is where you live. And if the mandatory radio tells you every morning in the same voice that it is a fine day, if the only newspaper – although several 'different' newspapers can serve up the same information. as in Guy Debord's *'Aujourd'hui toute information est un ordre'* (Today all news is an order) – publishes the orders of the authority in power, if the doctors work for central government and if the citizens are their own police force, this is simply the best of all possible worlds, 1984, your world, our world. McGoohan is a poet. So he addresses his cry to us in the form of a television work of art. The Prisoner tries to escape from the Village with the aid of an abstract sculpture that is in fact a sailing boat, the sail of which is a tapestry; he uses music to undermine Number 2, and is evidently well read. But he is an individualist, alone in the face of many people who represent hell. For him Sartre's epigram is incomplete. Clearly: 'Hell is the herd of people', the herd that suppresses any elite and turns an individual deed into society's deed.

We see the inhabitants of the Village wandering aimlessly in their striped shirts and boaters, the braggart Number 2s quaking before the telephone that links them with Number 1, and the cowardly collaborators, the inept remote-controlled resisters among the Number 2s. We witness the massive disinformation exercises carried out by the very victims of those exercises and note the citizens' lack of commitment. We observe what masquerades as a social life, its sole aim being to enslave its participants a little more; this pitiful society of pathetic and carefully calculated leisure activities, these classified people make us realise that Patrick McGoohan has produced not just a mere television series but a work of art that stands somewhere between Swift and Debord. It is truly great commentary on our age, and certainly the finest and most intelligent satire of the post-war era. The problem is that, like all truly great works of art, it has not really been understood, and therefore has not, apparently, changed anything . . .

# Why?

## FRANÇOIS RIVIÈRE

'*Why?*' asks the Prisoner of the great computer in 'The General'.

The English have always taken delight in exploring the imaginary. A great, playful tradition, an inordinate taste for dreams and their labyrinthine constructions have encouraged the production of narrative Utopias, mischievously combined with the most adventurous philosophical ideas – those of Locke, Hume, etc. – indeed, with mathematical theories teetering on the absurd. In fact, the absurd has become the norm for storytellers and essayists and illuminated prophets of this genre and its colourful language. The great humorists of the 18th century – as defined by Thackeray – painted the first canvases of the fabulous imaginary landscape of literary Utopia.

The doyen Swift – it is often forgotten that he was related to William Godwin – was the most imaginative, most subversive Irishman of his era. He wrote the most savage satire, and with his *Gullivers' Travels* the most accomplished political, poetic and novelistic work of that same period. Swift's writing filtered through his deep misanthropy and took as its target the organization of society, present and future – no small subject. The horror distilled in some of his work, in a dizzying switch from the infinitely large to the infinitely small, remains unequalled. Congreve, Addison and Pope are drivelling old fools in comparison; their work is soporific.

In the 19th century, *Punch* gave contributors ample opportunity to display their love of character study. But it was minds which were even more marginal – that is to say, less confined to the London clubs, or the smoky rooms of the Café Royal – that came up with the most disruptive metaphors. The most claustrophobic Utopia was born of the brain of a timorous Oxford don, Charles Dodgson, better known by his pseudonym as Lewis Carroll. Thanks to him, those sinister nursery rhyme figures, often unbearably cruel, finally enjoyed their apotheosis. Carroll, minor chess genius that he was, swept aside all metaphysical problems by imposing the logic of dreams, unravelled and reknotted according to his very caustic humour. Age notwithstanding, Lewis Carroll, a cross between Beatrix Potter and Marcel Duchamp, could do no better than to involve us in a tense ironic game artfully intended to destabilise our image of the real world. More than an affectation – for the references relate solely to the world of childhood and its mythologies, and to that of the most sophisticated

knowledge – Carroll's literary enterprise turns out to be a *trompe-l'oeil* montage, a trip on the scenic railway of our innermost perceptions. A subversive work, too, that appeals to the child in each one of us; it appeals, in other words, to our freedom to invent another world. The crazy figure of Sylvie and Bruno's 'gardener' together with the Mad Hatter or those minor characters (beware!) that are like Martial's *aide-aux-fourrures* in Raymond Roussel's *Locus Solus* take us by the hand and transport us to a place that has certainly not since the beginning of this century met a more dazzling match than the Village...

G. K. Chesterton's vivid paradoxes, the fictional labyrinths of *The Man Who Was Thursday*, or the philosophical puzzles of Father Brown, which owe more to William Blake than to Carroll's confined, purely intellectual world, anticipate the terribly suggestive setting – deceptively welcoming and good-natured – of the nightmare envisaged by actor-director Patrick McGoohan. The word nightmare merits examination as the most appropriate term: it was used by Chesterton as the subtitle of *The Man Who Was Thursday*, which has a structure which is extremely close to that of *The Prisoner*. The investigation of Gabriel Syme, poet and secret agent, into the mysterious Council and in particular the nature of 'Number 1' of brotherhood of anarchists is strikingly similar to Number 6's dogged, nightmarish and increasingly dubious quest. Could not the voice heard in the Black Chamber be the echo of an inner voice resonating in the very heart of this individual witness called Syme – which, pronounced with a Cockney accent, sounds like 'same'.

Situated where the fantastic borders on modern science fiction and the spy story, McGoohan's postulate, like that of Kafka, Gustav Meyrink and Alfred Kubin, sets up a fictional structure that, like a Möbius strip, offers no purchase to the rationality of an innocent reading. Perhaps I should say *naive* reading, for the hero's total innocence, which is here at stake, justifies the childish philosophy. In Chesterton's novel Syme reflects: 'I would never have thought we were so close to London.' And at once the pressure of the real world falls away and the adventure resumes...

Often I have been tempted to *understand* McGoohan's work by taking the actual setting of his story as the first mystery to resolve. And this mystery at once deepened with the reflection mirrored in the water lying before it, that uncharted area Number 6 tries in vain to

cross, only to find himself on the other side of a mirror that has to be crossed yet again indefatigably.

I have tried to justify his behaviour by likening it to the solitude of a child, master and prisoner of his own coded universe, often confined to the family garden or the park, where he can hear sounds of a world at once near and far, incomprehensible and fascinating. The Village then seemed to me like the technological necropolis of a life entirely fashioned by the insanity of an individual trying to escape.

It was then that the word 'escape' imposed itself upon me. 'Why?' the Prisoner almost playfully asks of the absurd invention alleged to be the repository of all knowledge and supposed to know all the answers. This metal sphinx explodes and we are sent back to the first and last question around which McGoohan's whole fiction revolves.

Escape: all the literature that elaborates on this notion, inherited from the last century, has contrived to go beyond the often derisory form prescribed. New writers – Jules Verne, H. G. Wells, Rider Haggard, John Buchan, C. S. Lewis, to cite only a few – deliberately chose to transform the content of the adventure story into a coded message. Buchan is of special interest here, for it was he who invented the modern spy story, and he was the first writer of the genre to have given deep thought to the terrifying symbolism of the war in the shadows. Thanks to Buchan and his protagonist, Richard Hannay, the perfect precursor of Number 6, the secret agent has become the hero of an apocalyptic legend, protagonist in a titanic combat the setting for which more often than not is just a weekend cottage in Dorset. Having acceded to the status of myth, John Buchan's fiction never went out of fashion, while fictional spies continued to flourish. Then another myth, born of the Cold War and of the mind of another former Etonian, Ian Fleming, began to popularise beyond all expectation the picaresque adventures and romantic fortunes of an agent working for the British Secret Service. The proliferation of gadgets testified to an increasing willingness among intelligence services to regard science as an ally. But in a genre that had always favoured understatement, this flirtation with such extravagant accessories created new metaphors within a fetishist and cryptic universe. Ian Fleming's novels, when turned into films, made the public very much aware of the aesthetic rituals of the Manichean struggle between the CIA, the KGB, and their ilk.

In 1966, when Patrick McGoohan was about to film the first episode of *The Prisoner*, ideas were filtering into the public subconscious from the underworld of espionage – the idea, for instance, that the superpowers were governed by the secret services, that a veritable cryptocracy had come to power.

Portmeirion, in North Wales, became the theatrical setting for a fantastic parable that depicts the mental landscape of a man who from his recent involvement in the spy serial *Danger Man* had given the public food for thought of a kind undoubtedly unique in the world of television spectacle. McGoohan leaves nothing to chance; the key to the enigma he advances is totally encapsulated, down to the very last comma, in the first lines of dialogue. The complex Roussellian nature of his fiction, masterminded from start to finish by himself, contains allusions to the oldest Utopias, combined with ingredients from more recent fables as though to entice the viewer and at the same time keep him at a distance. But the enigma of very existence of Number 1 – as in Chesterton's *A Man Named Thursday* – is there to destabilise the rational world that this work of fiction is supposed to present; while imposing no order on the unfolding of the episodes, the script at the same time creates the greatest sense of vertigo precisely through the effect of a recurring, implacable prologue.

Right from the start, the circle is closed. The Village nightmare – said to be inspired by memories of the Scottish internment camps – becomes the image of a mind that goes on to explore all the modern world's systems of confinement. The characters of Swift and Carroll, Wells's mad scientists, Lewis's whimsical lunatics, the warders of Orwell and Kafka have donned costumes for an hallucinating masked ball. Confronted with them – in other words, with himself – Number 6, like some post-war Gulliver, methodically sets about trying all the exits. As it turns out, they are all false.

*Escape.* The concept comes back at us like a boomerang, personified by the extraordinary convincing vision of McGoohan, who has caused the character John Drake to take a great leap forward. The gadgets are no longer gadgets but weapons with which we hold normal reason at bay. The Village with its touristic atmosphere is a stage with carefully oiled traps. Even if an answer to that insistent question 'Why?' were to be found, it is now too late. Like some Oedipus of the technological era, a single being, for whom the wheel of destiny turns only once in a lifetime, does not know whether he is in the process of being born or dying, of possessing his mother or embracing the image of death in the mirror of a vanished world. Number 1 rises from the limbo of the life we dream in order to endure better the idea that we are already dead, whilst Number 6 changes once more, becoming Hamlet and Prometheus, the spent hero of an impossible adventure story.

The modernist literature of the '60s – what we in France pompously termed *'le nouveau roman'* – considered itself obliged to sacrifice characters. Its champions would have done better to remember the lesson of the great action story, a lesson given over a century ago by a number of enlightened minds, most of them English. The broad vision of McGoohan paved the way for the arrival of a post-modernist trend, whose representatives are as diverse as Manuel Puig, Christopher Priest or Umberto Eco, author of *The Name of the Rose*. But Number 6, author and actor of his own fiction, a story cast in a form

that reached the widest public, escaping the vigilance of a critical fraternity blinded by its snobbery, will remain the forerunner of an unparalleled genre. It leaves us now, fascinated and chilled, in possession of a message which is that of the first fiction of the year 2000.

June 1989

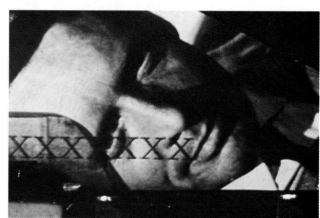

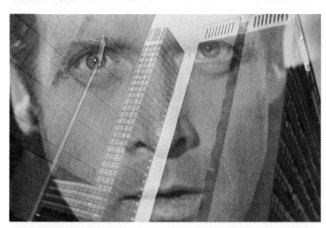
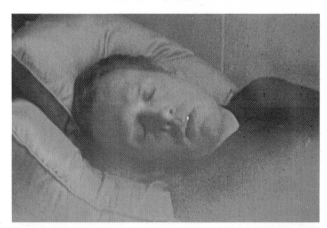

Where am I?
*In the Village.*

What do you want?
*Information.*

Whose side are you on?
*That would be telling.*
*We want information . . .*
*information . . . information . . .*

You won't get it.
*By hook or by crook we will.*

Who are you?
*The new Number 2.*

Who is Number 1?
*You are Number 6.*

I AM NOT A NUMBER,
I AM A FREE MAN!

# The Seventeen Episodes

The Prisoner *tells us, in seventeen episodes, the story of a man* apparently *cast adrift from history and separated from our world. All that we ever knew about him is that he is a former secret service agent who has resigned for reasons that he refuses to disclose; that he is in his thirties; that before his abduction he was living in London; that he owned a sports car, a Lotus 7; that he does not take sugar with his tea but lemon. We never discover his name and know him only by his number, 6, which in any case he never accepts. The series tells the story of his resistance against mental destruction and of his successive attempts to escape from the place where he is held prisoner — a village whose name and whereabouts are unknown. The eternal loser — each episode ends with symbolic bars closing on his face — he nevertheless thwarts all the attempts of those seeking to break him and succeeds in preserving his mental integrity. During the final episode, he is addressed as 'Sir'. But will he succeed in escaping?*

# Episode One:
# Arrival

The man whom we will call 'the Prisoner' returns to his London home. In an outburst of anger he has just hurled his resignation onto his boss's desk. But a hearse has followed his Lotus and a sinister character who looks like an undertaker climbs up the steps behind him. A cloud of gas suddenly fills the room in which he is furiously packing his bags. The dreary apartment blocks opposite his flat dance before his eyes; he collapses onto his bed and falls asleep.

When he wakes up, dazed, his head is resting on the same pillow. He seems to be still in his own bedroom, but when he lifts the blinds, to his astonishment a totally unfamiliar scene greets his eyes: a square surrounded by tall trees and curiously coloured baroque buildings in the middle of a flower-filled village – strangely beautiful, quiet and deserted, on a fine summer's morning.

He does not meet a living soul; on climbing a tower he sees only a panorama of bizarre architecture. There is not a sound but the mournful sighing of the wind. Suddenly a bell seems to awaken the village and he hurries to the terrace of a café, where at last he meets an inhabitant: a waitress busy putting up parasols:

*WAITRESS: We'll be open in a minute.*
*PRISONER: What's the name of this place?*
*WAITRESS: You're new here, aren't you?*
*PRISONER: Where?*
*WAITRESS: D'you want breakfast?*
*PRISONER: Where is this?*
*WAITRESS: The village.*
*PRISONER: Yes.*
*WAITRESS: I'll see if coffee's ready.*
*PRISONER: Where's the police station?*
*WAITRESS: There isn't one.*
*PRISONER: Can I use your phone?*
*WAITRESS: We haven't got one.*
*PRISONER: Where can I make a call?*
*WAITRESS: Well, there's a phone box round the corner.*

Inside a phone booth he picks up the receiver of a strange cordless phone.* A woman's voice is heard on the other end:

*OPERATOR: Number please.*
*PRISONER: What exchange is this?*
*OPERATOR: Number please.*
*PRISONER: I want to make a call to ... London.*
*OPERATOR: Local calls only. What is your number sir?*
*PRISONER: I haven't got a number.*
*OPERATOR: No number. No call.*

Increasingly anxious, the Prisoner discovers that the taxis are also confined to a local service and that the village shop sells only maps of The Village:

* The cordless phone did not exist at the time the series was made.

identifying merely 'The Mountains', 'The Sea', 'The Beach', without mention of a single proper name. In fact from now on he will not hear or set eyes on any proper names. The inhabitants greet each other with an enigmatic 'Be seeing you!' accompanied by an equally enigmatic gesture, and he is perplexed to discover the sign *Private. 6* outside his new home, the door to which opens automatically.

Hardly has he entered when he receives a telephone call. A man who calls himself Number 2 invites him to come and have breakfast at the Green Dome.

The Prisoner is ushered into this imposing edifice, which dominates the whole village, by a dwarf butler, who leads him across an elegantly but conventionally furnished hall to a pair of double metal doors. Like all doors in the Village, they open automatically. The contrast is astounding. The Prisoner stands on the threshold of a huge circular room of an impossibly futuristic design. In the centre is a spherical chair in which a man is seated at a control panel which bristles with buttons and flashing coloured lights. He wears on his jacket lapel a badge decorated with a penny farthing on which is inscribed the number 2.

The Prisoner is served an appetizing breakfast by the admirably competent butler, then finally learns the explanation for his abduction and is told what is expected of him.

*NUMBER 2: I suppose you're wondering what you're doing here?*
*PRISONER: It had crossed my mind...*

The Masters of this place, of whom he will never be told anything, represented by Number 2, want to know reasons for the Prisoner's sudden resignation. They already seem to know everything about him: Number 2 projects on to a large screen images from his past life, public and private, that he believed he alone knew about. But his date of birth is missing. The Prisoner gives it: 4.31 a.m., 19 March 1928* – and says:

*PRISONER: I've nothing to say, is that clear... Absolutely nothing.*
*NUMBER 2: Now be reasonable old boy... it's just a matter of time. Sooner or later you'll tell me. You co-operate, tell us what we want to know and this can be a very nice place. You may even be given a position of authority.*
*PRISONER: I will not make any deals with you. I've resigned. I will not be pushed, filed, stamped, indexed, briefed, debriefed or numbered. My life is my own.*
*NUMBER 2: Is it?*
*PRISONER: Yes. You won't hold me.*
*NUMBER 2: Won't we? Let me prove that we will... come I'll show you... We can take this up later...*
Number 2 and the Prisoner climb into a helicopter, piloted by the butler, and fly over the Village.
*NUMBER 2: Are you receiving me...*
*PRISONER: Loud and clear.*
*NUMBER 2: Quite a beautiful place really, isn't it... Almost like a world of its own.*
*PRISONER: I shall miss it when I'm gone.*
*NUMBER 2: Oh it'll grow on you. We have everything here... water, electricity, there's the council building. We have our council, democratically elected... we also use it for public meetings, amateur theatricals.*
*PRISONER: Fascinating.*
*NUMBER 2: Yes indeed... There's the restaurant... But did you know we have our own little newspaper...*
*PRISONER: You must send me a copy.*
*NUMBER 2: You'll be the death of me. We also have our own graveyard...*

* This is Patrick McGoohan's date of birth.

The Village, which has the ambiance of a small seaside resort, appears to have acquired a lively crowd whose brightly coloured costumes complement the pretty little painted cottages. Brass band music contributes to the jolly atmosphere.

On leaving the helicopter, the Prisoner makes his way to the Village's picturesque central square – the one he saw completely deserted when he woke up. He stares in amazement at the bizarre multicoloured outfits of the carefree throng strolling in the square. A brass band parades past a notice instructing people to *Walk on the grass*. A cheery voice suddenly comes over the loud-speakers throughout the Village:

*VOICE: Good morning all, it's another beautiful day... Your attention please. Here are two announcements. Ice cream is now on sale for your enjoyment. The flavour of the day is strawberry. Here is a warning. There is a possibility of light intermittent showers later in the day. Thank you for your attention.*

But the dream-like quality of the Village will soon turn into a nightmare for the Prisoner.

From a balcony overlooking the square he witnesses a significant scene, orchestrated for his benefit by Number 2. Amplified by a megaphone, Number 2's voice suddenly rings out brutally, ordering the strollers to stop.

Everyone is instantly rooted to the spot, frozen like statues. The music dies and the oppressive silence makes the whole scene more unreal and disturbing.

One young man does not stop. The voice rings out again, calling him to order, whilst a little ball seems to materialize from the top of a jet of water gushing from the middle of the central fountain. We watch it bob up and down like a ping-pong ball. Then suddenly, inexplicably, an enormous white ball appears above the balcony and begins to hover over the square. Seized with panic, the recalcitrant young man takes flight, ignoring Number 2's repeated warnings. The scene then turns to outright horror: the giant ball, now apparently endowed with a life of its own, begins to roll along the ground towards the fugitive, emitting a strange whine. The rebel is quickly caught; we glimpse for a moment his terrified face suffocating under a whitish membrane before the palpitating mass engulfs him. Only a few seconds later it detaches itself from the now lifeless body of its victim. The Prisoner stares dumbfounded at the monstrous object which is already moving away, gently bouncing, still accompanied by the same lugubrious whine.

Then suddenly the scene changes and everything returns to normal: the band's joyful music bursts out once more, everyone starts to move again, resuming their interrupted gestures as though nothing had happened.

'What was that?' the Prisoner, still in a state of shock, asks Number 2. 'That would be telling,' the latter laconically replies.

Just at that moment the loudspeakers blare once more, calling Number 2 to the Labour Exchange. He takes along the Prisoner , who notices some of the Village's maxims posted on the walls of the reception hall:

QUESTIONS ARE A BURDEN TO OTHERS;
ANSWERS, A PRISON FOR ONESELF.

and:

A STILL TONGUE MAKES A HAPPY LIFE.

He is shown a circular room with a bewildering interior, where a jovial man wearing a suit and seated behind a fantastic wooden contraption resembling a giant toy sets about giving him an aptitude test:

*MANAGER: ... And now the questionnaire. If you just fill in your race, religion, hobbies ... What you like to read, what you like to eat. What you were, what you want to be ... any family illnesses ... any politics?*

The Prisoner's only response to the personal questions is to leap up and smash the contraption, so that pieces of it are scattered on the ground. Then without a word he makes straight for the metallic door.

*NUMBER 2:* (holding a file) *Never mind, you can get all you need from this ... I think we have a challenge.*

Too true! Moreover, the Prisoner will soon make his first attempt to escape. But first he will explore his new home, which is a replica of his London flat although it contains a few small differences – in particular, a radio broadcasting syrupy music at full volume. Having tried in vain to turn it off, he hurls it in exasperation to the ground and stamps on it in fury. But even in fragments, the radio continues to broadcast; the only result is the almost immediate appearance of a repairman.

Nor is he taken in by the trimly uniformed maid who has been assigned to him when she tries to get him to talk.

But he is unaware that all the while his every action has been observed by Number 2 and a disquieting bald-headed Supervisor on a giant screen in an impressive Control Room whose walls are covered with huge maps of the world, terrestial and celestial. A small army of cameramen work in shifts to keep the Village and its surroundings, including the inside of the houses, under constant surveillance.

*SUPERVISOR: She was most convincing. I felt sure she was going to pull it off.*
*NUMBER 2: He's no ordinary man. This has got to be handled very differently.*
*SUPERVISOR: That could be difficult.*
*NUMBER 2: You know how important this is ...*

The Prisoner's first attempt to escape will get similarly live coverage.

We see him running headlong through the woods, having bumped into a strange gardener who is the exact double of the man who came to mend his radio. He has to hide behind a bush to avoid the enormous white ball which is still producing its unnerving whine. He begins to run in the opposite direction, and enters a scene of surrealistic beauty; he runs between strange statues that appear to belong to all the world's cultures. As he passes, their heads swivel, their eyes of stone tracking the fugitive with empty gazes. Strange lights flash in the eyes of some of the statues, revealing the existence of hidden cameras. To escape the white sphere that continues to pursue him, perhaps under remote control, he flees towards the beach. Meanwhile in the Control Room:

*SUPERVISOR: Attention post 14 ... attention post 14, yellow alert ... Yellow alert ... yellow alert ... Now leaving Northern perimeter. Number 6, repeat Number 6. Now approaching ... contact imminent, contact imminent ...*

Intercepted on the beach by a bunch of thugs, the Prisoner succeeds in putting them out of action and escapes at the wheel of their car. This time the response from the Control Room is decisive:

*SUPERVISOR: Northern Area Number 6, heading for outer zone ... in our vehicle ... orange alert, orange alert all units ...*

Looming up from the swirling sands, the enormous soft white ball comes rolling towards him at great speed. Thrown out of the car, he is overtaken by the monstrous palpitating mass that adheres to him and smothers him beneath its weight. It then moves away, leaving him motionless and unconscious on the sand. Almost instantaneous intervention seems to be the rule in the Village: an ambulance arrives immediately.

When the Prisoner wakes up he is in hospital – an imposing building reminiscent of a medieval fortress and a striking contrast to the pretty villas in the rest of the Village. He is astonished to recognize in the next bed a friend of his, a former colleague whom he calls Cobb. But the latter seems to be in a kind of trance and in reply to frantic questions manages only to stammer out fragments of a story of abduction similar to the Prisoner's experiences.

A few seconds later the Prisoner is taken from the room for a routine medical examination before being allowed to leave. He is amazed to see, down a long corridor bathed in red light, two rows of patients dressed in long tunics and sitting motionless on the ground opposite each other. 'Group therapy. Counteracts obsessional guilt complexes producing neurosis,' the doctor with him comments briefly.

Shortly afterwards, just as his check-up is completed, an alarm goes off and an assistant bursts in, shouting: 'The amnesia case sir – Cobb – he jumped out of the window. He's dead.'

On leaving hospital, the Prisoner appears for the first time in the outfit that he will wear from now on: the famous dark jacket with a white trim. Like most of the men in the Village , he has been given a boater, but immediately gets rid of it. He also wastes no time in tearing off the badge on his jacket lapel – a badge on which the Number 6 is inscribed in the middle of the large wheel of a penny-farthing that seems to be the ubiquitous emblem of the Village. He is given an identity card, an employment card, a credit card and a health and welfare card, but gives them only a cursory glance. Upset by the death of his friend Cobb, his face stamped with grim determination – an expression that will become familiar with succeeding episodes and which is as much the Prisoner's hallmark as his jacket with the white trim – he hurries off to the Green Dome to demand an explanation from Number 2. But he does not recognize the man now sitting in the spherical chair:

PRISONER: *Get him.*
NEW NO. 2: *I have taken his place. I am the new Number 2.*
PRISONER: *Get Number 1.*
NEW NO. 2: *As far as you're concerned I'm in charge. What can I do for you?*
PRISONER: *Cobb.*
NEW NO. 2: *What we do here has to be done. It's the law of survival, it's either them or us.*
PRISONER: *You imprison people, steal their minds, destroy them . . .*
NEW NO. 2: *It depends whose side you're on, doesn't it?*
PRISONER: *I'm on our side.*
NEW NO. 2: *Then we'll have to find out where your sympathies lie . . .*
PRISONER: *You know where they lie.*
NEW NO. 2: *Subject shows great enthusiasm for his work. He is utterly devoted and loyal. Is this a man that suddenly walks out?*
PRISONER: *I didn't walk out. I resigned.*
NEW NO. 2: *People change, exactly. So do loyalties.*
PRISONER: *Not mine.*
NEW NO. 2: *All very commendable. But let's be practical. I'm interested in facts. Your only chance to get out of here is to give them to me . . . and if you don't give them, I'll take them. It's up to you, think about it. Good day, Number 6.*
PRISONER: *Number what?*
NEW NO. 2: *Six. For official purposes. Everyone has a number. Yours is number 6.*
PRISONER: *I am not a number. I am a person.*

After he has gone, the new Number 2 dictates into a microphone:

*NEW NO. 2: Report on Number 6. Normal classification. On arrival subject showed shock symptoms followed by accepted behaviour pattern. Since then has been uncooperative and distinctly aggressive... attempted to escape... Subject proving exceptionally difficult, but in view of his importance no extreme measures to be taken yet.*

For his second escape bid, the Prisoner believes he has found help.

At Cobb's funeral – the coffin is escorted to the cemetry by a brass band playing the same cheery music that seems to accompany all events in the Village – he falls into conversation with woman whose sad and tearful face has attracted his attention.

Having revealed that she was a friend of Cobb, she then confides that they had planned to escape together and suggests that he take advantage of the plan. Her refusal to go with him – she says that without Cobb escape is no longer of any interest to her – at first makes the Prisoner suspicious, but eventually he decides to trust her. She gives him an electropass, a kind of wristwatch which will enable him to escape undetected in the helicopter, and he decides to use it.

He manages to get into the helicopter without provoking an attack from the mysterious white ball, which comes and prowls menacingly around him. (We will later learn that this monstrous object is called Rover.) Then he begins to fly over the Village towards freedom. But this turns out to be a cruel trick on the part of Number 2 who, his face lit up with sadistic joy, is following the whole scene on a screen. Suddenly he pulls a lever. In spite of his desperate efforts, the Prisoner loses control of the helicopter, which turns round and lands where it started.

Cobb's girlfriend was in fact being manipulated by Number 2. Only her grief was genuine: she too genuinely believed that Cobb was dead. Cobb appears dressed in ordinary clothes, standing beside Number 2 and apparently about to leave.

*NEW NO. 2: I think I'll let him keep the watch, Cobb, just to remind him that escape is not possible.*
*COBB: Don't be too hard on the girl. She was most upset at my funeral.*
*NEW NO. 2: Don't worry she'll be well taken care of.*
*COBB: Yes, that's what Im afraid of... Ah well I'd better be going... got a long journey mustn't keep my new masters waiting.*
*NEW NO. 2: They'll be delighted with you... give them our compliments.*
*COBB: I will... and I'll tell them there are no loopholes.*
*NEW NO. 2: I appreciate that. I do hope that your stay has had its lighter moments. Au revoir.*
*COBB: You'll find him a tough nut to crack... Auf Wiedersehen.*

This opening episode provides an introduction to the world in which the rest of the action will take place. But the Prisoner has much more to learn about the twisted game in which he is caught.

# Episode Two:
# The chimes of Big Ben

All the episodes of *The Prisoner* seem to take place in an eternal present and to tell an uncompromisingly cyclical story.

With very few exceptions, each starts by going back to the beginning of the story, with the appearance on the horizon – against a stormy sky and simultaneous with a resounding and ominous clap of thunder – of the Prisoner in his Lotus 7 on the way to submit his resignation. We are shown all the events up until the moment when he lifts the blinds of his duplicate bedroom and discovers the Village.

From this second episode onwards there is an additional title sequence constructed round a dialogue between Number 2 and the Prisoner:

*PRISONER: Where am I?*
*VOICE: In the Village.*
*PRISONER: What do you want?*
*VOICE: Information.*
*PRISONER: Whose side are you on?*
*VOICE: That would be telling... we want information... information... information...*
*PRISONER: Well you won't get it.*
*VOICE: By hook or by crook we will.*
*PRISONER: Who are you?*
*VOICE: The new Number Two.*
*PRISONER: Who is Number One?*
*VOICE: You are Number Six.*
*PRISONER: I am not a number, I AM A FREE MAN!*

The whole sequence, the first part of which is punctuated by some unforgettable music is in fact a condensed version of the 'Arrival' episode. Today we could use the term 'clip' a word unknown at the time of filming but it seems inadequate; there is still no word to describe a 'television poem'.

As usual, it is a lovely morning in the Village. A cheery voice issues from the loud-speakers and radios:

*VOICE: Good morning, good morning, good morning... and what a lovely day it is. Rise and shine, rise and shine. Before our programme of early morning music, here are two announcements... the long range weather forecast is that the fine spell will continue for at least another month... your local council, and remember it is your local council democratically elected by you, have decided to organize a great new competition. Can you paint? Can you draw? Can you model in clay? If you can then your day is just six weeks today. All about it later but now music...*

Syrupy music invades the Prisoner's bedroom. He has just woken, evidently in an extremely bad mood. As he gets up, yet another Number 2 observes him on the screen in his impressive circular office.

*NUMBER 2: He can make even the act of putting on his dressing gown appear as an act of defiance.*
*ASSISTANT: There are methods we haven't used yet of course.*


As the Prisoner gets his breakfast the music becomes more and more intrusive, and his face shows increasing exasperation. Suddenly, seized with inspiration, he opens his refrigerator and shoves the radio inside it.


*NUMBER 2: Fascinating.*
*ASSISTANT: He doesn't even bend a little.*
*NUMBER 2: That's why he'll break. It only needs one small thing. If he will answer one simple question the rest will follow. Why did he resign?*


Later the Prisoner, who seems to be taking part in Village life, finishes a game of chess with an old gentleman in seaside garb, a retired general of some unspecified army. He is joined by the new Number 2, a plump, jovial man with a booming laugh, who seems to have a stronger personality, and on initial contact a more sympathetic one, than his predecessors.


*NUMBER 2: We must play some time.*
*PRISONER: Certainly we must... by post.*
*NUMBER 2: I must add 'sense of humour' to your file... they tend to leave out things like that... very important.*


A helicopter lands not far from them and two nurses bring out of it an unconscious woman, whom they place on a stretcher.


*PRISONER: What crime did she commit?*
*NUMBER 2: Nervous tension, that's all. She's come here to recuperate.*
*PRISONER: How much are you charging her?*
*NUMBER 2: I really must bring your file up to date.*


A little later in Number 2's huge circular office:


*NUMBER 2: Sit down my dear fellow.*
*PRISONER: Thank you.*
*NUMBER 2: File Number 6. Section 42, subsection 6, paragraph 3. Add, sense of humour, strong and unimpaired... I can never remember – one lump or two?*
*PRISONER: It's in the file...*
*NUMBER 2: Yes. As a matter of fact, yes. But it would save time if you just answered.*
*PRISONER: Why? Are you running out of time?*
*NUMBER 2: Does not take sugar. Frightened of putting on weight?*
*PRISONER: No. Nor of being reduced.*
*NUMBER 2: Oh, that's excellent. I am glad you're here. You really are a model.*
*PRISONER: But I don't run on clockwork.*
*NUMBER 2: You will, my dear chap, you will.*
*PRISONER: Do you think so?*
*NUMBER 2: Do you still think you can escape, No. 6?*


The conversation, which has so far been conducted with guarded humour, abruptly changes tone:

*PRISONER: I'm going to do better than that.*
*NUMBER 2: Oh?*
*PRISONER: I'm going to escape and come back.*
*NUMBER 2: Come back.*
*PRISONER: Escape and come back and wipe this place off the face of the earth.*
*NUMBER 2: Oh... subsection 6, paragraph 4. Add* on the other hand per-secution complex amounting to mania. Paranoid delusions of grandeur.

But he is all at once rendered speechless when he notices the Prisoner staring at him defiantly, dropping four lumps of sugar, one by one, into his cup...

*NUMBER 2: Don't worry, Number 6. You'll be cured. I'll see to it. No more nightmares. If you have so much as a bad dream, you'll come whimper-ing to me. Whimpering.*

At this point we can see on the control screen an elegantly furnished bedroom. The nurses are laying on the bed the young woman they carried unconscious out of the helicopter.

*NUMBER 2: She's your new neighbour, that's all. I thought you might be interested. The new Number 8.*
*PRISONER: What happened to the old one?*
*NUMBER 2: He vacated the premises. You noticed surely.*
*PRISONER: Did he escape? There was no funeral.*
*NUMBER 2: It's not always possible. You need a body. Oh look, she's get-ting up. It's quite like old times, isn't it. D'you remember your first day...*

When he gets back home, the Prisoner meets his new neighbour, who is obviously in the grip of the same panic he suffered on his arrival in the Village. She tells him her name, Nadia Rokowski, and reveals that she is Estonian and has resigned from her job. Wary, the Prisoner refuses to exchange confiden-cies. But the next day Nadia's insane attempt to escape will make him change his mind.
He is sitting on the terrace overlooking the beach when he is joined by Number 2:

*NUMBER 2: May I join you? You're good neighbours I hope? There are some people who talk and some people who don't. Which means that there are some people who leave this place, and some who do not leave. You are obviously staying.*
*PRISONER: Has it ever occurred to you that you're just as much a pris-oner as I am?*
*NUMBER 2: My dear chap, of course, I know too much. We're both Lifers. I am definitely an optimist, that's why it doesn't matter who Number 1 is... It doesn't matter which side runs the Village.*
*PRISONER: It's run by one side or the other.*
*NUMBER 2: Oh certainly, but both sides are becoming identical. A perfect blueprint for World Order. When the sides facing each other suddenly realize that they're looking into a mirror, they'll see that this is the pat-tern for the future.*
*PRISONER: The whole earth as the Village.*
*NUMBER 2: That is my hope. What's yours?*
*PRISONER: I'd like to be the first man on the moon.*

During the conversation Nadia has arrived on the beach in a swimsuit. She goes into the water and starts to swim with a strong, regular stroke. Soon she has swum some distance from the shore and continues to advance towards the open sea. Simultaneously the Prisoner and Number 2 realize what her true crazy intention is. Number 2 rushes off to the Green Dome... and suddenly the mysterious and monstrous Rover appears rolling on the water towards the fugitive. It catches her, smothers her by sticking to her face, and brings her back unconscious to the beach. The Prisoner hurries towards her, but the nurses are already there.

Shortly afterwards the Prisoner is summoned to the hospital by Number 2 and finds the latter there watching the dreadful interrogation, in fact, real psychological torture, that Nadia undergoes on regaining consciousness – torture so dreadful that she tries to put an end to it by attempting suicide. Overwhelmed by her suffering, the Prisoner for the first time abandons his sarcastic impassiveness and offers to do a deal with Number 2. If they let Nadia go, he, the Prisoner will co-operate; not by supplying information but by trying to become integrated in the Village community. He offers to take part in the arts and crafts exhibition; Number 2 agrees.

A relationship of friendship and trust begins to develop between Nadia and the Prisoner. We see them having breakfast together, and almost have the impression of a couple who are happy to be alive. Then, at nightfall:

*VOICE: Hello and good evening... curfew time, sleep time, fifteen minutes from now to curfew... Meanwhile allow us to lull you away with...*

Nadia joins the Prisoner on the terraces of Cottage Number 6. He brings out his radio; the usual syrupy music serves to cover their whispered conversation. They act out an amazing love scene, something never seen in the Village; a piece of bluff intended for the control screens.

*PRISONER: Tell me...*
*VOICE: Curfew in five minutes... to curfew the minutes are five...*
*NUMBER 2: The language of love...*
*NADIA: I do know where the Village is...*

She then tells the Prisoner that when she was working for 'her' government (she does not specify which) she discovered in a secret file the location of the Village. It is, she says, in Lithuania, only thirty miles from the Polish border where she has friends in a little fishing village. If they manage to get that far a 'contact' of hers will be able to help them. The Prisoner agrees to take her there and gives his word that he will do his best to ensure her safety.

*NADIA: Do you really know what I want... to hear the chimes of Big Ben.*
*PRISONER: Big Ben...*

The Prisoner will now work on their escape, at the same time producing his entry for the Village art competition. His contribution, an arrangement of three pieces of wood, gradually takes on the shape of a boat. He presents it as an abstract work to Number 2, when he comes to give the Prisoner some 'friendly' encouragement. Though glaringly obvious the nautical resemblance seems to escape Number 2.

The big day of the contest arrives at last. The brass band strikes up and in a joyous whirl of coloured umbrellas the inhabitants of the Village converge on the recreation hall, where Nadia and the Prisoner are greeted by Number 2.

*NUMBER 2: The awards committee are intrigued with your abstracts, but they're a little mystified... could you spare a moment to give them a word?*

The Prisoner agrees and together they enter the exhibition room. By contrast with that of the Prisoner, all the works are plainly 'figurative'; every one of them a portrait of Number 2.

NUMBER 2: *Remarkably high standard don't you agree?*
PRISONER: *Highly original.*

The Prisoner then offers the awards committee some explanation of his work.

MAN 1: *We're not quite sure what it means.*
PRISONER: *It means what it is.*
NUMBER 2: *Brilliant. It means what it is. Brilliant. Oh no you mustn't let me influence you... you are the awards committee.*
WOMAN: *What puzzled me Number 6 was the fact that you'd given the group a title... Escape.*
PRISONER: *This piece. What does it represent to you?*
MAN 2: *A church door?*
PRISONER: *Right first time.*
WOMAN: *I think I see what he's getting at...*
PRISONER: *Now this other piece here, the same general line, somewhat more abstract as you'll notice, representing freedom or a barrier depending how you look at it... The barriers down the door is open, you're free, free to go, free to escape, to escape to this... symbol of human aspirations... Knowledge, freedom, escape.*
MAN 1: *Why the cross piece?*
PRISONER: *Why not?*
WOMAN: *Oh good, splendid... I was really quite worried for a moment. The only thing I really don't understand...*
PRISONER: *Yes?*
WOMAN: *Where is Number 2?*

The Prisoner's brilliant exposé of his work is in fact a parable that shows the artist expressing a blinding truth which everyone refuses to see. But he is interrupted by the prize-giving ceremony. Number 38, a charming old lady like some character from an Agatha Christie novel is, to her confusion and delight, awarded 'the special prize for the over-sixty group' for her magnificent tapestry depicting Number 2. But it is the Prisoner who wins the special merit award of 2000 work units (the Village currency). With a beaming smile, showing all signs of being perfectly intergrated, he offers a few well-worn words of thanks. He decides to spend all his prize money at once on buying Number 38's award-winning tapestry – a tapestry that will put the final touch to the Prisoner's own masterpiece. After nightfall this improvised sail, emblazoned with the image of Number 2, will bear Nadia and himself towards the open sea in his craft.

But the fugitives do not elude the Supervisor's battery of cameras, which set off an orange alert; it is not long before Rover appears on the scene. Just as it reaches their frail craft, they jump into the water and manage to swim to the shore where Nadia's 'contact' awaits them.

The contact, who converses with Nadia in Russian, has organized the rest of their escape route, which will take them to London via Danzig and Copenhagen. The Prisoner gives him a message for his bosses, and before leaving asks a favour: the loan of his watch to replace his own which has been damaged by sea water.

Measuring time will in fact be a necessity throughout the long and difficult journey ahead of them. They get into a large wooden box separated into two compartments. Karel, Nadia's friend, places the lid on top of them, and nails it down. They are driven through the countryside, then the box is transferred on to a boat.

The Prisoner, wrapped up in a blanket, tries to sleep, but he is frequently disturbed by Nadia, who seems to find the journey rather long. He comforts her by telling her how soon it will be before they finally hear the chimes of Big Ben. But not content with that, she tries to put their conversation on a more intimate level. Her friendship towards him is, it seems, beginning to turn into something more – a feeling which is apparently not mutual.

We see a plane taking off. Meanwhile, in a typical London government office, a man who is evidently a senior Secret Service official picks up the receiver of a red phone:

FOTHERINGAY: *Fotheringay here. Yes. Yes. I've seen a copy of the deciphered message... What time would you say? Good... my dear sir, I can't wait to see him...*

We see a second plane take off, bringing the wooden box to London and Big Ben.

At last, bruised all over from being shaken around in their box, stiff and aching, exhausted and dazed, the Prisoner and Nadia are released and find themselves in the same London office, in which the sound of the traffic can be heard very distinctly. It is the end of a nightmare. As he greets the two men there to welcome them the Prisoner betrays his emotion.

PRISONER: *Colonel...*
COLONEL: *Alright.*
FOTHERINGAY: *Hello old man.*
PRISONER: *Allow me to introduce you to Nadia...*

Outside, slowly and magically, the long-awaited chimes of Big Ben start to ring out...

NADIA: *Is this London?*
PRISONER: *Sh... that's it.*

At the Colonel's request Fotheringay leaves the room, then Nadia, welcoming with relief the idea of at last being able to have a bath departs; left alone with the Colonel, the Prisoner seems disappointed: obviously he was expecting a completely different reception:

PRISONER: *I don't see any fatted calf.*
COLONEL: *Did you expect one?*
PRISONER: *No.*

Then he answers the Colonel's suspicious questions about Nadia, and tries to explain the Village to him:

PRISONER: *...a place where people turn up... people who have resigned from a certain sort of job, have defected, or been extracted... the specialized knowledge in their heads is of great value to one side or the other... Are you sure you haven't got a village here?*
COLONEL: *Where is the village?*
PRISONER: *Lithuania, on the Baltic. Thirty miles from the Polish border.*
COLONEL: *How did you find out?*
PRISONER: *Nadia told me.*
COLONEL: *How did she know?*
PRISONER: *She worked for their government... she came across a secret file...*
COLONEL: *On how to catch a spy in six lessons.*
PRISONER: *I risked my life and hers to come back here because I thought it was different... it is isn't it, isn't it different?*
COLONEL: *My dear chap, I do apologize. You've had a long journey, you must be exhausted.*

The Colonel offers him a whiskey, while the chimes of Big Ben resound once more. The interrogation continues...

*COLONEL: But let's start at square one, shall we... First why did you resign?*
*PRISONER: It was a matter of conscience.*

While Big Ben slowly strikes the hour, the Colonel returns to the attack. He finally promises that Nadia will be given political asylum if he agrees to explain himself a bit more, and tell them why he resigned.

The chimes of Big Ben ring out once more. The Prisoner, who is about to reply, cannot help listening, counting the strokes.

*PRISONER: I resigned because for a very long time... just a minute... eight o'clock...*

Then, with a change of tone:

*PRISONER: Big Ben has just struck eight. My watch says eight... I was given this watch by a man in Poland. Would you like to explain to me, how a man in Poland came to have a watch showing English time when there's one hour's difference?*

He already understands. He inspects the room and roughly disconnects an electric wire leading to a tape-recorder concealed in a drawer. The sound of traffic abruptly ceases. Utterly dejected, he turns away without a word from the Colonel's embarrassed gaze, and as though in a trance slowly walks out of the room and down a corridor. He opens another door: outside he sees radiant sunshine, and multicoloured umbrellas twirling to the familiar sound of a brass band.

As he goes by, the Prisoner waves ironically to a group of three people – Number 2, Fotheringay and Nadia. Then exchanging the traditional 'Be seeing you!' with a few passers-by on his way, he enters his quaint little ochre cottage. The door opens and shuts automatically behind him.

*NUMBER 2: Well done Fotheringay. Now get back to London before any embarrassing questions are asked.*
*FOTHERINGAY: What's my next assignment?*
*NUMBER 2: The Colonel will give you your orders when he returns.*

At this point the cheery Village Voice makes an announcement:

*VOICE: Good evening citizens, your local council wishes to announce an exciting competition... the subject this time, Sea Escapes...*

In the Control Room Number 2, who is with Nadia, is dictating:

*NUMBER 2: File 6, subsection 1, paragraph 1... Back to the beginning.*
*NADIA: You were right about him.*
*NUMBER 2: I told you.*

Nadia, dressed in civilian clothes with a fur coat thrown over her shoulders says:

*NADIA: Don't worry. It was a good idea and you did your best. I'll stress it in my report.*

✳

The trap that has just been closed round the Prisoner makes gripping, captivating viewing. If the first episode acquainted the viewer somewhat with the peculiar world of the Village, the second initially led him to believe that he was going to be able to situate it in a coherent framework formimg part of our own world. But eventually the Prisoner begins to realize that he knows nothing; the programme demands of the viewer that he tries to understand, and follow the series through to its conclusion.

# Episode Three:

## A, B & C

In the circular office of the Great Dome, the strange red telephone suddenly starts bleeping. Yet another Number 2, who has been lost in thought, jumps and anxiously picks up the receiver.

*NUMBER 2: Number 2 here. Yes sir, I am doing my best. He's very difficult. I know it's important, sir. He's no ordinary person sir, but if I had a free hand... I know sir, yes... I know I'm not indispensable.*

He replaces the receiver with a unsteady hand and pours himself a glass of milk. Unlike his jovial predecessor, this Number 2, who looks like a junior civil servant, gives the impression of being a neurotic apparatchik, drinking milk for his ulcer and terrified by his mysterious superiors. Nevertheless he recovers his authority when addressing his subordinates:

*NUMBER 2: Get me Number 14. Number 14? The experiment must come forward.*
*NUMBER 14: Impossible. I need all of a week.*
*NUMBER 2: I haven't got a week.*
*NUMBER 14: I haven't even finished testing it on animals, let alone people.*
*NUMBER 2: Then now's your chance.*
*NUMBER 14: When?*
*NUMBER 2: Tonight.*

A flash of lightning illuminates the sky. Fine weather seems to reign eternal in the Village, despite the 'light showers towards the end of the day' sometimes announced on the loud-speakers, but tonight is dark and stormy and in the background is the sound of rolling thunder and pouring rain.

A metal door opens at the end of a corridor and two men, their black oilskins streaming wet, appear, pushing a trolley with a sheet covering what is obviously a body. They enter a huge laboratory equipped with a vast amount of electronic apparatus of every kind (mostly of an unfamiliar kind), where they are awaited by Number 2 and a young woman in a white coat. They draw back the sheet to reveal the inert body of the Prisoner, apparently in a deep, artificially induced sleep.

Once the orderlies have departed, the young woman, who wears a badge inscribed with the number 14 on her white coat, adjusts various pieces of equipment, then places electrodes on the 'patient's' temples.

*NUMBER 2: This brainchild of yours had better work. For your sake. If this man is damaged, I shall hold you responsible.*
*NUMBER 14: You know I haven't had time to prove the drug.*
*NUMBER 2: Just get it right or I'll see that it's proved on you. What's all that about?*

*NUMBER 14: Energy from his brain. Thoughts, like sound waves converted into electrical impulses and finally... into pictures.*

A succession of images appears on what looks like a television screen. They build up into a familiar scene: that of the Prisoner's resignation, the key scene of the series, which he seems to be reliving over and over again in his dreams.

*NUMBER 2: Extraordinary... how very single minded.*
*NUMBER 14: I sometimes think he's not human.*

Number 14 opens a metal box containing three syringes filled with a reddish liquid and she explains the experiment she is about to carry out.

This drug, which she has invented, will, along with some sophisticated equipment, make it possible to enter the subject's dream, projected on to a screen, and to control it by introducing extraneous elements, settings and characters that belong to his past. But the patient cannot take any more than three injections, a maximum that already involves a serious risk.

The Prisoner is injected with the contents of syringe number 1:

*NUMBER 14: His mind is now yours. What do you want from it?*
*NUMBER 2: Why he resigned. I believe that he was going to sell. I want to know what he was going to sell and to whom he was going to sell it. We've researched and computed his whole life and it boils down to three people... A, B and C... He must meet each one of them, we shall then know what would have happened if we had not got to him first.*
*NUMBER 14: Where do you want them to meet?*
*NUMBER 2: Paris. They've got one thing in common. They all attended Madame Engadine's celebrated parties. Here's some film from the most recent.*

Number 14 places a circular tape canister on the 'dream machine', and presses a button. A waltz tune fills the laboratory while on the screen men and women in evening dress are gathered round a fountain in the gardens of what seems to be a very grand house. 'The moment of truth,' she says, and turns up the current.

An image of the Prisoner in black tie suddenly comes into focus on the screen. Initially incredulous, Number 14 and Number 2 watch him with delight. They are beginning to believe in the success of their enterprise.

The elegant man whom we now see moving easily amongst Madame Engadine's guests is a very different person from the Prisoner whom we have often seen in the grip of suppressed fury, pacing the streets of the Village or the rooms of his villa like some wild animal in a cage.

Smiling and relaxed, with all the assurance of the perfect *homme du monde*, he exchanges a few friendly words in passing with one or two of the guests, then suddenly:

*PRISONER: Good evening... Engadine.*
*ENGADINE: Darling... I am so happy you are here.*
*PRISONER: You look as wonderful as ever.*
*ENGADINE: I should. What it cost... You look tired, darling. Things are bad.*

Indeed a shadow has darkened the face of her elegant guest, and we glimpse for a moment an expression in which we recognize the Prisoner we know. But it quickly passes.

*PRISONER: Not now. I'm starting a holiday.*
*ENGADINE: Oh, the English holiday. Big boots and fishing sticks.*
*PRISONER: Not quite like that.*
*ENGADINE: Where then?*

*PRISONER: Somewhere different, somewhere quiet, where I can think.*
*ENGADINE: Oh there is no quiet anywhere. Hello... ah and remember.*
*You're mine. Be horrible to other women.*
*PRISONER: I promise.*

As he becomes further and further removed from the austere Prisoner of the Village, we begin to forget that this is only a fabricated dream controlled in a laboratory. But we are suddenly brought back to reality:

*NUMBER 2: I think it's time we introduced A.*
*NUMBER 14: His face looks vaguely familiar. What's his real name?*
*NUMBER 2: I'm surprised you don't remember him. He made world news a few years ago.*

He opens a file and takes out a film and the photograph of a dark-haired fellow with a moustache and the worldly charm of a successful ladies' man.
Number 14 projects film A. On the screen the Prisoner exclaims:

*PRISONER: I'm surprised.*
*A: Not unpleasantly, I trust.*

The veneer of small talk scarcely conceals the hostility between the two men. Everything, including their different physiques, seems to set them apart. Their conversation is carried on in an often sarcastic tone and is not devoid of threatening insinuations.

*A: To us.*
*PRISONER: As we are, or as we were?*
*NUMBER 14: Oh, I remember him. He defected about six years ago.*
*A: It's been a long time.*
*PRISONER: Not long enough.*
*A: We used to be friends.*
*PRISONER: Once.*
*A: With a lot in common.*
*PRISONER: That's in the past.*
*A: Then let us think of the future. We're still the same people.*
*PRISONER: Working for different sides.*
*A: Sides don't matter. Only success.*
*PRISONER: In that case we should have a great deal in common.*
*A: We do the same jobs.*
*PRISONER: For different reasons.*
*A: I see you still overrate absolute truth. Whatever way you look at it we both want to conquer the world. I hope you're happy in your new life.*
*PRISONER: New life?*
*A: News of old friends travels quickly.*
*PRISONER: In a few hours.*
*A: To you and me, news is like air. We breathe it deeply, draw it from far and wide.*
*PRISONER: If it's interesting.*
*A: What are you going to do with your freedom?*
*PRISONER: Go fishing.*
*A: Perhaps you're fishing now. What's your price?*
*PRISONER: What am I selling?*
*A: I'm anxious to find out.*
*PRISONER: Madame's wine is always excellent.*
*A: If you haven't got a price, you must have a reason.*
*PRISONER: They're not always the same thing. Excuse me.*

With these words he walks off and disappears in the crowd.
Meanwhile in the laboratory:


NUMBER 2: *He's going. We haven't found out a thing, he must not go.*
NUMBER 14: *He's only doing what he should have done. I can only create a situation.*
NUMBER 2: *Get him back.*
NUMBER 14: *It's his dream. It must take its course.*


On the screen, the Prisoner is now on the point of leaving the party. Two liveried footman hand him his coat and open the door for him. But on the other side of the door A, now openly hostile, bars his way, and at his signal the two footmen in powdered wigs reveal themselves to be no more than a couple of thugs. A few seconds later the Prisoner finds himself squashed between them in the back of a white Citroen speeding through the night. In the laboratory Number 2 wonders what their destination might be . . .

A little later the Citroen stops in the grounds of a country house. A and his henchmen get the Prisoner out of the car.


A: *You're in my country now.*
PRISONER: *Diplomatic immunity? I like travel, it broadens the mind.*


He then turns on them, fists flying. To the accompaniment of jazz music of the kind often associated with *film noir*, a spectacular fight now ensues. The Prisoner, despite being one against three, succeeds in neutralizing his adversaries. But by the end, elements of the series' very distinctive usual music pervert the jazz rhythms. If the Prisoner seems groggy, this is not simply because of the beating he has taken. With a peculiar smile on his lips, he straightens his bow-tie and comes out with a misplaced 'Be seeing you!' This is no longer Madame Engadine's guest talking . . .

In the laboratory Number 14 begins to switch off the equipment. Number 2 – who has learned only that A was not the buyer – looks disappointed and would like to continue the experiment there and then. But Number 14 insists that her subject should rest for at least twenty-four hours. She removes the electrodes from his temples while Number 2 stares anxiously at the red telephone.


The next morning when he wakes up, the Prisoner seems ill and staggers to the door to get some air. In the street opposite him, Number 14, dressed now in the pretty multicoloured cape worn by the Village's inhabitants, is buying some flowers. The Prisoner starts, then stares at her, perplexed. Number 14's face, and more particularly the number on her badge, seem to remind him of something. Suddenly, he makes the connection, and looking down at the inside of his wrist, he is amazed to discover the reddish mark left by the experiment carried out during the night. Shortly afterwards he joins Number 14 on a terrace, where she is immersed in reading the local newspaper, the *Tally Ho*.


PRISONER: *My handbook on social etiquette doesn't deal with this. How does one talk to someone that one has met in a dream?*
NUMBER 14: *Look, number . . .*
PRISONER: *6.*
NUMBER 14: *6. I'm usually a social animal, but not now. Another time?*
PRISONER: *Last week, Number 14 was an old lady in a wheel chair. You're new here, and you're one of them.*

Her sole response is to fold her newspaper and get to her feet...

The Prisoner will get nothing out of Number 2 either, although he makes a point of showing him the inside of his wrist as he pours himself a glass of milk. And that evening he accepts, apparently without suspicion, the drink brought to him by his maid. Almost instantly he falls unconscious to the ground.

A little later we see him in a setting now familiar to us: the laboratory where Number 14, again wearing an austere white coat, injects him with the contents of the second syringe.

He appears on the screen, deep in conversation with Madame Engadine, in the gardens where the party is in full swing. But his former social self-confidence seems to have deserted him; he even seems a little lost. Yet he manages to get a grip on himself and respond lightheartedly to his hostess's playful remarks.

Meanwhile in the laboratory Number 2 takes out a second film and it is not long before character B appears on the screen. She is a young woman, attractive despite her disquieting appearance. 'She even looks like a spy,' remarks Number 14.

Indeed she does. B seems like a caricature of a female spy, straight out of a Cold War B-movie. But it is a while before she enters the Prisoner's dream; his mind seems less malleable than it was during the episode with A.

However, his dream scenario, which has become rather disjointed, eventually has him meet her. B sits alone at a table in an arbour waiting for him, away from the rest of the party. She seems to be an old friend, but also an ex-colleague. They swop a few reminiscences, then the Prisoner invites her to dance.

Number 14 then decides to speed things up and to intervene directly in the dream, by feeding him words as well as images. She picks up a phone and begins to dictate things to B that will eventually rouse the Prisoner from his dreaminess within his dream.

What B tells him is as disturbing as it is surprising. She claims she is being threatened by A's henchmen, who have, she says, followed her to this party and will spare her life only in exchange for information: the reason for the Prisoner's resignation.

In the laboratory, witnessing the Prisoner's perplexity, Number 14 starts to dictate more and more melodramatic statements to B. But this crass performance serves only to increase the Prisoner's mistrust.

PRISONER: *Have you the feeling that you're being manipulated?*
B: *Manipulated?*
PRISONER: *Who are you?*

To create a diversion, a new element is introduced into the dream. Two sinister characters in evening dress emerge dramatically from the bushes:

B: *They're here. If you don't tell them they'll kill me.*
PRISONER: *You are not who you pretend to be. Excuse me.*

He walks off, but the two thugs jump on him. After a brief scuffle, he manages to free himself, but the incident is not yet over. A third man now holds the barrel of his gun to B's temple.

B: *Tell him! He'll kill me!*
PRISONER: *I don't believe in you.*
B: *He'll kill me.*
PRISONER: *How long has your husband been dead?*

His question creates a momentary flurry in the laboratory, but Number 2, rapidly consults a file. He whispers the response to Number 14, who transmits it to B.

*B: Four years.*
*PRISONER: How old is your son now?*
*NUMBER 2: Son? Husband, yes. There's no son . . .*
*NUMBER 14: Help me please.*
*B: Help me please.*
*PRISONER: What is your son's name? That's an easier question. I thought you wouldn't answer.*

He turns his back on her, resolutely deaf to her increasingly histrionic pleas, and walks away, out of his dream . . . and off the screen. In the laboratory where he is still lying unconscious, with electrodes on his temples, Number 14 and, more especially, Number 2 have suffered another setback. Number 2 cannot help darting a terrified glance at the red telephone, whose menacing presence reminds him that he has only one more chance.

The next morning the Prisoner again wakes up in some discomfort. But this time fragments of his dream undoubtedly linger in his mind, for his eyes go straight to the inside of his wrist where there are now two red marks.

His suspicions aroused now, he remains wary, and later in the morning he tails Number 14. She leads him straight to the laboratory where he has spent the two previous nights dreaming.

She stays only a few moments and after she has gone he slips in and thoroughly examines the various electronic devices. After fiddling around with some electric wires, he manages, through a process of trial and error, to get the 'dream machine' working. Images from Madame Engadine's party start to come up on the screen. It is to the romantic waltz tune it plays that he continues his investigations. Eventually he pieces together the psychological manipulation to which he has been subject during his sleep. In the space of a few seconds, he works out a strategy for turning the tables, and replaces with water most of the contents of the one syringe remaining in the metal box that obviously contained three.

It is this diluted liquid with which he is injected that same evening. His dream once again takes him to Madame Engadine's, but the atmosphere of the party is dramatically changed; now the guests are gyrating to the wild beat of deafening disco music. Moreover, the image on the screen appears distorted and unstable. Fearing for the Prisoner's life, Number 14 is on the point of breaking off the experiment, but Number 2, who is worried more on his own account, forces her to continue.

Looking drunk or drugged, the Prisoner staggers among the frenzied guests. Eventually he meets his hostess and in a curiously emphatic tone of voice, he exchanges a few disjointed remarks with her. Suddenly, apparently in a fit of madness, he goes up to a crooked wall mirror and seizes it with both hands. Distraughtly, he stares at his distorted face. As he straightens the glass, the room and the party guests become upright again. The image on the screen is no longer distorted.

In the laboratory Number 14 and Number 2 – who have no photograph of the character C – grow more and more impatient as they wait for the Prisoner to identify the right person among the guests.

On the screen Madame Engadine introduces the Prisoner to one of her friends, a blonde woman, still young and quite attractive.

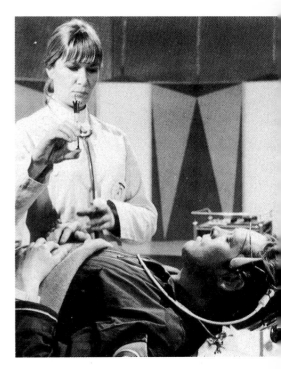

*ENGADINE: Watch him for me, will you darling... he's the last sane man in the world.*
*BLONDE: I like sane men. Are you in business?*
*PRISONER: I was.*
*BLONDE: You're young to retire.*
*PRISONER: Age is relative.*
*BLONDE: Meaning you're free.*
*PRISONER: Possibly.*
*BLONDE: I know of something and the pay's very good.*

She takes off one of her diamond earrings and gives it to him:

*BLONDE: Number 6. I'm sure it's your lucky number.*

His interest caught, the Prisoner heads for the gaming table, where he places the earring on the black 6. The wheel turns. The croupier calls: 'black 6, even and manque' – and changes the earring for a key. The Prisoner walks away from the gaming table, and Madame Engadine holds out to him another key, identical in every respect.
It is with amazement that Number 2 learns the identity of C.

*ENGADINE: It takes you a long time to sell yourself darling.*
*PRISONER: It took a lot of thought.*
*ENGADINE: Come on this way...*
*NUMBER 2: She's fooled us for years. But not any longer.*
*NUMBER 14: You'll bring her to the Village?*
*NUMBER 2: Yes...*

The Prisoner and Madame Engadine, having walked across the garden where the party is getting into full swing, have now come to a door. They each of them insert a key into one of its two locks. But first Madame Engadine gives him a final warning:

*ENGADINE: If you want to go back, you can. Back to the party. Back to your life. But once through this door, you can never return.*

At this point, back in the laboratory, the Prisoner begins to stir restlessly in his sleep. He groans and suddenly the screen is a total blank. 'He's collapsed!' cries Number 14, who has been getting increasingly worried, and promptly places an oxygen mask over his face. On the screen the dream resumes its course. It is that same night, and the Prisoner and Madame Engadine, still in evening dress, are driving down the Champs-Élysées in a dream car, a luxury Alfa-Romeo convertible. They are on their way to meet a mysterious 'someone else' – the real boss.
Hanging on their every word Number 2 watches the screen with shining eyes and slackened jaw, eagerly waiting for the identity of this fourth character to be revealed. This is a person whose existence he admits he has never even suspected; with a touch of irony Number 14 suggests calling him 'D'.
The Alfa-Romeo is now driving through a fantastic landscape. After passing under a stone arch, it finally comes to a halt outside an imposing medieval-style building. The setting has become completely dream-like, which is not totally lacking in a certain logic...
Her mission accomplished, Madame Engadine then wishes the Prisoner good luck. He gets out of the car, and climbs the steps to the building whose gothic porch is like that of a church. The enigmatic sound of an express train can be heard in the distance. He pushes open the heavy double doors, which swing back to reveal a dark and deserted square in a quiet, expensive-looking residential quarter of, perhaps, Paris or London. A loud male voice that seems to emanate from everywhere and nowhere suddenly rings out:

*VOICE: I'm glad you could come.*
*PRISONER: Where are you?*
*VOICE: It doesn't matter.*
*PRISONER: I want to see you. I've been dying to see you.*

The same might be said by Number 2, who is sitting wild-eyed before the screen. He looks as if he is on the point of succumbing to a paroxysm of curiosity. A bell, reminiscent of the one in the Village, chimes several times. This is the final act: the intolerable suspense will soon be over for Number 2. At the far end of what looks more and more like a stage set, a sinister dark silhouette appears and comes towards the Prisoner, towards Number 2 in front of his screen, towards the viewer in front of his . . . It is the figure of a masked man, whose evening dress, top hat, black gloves and full black cloak with red lining call to mind the Phantom, or the Devil.

*PRISONER: I didn't know you existed.*
*D: It is is often the case with really important people. Anonymity is the best disguise.*
*PRISONER: You are afraid. This is very important to me.*
*D: It is only a commodity.*
*PRISONER: No. It's my future.*
*D: You belong to me now. You were told there is no return.*
*PRISONER: Not until I know who you are. I've never liked secrets.*
*NUMBER 2: Nor have I. I want to see him.*
*D: No-one will ever see me.*
*PRISONER: I will. I want to know who I'm selling out to. We must all know.*
*D: All? Aren't you alone?*
*PRISONER: No. But you are.*
*D: Violence will do no good.*
*PRISONER: It relieves the feelings.*
*D: Does it matter?*
*PRISONER: It does to them. We musn't disappoint them. The people you are watching . . .*

The Prisoner then tears off his mask and forces him to turn towards us, towards Number 2, who stares, wide-eyed in amazement, at his own face. Number 14 stifles a cry. Distraught, on the verge of collapse, Number 2 reels as he watches his double on the screen tottering down the steps.

As for the Prisoner, once again he pushes against the double doors, which open this time on a very familiar scene: that of the Village.

*NUMBER 14: He knew all the time. He was playing with you.*

On the screen the Prisoner now appears in his dark, white-trimmed jacket and with a malicious smile, addresses Number 2 in the laboratory.

*NUMBER 2: Your drug failed.*
*NUMBER 14: No. He succeeded.*

But her subject's dream – which has become Number 2's waking nightmare – is not over. On the screen the Prisoner now walks towards a metal door which opens before him leading to a gangway that takes him into the laboratory, where in his dream, he finds Number 2 and Number 14. In reality, these two cannot help glancing anxiously towards the real door, which remains firmly closed.

In the dream laboratory the Prisoner holds out an envelope to Number 2's double.

*PRISONER: I forgot to give you this. A bargain's a bargain.*
*NUMBER 2: Open it you fool, open it ... I must see the reason he resigned ...*

On the screen his double opens the envelope and takes out some illustrated holiday brochures for Italy and Greece ...

*NUMBER 14: He was going on holiday.*
*PRISONER: I wasn't selling out. That wasn't the reason I resigned.*

With these words the Prisoner's double on the screen lies down in the same position as his body in the real laboratory, closes his eyes and falls asleep, his secret intact.

Once more the screen goes dark. Then images from the scene of his resignation appear.

By the end of this 'optimistic' episode, even drugged, even in his dreams, the Prisoner has succeeded in preserving his secret, thereby safeguarding his integrity, and possibly his soul. Though still a captive of the Masters of the Village, he has nevertheless managed not only to resist them but also, by turning their experiment against them, to hold up to ridicule the sinister scientific manipulation of his mind.

The cosy status of the viewer as a consumer of escapist television has, meanwhile, been altered beyond recognition. For far from being escapist, what he is watching is designed to involve him in the world of *The Prisoner*. He is not soothed or amused; he begins to feel a nagging anxiety that, even on his side of the television screen, he is being drawn into the psychological maze.

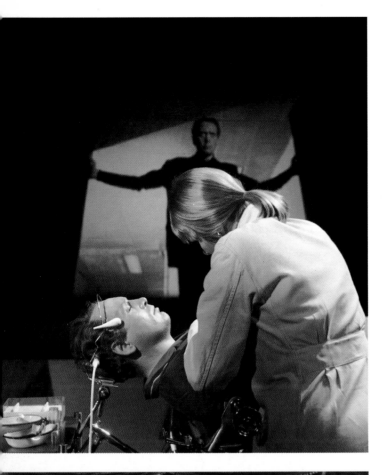

# Episode Four:
## Free for All

It is morning, another fine day in the Village.

While still struggling into his blazer, the Prisoner picks up the receiver of a phone marked number 6.

PRISONER: *What do you want?*
VOICE: *Number 6?*
PRISONER: *I said what do you want?*
VOICE: *You are Number 6.*
PRISONER: *That is the number of this place.*
VOICE: *Call from Number 2.*

As his voice comes over the receiver, Number 2's face appears on the screen of a television set.

NUMBER 2: *Good morning, good morning, any complaints?*
PRISONER: *Yes. I'd like to mind my own business.*
NUMBER 2: *So do we. Do you fancy a chat?*
PRISONER: *The mountain can come to Mahomet.*

No sooner has the Prisoner slammed down the receiver than the door to his house opens to let in Number 2, an affable smiling fellow in his fifties.

NUMBER 2: *Mahomet?*
PRISONER: *Everest, I presume?*

The conversation continues in this ironic vein until a shy young maid – whom Number 2 introduces to the Prisoner as having 'a wonderful gift . . . photographic memory, you know', although 'a mere Number 58' – serves breakfast.

Whilst the two men begin to eat, the suave voice on the Village radio informs them that the weather will be 'fine and dry' on yet another day to enjoy. This day, however, is not quite like any other, for Number 2 tells the Prisoner that this is the first day of the election campaign. In the face of his disbelief, Number 2 explains that the Village's inhabitants exercise their democratic vote every twelve months; he suggests that the Prisoner runs for election.

NUMBER 2: *I meant, run for office.*
PRISONER: *Whose?*
NUMBER 2: *Mine, for instance.*
PRISONER: *You have a delicate sense of humour.*
NUMBER 2: *Naturally. Humour is the very essence of a democratic society.*

But their conversation is suddenly interrupted by the sound of brass band music. Followed by the Prisoner, Number 2 goes to the balcony, where he waves to the joyous colourful throng of Villagers in the street. The Villagers cheer him enthusiastically, rhythmically raising and lowering their big multi-coloured umbrellas as they chant his number.

*PRISONER: It looks like a unanimous majority.*
*NUMBER 2: Exactly. That's what's worrying me. Very bad for morale. Some of these people don't seem to appreciate the value of free elections... they think it's a game.*
*PRISONER: Everyone votes for a dictator.*
*NUMBER 2: Not at all. It's just that their resistance is low. Frankly, my dear fellow, you are just the sort of candidate we need...*
*PRISONER: What happens if I run against you? I might as well while I'm waiting.*
*NUMBER 2: Delighted.*
*PRISONER: What physically happens if I win?*
*NUMBER 2: You're the boss.*
*PRISONER: Number 1 is the boss.*
*NUMBER 2: Join me... if you win Number 1 will no longer be a mystery to you...*

Number 2 leads the Prisoner to one of the litte mini-moke taxis that takes them to the Village's central square. They are followed by the crowd of enthusiastic Villagers in the grip of pre-election hysteria. The noisy colourful procession moving to the rhythm of deafening brass band music is in striking contrast with the silent diminutive figure, dressed in black and carrying a huge black-and-white umbrella, who brings up the rear. This is the mysterious butler whom we have already seen serving in the Green Dome and at the controls of a helicopter.

Speaking into a megaphone, Number 2 addresses the crowd gathered round the fountain in the square:

*NUMBER 2: Good people of our community...*

He is interrupted by frenzied applause. But we notice that the Villagers' 'spontaneous' cries are in fact being read from a cueboard held aloft by the butler.

*NUMBER 2: There is recently a lack of opposition in the matter of free elections. This is not good for our community and reflects an acceptance of things as they are. We know what we must do... What must we do?*
*CROWD: Progress, progress etc...*
*NUMBER 2: Exactly... we are however fortunate in having with us recent recruit, whose outlook is particularly militant and individualistic...*

Waiting until the 'spontaneous' applause has died away, the Prisoner then begins to speak:

*PRISONER: I am not a number... I am a person...*

He is unable to continue: the crowd's great burst of laughter drowns his voice. But examined one by one, the Villagers look as though they have stepped straight out of a Goya painting. There is no gaiety in their stupid, prematurely aged and distorted faces. Their vacant eyes show no light but only the unspeakable suffering of those who have irrevocably lost their souls...

*PRISONER: In some place, at some time, all of you held positions of a secret nature, and had knowledge that was invaluable to an enemy... Like me you are here to have that knowledge protected or extracted...*

*NUMBER 2: That's the stuff to give 'em.*
*PRISONER: Unlike me, many of you have accepted the situation of your imprisonment and will die here like rotten cabbages.*
*NUMBER 2: Keep going. They love it.*
*PRISONER: The rest of you have gone over to the side of our keepers. Which is which? How many of each? Who's standing beside you now? I intend to discover who are the Prisoners and who're the Warders . . . I shall be running for Office in this election.*
*NUMBER 2: Good people. Let us applaud a citizen of character. May the better man win and a big hand for Number 6. Be seeing you . . .*

The crowd, of course, at once duly obliges, cheering all the louder and brandishing placards with emblazoned Number 2's portrait. Suddenly, to his great astonishment, the Prisoner sees other placards raised behind these, placards bearing his own portrait and the words 'Vote for No. 6' in large letters.

From now on, the Prisoner, having become candidate Number 6 – he even wears a rosette with his number on it – plays an active part in the election campaign. Although he has freely chosen this role, he seems to find it very difficult to remain in control.

A taxi is placed at his disposal for the duration of the campaign; he soon realizes that the driver is nothing but a nuisance. She is in fact Number 58, the young maid who served him breakfast that same morning; still in her smart uniform, she dogs his heels. Completely stupid, she seems incapable of any response other than silly chuckles and mechanical cries of enthusiasm.

The Prisoner is summoned to the Town Hall to be present at the dissolution of the outgoing Council. On his way there in his open-top taxi, which carries a huge placard with his picture on it, he makes the acquaintance of the Village's Press.

With all the cheek typical of their profession, a journalist and a photographer jump onto the car as it is moving, one on the bonnet, the other at the rear.

*FIRST MAN: Congratulations.*
*NUMBER 2: Come again.*
*FIRST MAN: Allow me to introduce myself. I am Number 113 and this is my photographic colleague Number 113B.*
*NO. 113B: Smile . . .*
*FIRST MAN: We contribute to the local newspaper. The* Tally Ho *you know.*
*PRISONER: Drive on . . .*
*FIRST MAN: This is red hot stuff, you know. Haven't had a candidate of your calibre for ages.*
*PRISONER: Congratulations.*
*FIRST MAN: How are you going to handle your campaign?*
*PRISONER: No comment.*
*FIRST MAN: Intends to fight for freedom at all costs . . .*
*NO. 113B: Smile . . .*
*FIRST MAN: How about internal policy?*
*PRISONER: No comment.*
*FIRST MAN: Will tighten up on village security.*
*NO. 113B: Smile . . .*
*FIRST MAN: How about your external policy?*
*PRISONER: No comment.*
*FIRST MAN: Our exports will operate in every corner of the globe. How do you feel about life and death?*
*PRISONER: Mind your own business.*
*FIRST MAN: No comment.*

Having taken one last photograph, the supposed journalists jump off the taxi and no more than a few seconds later the Prisoner is stunned to discover the text of his interview already printed in the *Tally Ho* and on sale for all to read. Furious, he is on the verge of going away again, but the sudden appearance of Rover is enough to change his mind. He comes to the Council Chambers, an impressive underground room, which, as is often the case in the Village, seems to have been designed according to a 'different' geometry. He is welcomed by Number 2, who presides over a surprising assembly of Villagers in striped sailor-shirts and top hats. Behind him a large light in the shape of an eye flashes at the top of a strange pyramid, almost masonic in style.

*NUMBER 2: Good show, come ahead my dear fellow. You are formally welcomed to this gathering as the prospective Opposition candidate. Kindly approach the centre dais. Play the game.*
*PRISONER: According to Hoyle?*
*NUMBER 2: According to the laws of a Democratic society. These are designed for the protection of the citizens. You are a civilized man and would not, I'm sure, deny the right of proper Procedure. The final resolution of this outgoing Council is a vote of thanks to Number 6. It is carried unanimously and there is no further business at this time.*

The Prisoner then very politely requests permission to ask a question. Equally politely, permission is granted by Number 2.

*PRISONER: Where did you get this bunch of tailor's dummies?*
*NUMBER 2: They were here when I arrived. Do you wish to question them?*

The Prisoner says he does. Number 2 then presses a button and the central dais on which the Prisoner is standing begins to rotate. The blank-eyed faces of the Council members pass by before him.

*PRISONER: Who do you represent? Who elected you? To what race or country do you owe allegiance? Whose side are you on?*
*NUMBER 2: Mustn't get too personal, my dear fellow. Any further questions?*
*PRISONER: This farce... This twentieth-century Bastille that pretends to be a pocket Democracy ... Why don't you put us all into solitary confinement until you get what you're after and have done with it? Look at them. Brainwashed imbeciles... can you laugh? Can you cry? Can you think? Is this what they did to you? Is this how they tried to break you 'til they got what they were after? In your heads there must still be the remnants of the brain. In your hearts there must still be the desire to be a human being again.*

The Prisoner's face is then caught in a violent purple light emanating from the 'eye' situated behind Number 2. Simultaneously a bizarre whistling noise rents the air. His stand begins to spin faster and faster, and overcome with giddiness he sees the red walls of the Council Chambers revolving at fantastic speed. Then he is brutally catapulted on to a sloping gangway, flooded with a hallucinatory red light. We see him staggering about until he comes to a strange room. He collapses in a daze at the feet of a man in a suit whose appearance is both formal and disquieting. This is the new Director of the Labour Exchange. Having helped the Prisoner to his feet, he installs his guest, still in a state of shock, in something that looks rather like a dentist's chair. Very courteously he offers the Prisoner some tea, assuring him of his friendship.

But after a telephone conversation with Number 2, in which reference is made to a mysterious 'first stage only', this affable fellow unexpectedly changes into a ruthless operator, who subjects the Prisoner to a 'Truth Test' by means of an extraordinary lie-detector that reacts directly to the individual's thoughts.

The Director's subject is strapped into a kind of electric chair. We see the Prisoner's face contort in response to a series of powerful electric shocks. A silhouette of his body appears on a giant screen bathed in blue light. In response to the questions asked, a square and a circle move alternatively along two sides of a triangle that join at the apex, which is on a level with the victim's eyes. When the square and the circle meet, the Prisoner loses consciousness.

He undergoes a thorough brainwashing, and when he gets up a few moments later he evidently has no memory of the experiences; his sole concern is to find out whether his host will vote for him. With a stupid smile on his lips, the Prisoner takes his leave, thanking the Director kindly for the tea.

He is now a suitable candidate for the democratic game; the jubilant crowd of Villagers cheer him as he leaves the Town Hall.

He now gives with good grace glib answers to the journalist's stereotyped questions. Back at home he watches himself giving his speech on television – a speech that is wooden and lifeless.

PRISONER: *The Community can rest assured that their interests are very much my own and that anything I can do to maintain the security of the Citizens will be my primary objective. Be seeing you... Although you've only been here a short time my dear, there is only one thing to learn and it can be learnt very quickly... Obey the rules and we will take good care of you...*

But occasionally the effects of the brainwashing seem to weaken and flashes of lucidity break through his conditioned mind. Suddenly, his face twitching, he experiences with horror flashbacks of the incoherent remarks in some unknown foreign language of Number 58. The discovery of the rosette marked Number 6 pinned to his jacket brings his mental distress to a climax. He tears it off and takes flight at the wheel of his taxi.

The Prisoner is no longer the secret agent we knew, the man with nerves of steel; in his frantic attempt to escape he is confused, and in the grip of an almost animal-like panic.

He will not get far. A crowd of his joyous supporters block the road and he flees towards what still seems the only possible way out of the Village: the sea.

On the shore, he forces a motor boat from its occupants, and roars off in it at great speed towards the open sea. But the powers that be are not slow to react. A helicopter, piloted by Number 2, hovers over the fugitive's craft; Rover appears on the scene.

A few seconds later the Prisoner's face is being smothered beneath a white membrane.

Amid foaming waters, the Village's fearsome guardian returns to the seabed until the next orange alert and an ambulance takes the Prisoner to hospital. And when he emerges after treatment, or rather reprogramming, he resumes his campaign quite normally.

From the top of the stone boat in which, under normal circumstances, the inhabitants of the Village play at seafaring, he now addresses the crowd in a voice vibrant with enthusiasm:

*PRISONER: There are those who come in here and deny that we can supply every conceivable civilised amenity within our boundaries ... you can enjoy yourselves and you will ... you can partake of the most hazardous sports and you will. The price is cheap. All you have to do in exchange is give us information. You are then eligible for promotion to other spheres. Where do you desire to go? What has been your dream? I can supply it. Winter, Spring, Summer or Fall. They can all be yours at any time. Apply to me and it will be easier and better.*

After this brilliant flight of electoral rhetoric Number 2's more down-to-earth speech seems rather lacking in surprises. He contents himself merely with warning the voters against the empty promises of the Opposition and with stressing his opponent's lack of experience.

The Prisoner, addressing the increasingly large crowd of supporters from his buggy, now seems more inspired. He promises the Villagers more leisure if they vote for FREE, FOR ALL!

*PRISONER: Place your trust in the old regime. The qualities are divine, the future certain, the old regime forever ... the old Number 2 forever... Confusion by coercion is that what you want?... Vote for him and you'll have it ... Or ... stand firm upon this electoral platform and speak a word without fear ... the word is, Freedom ... They say six of one and half a dozen of the other, but not here... It's six for two and two for nothing, and six for free for all, for free for all. Vote, vote...*

That same evening the Prisoner's conditioning once again starts to show signs of weakening. His behaviour becomes incoherent: one minute, a stupid smile on his lips, he is mechanically repeating electoral slogans, the next he is alert, aware of the situation and angry.

At the Cat and Mouse nightclub, he creates a scene by violently refusing the choice, albeit a large one, of non-alcoholic drinks, all of which look and taste identical to their alcoholic namesakes, offered to him by the barmaid.

Number 58, his faithful and devoted assistant, still in her maid's uniform, takes him off to a secret place: a cave in the cliffs outside the Village, where, in a smoky atmosphere, a curious character presides over a still. The only other customer in this strange speak-easy is Number 2; already rather tipsy, he invites the Prisoner to have a drink with him. He reveals to the Prisoner that this extraordinary place, which he calls the 'Therapy Zone' is not under the surveillance of the Control Room. The Prisoner gladly accepts the alcohol he is served, but his behaviour is as bizarre as ever. Suddenly he starts shouting:

*PRISONER: Clever, aren't they...*
*NUMBER 2: They are... damned clever. Think of it. if you want to be an alcoholic, you can be one here in perfect privacy ... as long as you rejoin the flock in good time.*
*PRISONER: You don't approve?*
*NUMBER 2: Of the Village?*
*PRISONER: Yes.*
*NUMBER 2: Hell to the Village. Cheers.*

They continue to drink, to toast each other, to talk in slurred voices, like any two drinkers who chance to meet in the cosy atmosphere of a bar. Number 2 explains to the Prisoner that the man he saw presiding over the still is in fact a brilliant scientist and the formulaes and diagrams on a board at the far end of the room are photographed every week, then wiped out so that he can tackle another problem. The two men seem increasingly drunk. In a broken voice Number 2 hums the words of a drinking song. Suddenly the Prisoner falls to the ground. His drinking companion instantly stands up, quickly tidies his thinning hair and in a perfectly clear, commanding voice addresses the scientist, whose knowledge of chemistry has in fact been applied to drugging the Prisoner's drink. The scientist tells him that the dose was very precisely calculated 'to take him right through the election'.

On voting day the ballot box marked number 6 is overflowing with ballot papers, whilst that of Number 2 seems almost empty. The jubilant crowd chants the number of the winner: 6!

Playing the good loser, Number 2 then presents his successor to the people of the Village. Inexplicably, the cheering suddenly dies down, the brass band music stops, the faces of the crowd become frozen, the party seems to be well and truly over. And before the vacant, indifferent stares of the Villages, Number 2 leads the Prisoner, now wearing a rosette with the number 2 inscribed on it, and his faithful assistant, Number 58, still trailing after him, to the Green Dome. In the anteroom, he takes leave of them; oddly, he addresses the young woman in that strange foreign language of hers.

In Number 2's huge circular office one of the most insane scenes in the whole series now unfolds.

The Prisoner, far from his old self, and Number 58, as hysterically stupid as ever, suddenly begin to lark about like lunatics – or rather, like children left alone by their parents. Number 58 especially runs completely wild; giving little squeals of joy, she presses all the buttons on the control panel, making scenes of the Village appear, the disappear, on the giant screen. Chairs rise automatically out of the ground, then sink back again in some crazy routine. The Prisoner, still apparently in some kind of trance, plays more timidly with the telephones.

But the unreality of this completely crazy scene is abruptly swept aside by the intrusion of the malevolent reality of the Village.

The young woman's eyes which are shining with childish joy instantly turn into narrowed, ruthless slits. Her silly smile is no more than a memory; her face is now terribly serious. With a few precise and rapid movements, punctuated by some peculiar sounds, she brings the Prisoner out of the state of hypnosis in which he has been since leaving hospital. Violently, methodically, sadistically, she strikes him several times.

This treatment produces dramatic results: the Prisoner, no longer in a trance, rushes to the control panel. Frenetically he presses all the buttons, picks up all the cordless telephones and harangues the inhabitants of the Village, who appear one after the other on the control screen:


*PRISONER: This is our chance ... this is our chance, take it now. I have command. I will immobilise all electronic controls ... Listen to me ... you are free to go ... you are free to go ...*


His speech, which comes over the loud-speakers, meets with utter indifference from the Village's inhabitants, whose futile to-ing and fro-ing continues as though nothing were wrong.


*PRISONER: Free to go ... free to go ... You are free to go ... You are free free free to go ... I am in command, obey me and be free ... you are free to go ... you are free to go ... you are free to go ... free to go ...*

But he has failed to notice the appearance of two security guards in grey tunics standing on platforms that rise up from the floor. When he makes a dash for the door, it opens not on the Village and the prospect of freedom but onto a wierd cavern, the floor of which is strewn with straw. The unexpected, the sinister – the Prisoner's usual experience since his arrival in the Community – this time approaches the inconceivable. In the shadows at the back of the cavern four novices, wearing overalls and dark glasses, are seated, their arms folded, round the luminescent and palpitating mass of the Village Guardian. They give the impression of having been caught unawares, engaged in the bizarre worship of this monstrous entity.

The ominous characters all rush at the Prisoner and with sickening violence, assault him. They drag him into the circular room where they throw him onto a stretcher at the feet of the new Number 2, who is none other than Number 58.

The young woman, still in her maid's uniform, now wears a badge with the number 2 inscribed on it. Speaking this time in a language that is completely intelligible, with perfectly clear diction, she addresses the Prisoner in a severe and menacing tone:

*NEW NUMBER 2: Will you never learn … this is only the beginning … We have many ways and means but we don't wish to damage you permanently … Are you ready to talk?*

The Prisoner, his face swollen, his lips bleeding, makes no response; he merely looks at her blankly from the stretcher on which he is held down by the security men.

While he is taken back unconscious to his villa, the former Number 2, on the point of departure, calls the new Number 2 from the helicopter.

*NUMBER 2: Just on my way. Everything go according to plan?*
*NEW NUMBER 2: Don't worry. All will be satisfactory in the end. Give my regards to the homeland.*

This time the Prisoner's defeat is almost total. In the course of this pessimistic episode, in which he is the victim of one of the most elaborate schemes in the whole series, he experiences the *absolute* violence – aimed at destroying every level of his being – of an *absolute* power.

This key episode is one of the finest in the whole series, an episode which questions basic ideas about the democratic process. Does it really concern us all? Its impact on the viewer is enormous, prompting queries about the very nature of freedom.

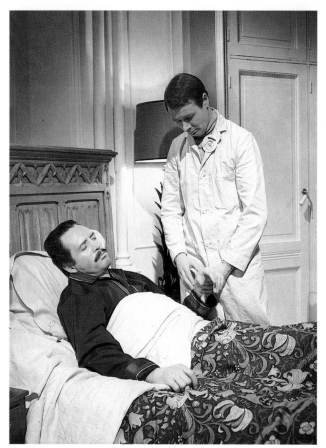

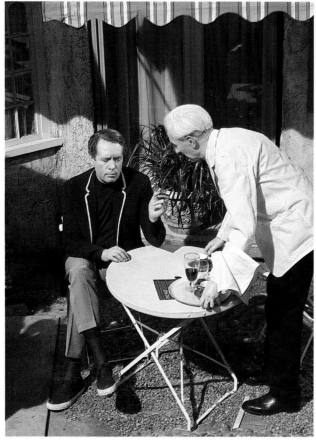

# Episode Five:
# The Schizoid Man

It is the evening of another 'lovely day'. For the Prisoner, the coming night will be less than lovely.

Right now, in House Number 6, the atmosphere is, for once, quite relaxed, even friendly. The Prisoner is with a young girl – she has a sensible intelligent face – and both are deeply involved in a telepathic experiment. In fact he is helping Alison (oddly, the girl, who wears a badge with the number 24 on it, has told him her name) to practise a mind-reading act that she intends to perform at the next Village Festival. She is using cards – the classic aid in this type of experiment – showing simple geometric shapes, on which the Prisoner is invited to concentrate; she then attempts to tell him which card he has in mind. She seems to have a gift for it, and gets a high proportion of them right. But she also explains her success on the grounds that they are 'simpatico'. The thought that the Prisoner's loneliness might be at an end crosses the viewer's mind. But not his! Though he appears friendly and indulgent towards young Alison, he does not go so far as to abandon his slightly distant attitude, and it is he who brings their evening to an end, on the grounds that it is getting late. However, he agrees to Alison's taking a few last photographs of him to enter in the Festival's photographic section.

But just before she presses the button on the camera, she clumsily knocks a heavy soda siphon onto her companion's hand. 'It's a mortal injury, wounded for life,' he kindly jokes in the face of her confusion. The small dark bruise at the base of the nail on his left index finger, caused by the knock, is visible on the polaroid snap; the Prisoner is unaware that this tiny injury will save more than his life. And he is equally unaware of what the night ahead, and the coming days, and the new Number 2 have in store for him . . .

Also visible on the photograph, very distinctly, is the date on his calendar: 10th February. This is the first time the viewer will encounter any temporal landmark; he would be wrong to set any great store by it. The same goes for the Prisoner, for whom this 10th February is going to seem endless.

When he falls asleep, having said a friendly good-night to Alison, it is the beginning of a long night's work for Number 2, and a long nightmare for the Prisoner.

Number 2, an undistinguished-looking man of about thirty, will direct against the Prisoner an amazing operation aimed at destroying his personality. And he will have considerable resources at his disposal to carry it out. We see, first of all, an alarming medical team acting under his orders.

The face of the sleeping Prisoner is on the screen in the Control Room; it is bathed at regular intervals by his face at regular intervals a dazzling light from above his bed. The apparent effect of these strange luminous pulsations is to make him sleep even more deeply, for he does not react when two men in white coats come into his room and give him an injection before carrying him out on a stretcher, scrupulously taking along his watch and his calendar. During the next stage of treatment, the Prisoner is subjected over and over again to powerful electric shocks intended to change his reflexes from those of a right-handed person into those of a left-hander.

Some time later, a man who bears a remarkable resemblance to the Prisoner wakes up in bed, judging by his look of alarm, an unfamiliar room. With its old-fashioned décor and furniture, it is totally different from the Prisoner's spartan, modern bedroom. The man, on the other hand, is his spitting image, except in a few minor details: his hair is dark instead of fair, and he has a thick moustache. His hairstyle too is different from that of the Prisoner. Only the date has not changed: beside the bed, a calendar still shows that it is Wednesday, 10th February.

Unnerved, the man whom we will assume to be the Prisoner raises his hands to his face and disbelieving feels 'his' moustache. He rushes to a mirror, where he earnestly examines his features. To his amazement he then finds hanging in the wardrobe a familiar-looking jacket – dark, with a light trim – to which is pinned a badge inscribed with the number 12. Just as he is beginning to show signs of panicking, he receives a telephone call from Number 2. Having greeted him in a friendly manner as 'Number 12', and asked him if he has slept well 'after your flight', he invites him over to the Green Dome.

When he goes out, he finds that 'his' house, which is not the Prisoner's, has the same number – 12. And all the inhabitants of the Village also address him as Number 12, and greet him with the ritual 'Be seeing you!'

On arrival at the Green Dome, he is very warmly welcomed by Number 2, who tells him that he has had to 'pull every string we could in order to get you seconded to us'. He is offered a sumptuous breakfast, and it becomes clear that not only is his physical appearance no longer entirely the same but that his behaviour too has changed, revealing different tastes. So that despite his state of confusion, he shows an excessive interest in food that is quite out of character. Abruptly giving way to temptation, he serves himself generously, having lifted the lids on the dishes with his left hand. He then asks, 'What's it all about?' In the same friendly tone, Number 2 answers his careful, hesitant questions.

*PRISONER: I'm sorry I didn't shave . . . couldn't find a razor.*
*NUMBER 2: My dear chap, I'm so sorry . . .*
*PRISONER: Must have been mislaid . . . strange apartment.*
*NUMBER 2: And after all that flying.*
*PRISONER: Yes.*
*NUMBER 2: You must feel a little disoriented.*
*PRISONER: What's it all about?*
*NUMBER 2: It's our prize prisoner. The one we call No. 6. Toughest case I've ever handled. I could crack him, of course. But I can't use the normal techniques. He's too valuable. Mustn't damage him permanently say our Masters. That's why I need you.*
*PRISONER: Why do you need me?*
*NUMBER 2: You bring two great gifts to bear. Firstly your ability as an agent.*
*PRISONER: Oh yes. Secondly.*
*NUMBER 2: You have a unique physical advantage.*
*PRISONER: Physical advantage of growing a moustache overnight?*
*NUMBER 2: No, not quite. You took longer that time in Bucharest.*
*PRISONER: Bucharest.*
*NUMBER 2: You remember how Susan hated you without it? She told me she wouldn't kiss you till you grew it again.*
*PRISONER: Good for Susan.*

Then while he examines a copy of the *Tally Ho* that 'happens' to be lying on Number 2's desk, and which bears the date of 10th February, Number 2 studies him with an air of satisfaction:

*NUMBER 2: You know, you really do bear a remarkable resemblance, remarkable ... Your job, Number 12, is to impersonate him. Take his sense of reality away. Once he begins to doubt his own identity, he'll crack ... What do you think of the idea?*
*PRISONER: I think it has fascinating possibilities, that we shall have an awful job convincing me that I am not your Number 6.*
*NUMBER 2: Ah excellent Number 12, of course. Always the professional. You've started living the part already eh? Oh that reminds me ... Allow me. You're now officially Number 6.*
*PRISONER: I shan't need this to remind me that I'm your Number 6.*

But apparently continuing to believe that he is joking, Number 2 retains his good humour and throws him a file at Number 6. The Prisoner catches it in the air with his left hand; Number 2 draws his attention to the fact that the Number 6 is right-handed.

A little later the Prisoner is placed in the hands of some pretty stylists who do a very professional job on the so-called Number 12, giving him the same physical appearance as Number 6, whose part he is supposed to play.

When they have finished with him, the man who comes back to Number 2 is indeed in every respect identical now to the Prisoner. His hair is once again fair, his moustache has disappeared and he has a side-parting. 'You'd hardly know yourself, would you, Number 12?' remarks Number 2, evidently very pleased with the result. He takes the Prisoner off to Villa Number 6, and he tells him to familiarise himself with the place before Number 6, who has gone out for a walk, gets back. Then he leaves him, giving him a password, 'Gemini'. This will be essential in order to identify himself once the experiment is under way.

A few seconds later a man in a white blazer with black edging wearing a badge inscribed with the number 6, comes in, whistling. He abruptly stops on seeing the Prisoner, his exact double. Indeed, not only is the resemblance in their build and features complete, but their bearing, mannerisms and the expressions on their faces are absolutely identical. And it is in the same voice as his, with the same intonation, that the Prisoner's double addresses his alter ego.

*DOUBLE: What the devil – oh very good, very good indeed. One of Number 2's little ideas, I suppose. Where'd they get you? A people copying service? or are you one of those double agents we hear so much about these days?*
*PRISONER: Seeing that you've gone to so much trouble the least I can do is offer you a drink.*
*DOUBLE: Scotch. I take it I'm supposed to go all fuzzy round the edges and run off into the distance screaming, Who am I?*
*PRISONER: Probably, no idea ... would you like some ice?*

The conversation continues for a while in this sparring vein. But what is actually taking place is a verbal duel, in which each of the two characters – the black and the white, the left-hander and the right-hander, the real and the fake – tries to counter his mirror-image, to catch him out on the smallest detail of everyday life. Tobacco, for instance. Each of them scores points: while the Prisoner is incapable of holding one of 'his' cigars in his right hand and coughs as soon as he starts to smoke it, his counterpart does not know how to light it properly.

The one we know to be the Prisoner does not in any case allow himself to be thrown off balance by this absurd situation and remains perfectly calm. And when his double in the white jacket suggests a duel with pistols, as a gentlemanly way of settling who is who, he readily agrees, confident of his ability (he claims to have an average of 90 percent) to expose the imposter once and for all.

But a little later, facing the targets in the Recreation Room, he is obliged, in order to prove to his adversary that he is himself, to shoot with his right hand. His double then very quickly proves to be a much better shot than himself.

DOUBLE: *Well, I certainly shoot more like me than you do...*
PRISONER: *What has all that proved?*

The whole scene is followed, on the screen in the Control Room, by Number 2 and the Supervisor, a man whom we see in this role for the first time.

The Prisoner's double then suggests fencing. But before crossing swords, the twin enemies briefly fight it out with quotations from *Hamlet*. This time they are on equal terms.

But the fencing duel proves a total disaster for the Prisoner, and his double, cruelly triumphant, sneeringly advises him to choose as his weapon in any subsequent duel 'battle axes in a very dark cellar'.

While persisting in his claim to be Number 6, the Prisoner is beginning to lose his composure and as the two men leave the Recreation Room he aggressively challenges his adversary to box.

The viewer sees his double's self-confidence take a slight dip. A doubt crosses his mind: could he have neglected some give-away detail?

The bare-fisted boxing match, as brief as it is violent, also ends in humiliating defeat for the Prisoner in his dark jacket. As he gets to his feet, to the sarcastic remarks of his counterpart in the white jacket, Rover appears on the scene:

DOUBLE: *Oh dear, looks as if we're in trouble with the headmaster. Must be confusing for it, not knowing which one of us to bite ... this way...*

But the massive, menacing white ball simply urges them in the direction of the Green Dome, by gently rolling along behind them.

As they enter the enormous circular room, two henchmen brutally seize the man in the white jacket, whilst Number 2 warmly welcomes the man in the black jacket, calling him Number 6.

This shift in perspective is a difficult one for the viewer; questions arise ...

The man in the white jacket is now subjected to interrogation in one of those pseudo-scientific psychological torture sessions in which the Masters of the Village excel. But he will not give in.

A strange patch of light wanders over his forehead. Gritting his teeth, sweat pouring from his forehead, he continues to shout out his identity as Number 6. Suddenly he collapses, unconscious.

PRISONER: *Your boy's dedicated to his work.*
NUMBER 2: *I told you he was a tough nut, Number 12.*
PRISONER: *Number 6. Number 6.*
NUMBER 2: *You're quite right, of course, careless of me. He might have heard.*

Then, addressing the man in the white jacket, who has come round but seems in a pretty bad way, still securely surrounded by his minders:

*NUMBER 2: You still insist you're Number 6?*
*DOUBLE: Yes...*

And while the two thugs drag him away, he says to the man in the dark jacket:

*NUMBER 2: Your mind can lie, but your body can't. You'll see. By the time we've finished with him, he won't know whether he's Number 6 or the cube root of infinity.*

Number 2 then decides to put the two claimants to Number 6's identity to the decisive test: fingerprints. This seems to prove that the man in the dark jacket is indeed the Prisoner, but these odd twins for once find themselves in agreement in disputing the result.

*DOUBLE: Very ingenious and scientific. But the trouble with science is that it can be perverted.*
*PRISONER: I'm inclined to agree, Number 2.*
*NUMBER 2: You agree?*
*PRISONER: I'm inclined to believe in human instinct.*
*NUMBER 2: How do you mean?*
*PRISONER: Well, I mean that, if I were in his shoes I'd rather be convinced by a human being, than by a piece of machinery.*

The Prisoner then suggests they try an experiment, with the assistance of Alison. He asks her over the phone if she would come and join them, and bring her cards. Having shown very understandable amazement on entering the room, at the sight of the extraordinary resemblance between the two men, she agrees to give them the mind-reading test. The mental rapport she has previously established with the Prisoner ought, in effect, to allow her to identify him once and for all.

The experiment ends in a real débâcle for the Prisoner in the black jacket, while the viewer feels increasingly disoriented, his mind oddly divided.

The triumphant man in white then draws from his pocket the photograph taken by Alison at the time of their practice session, saying that he could have proved his identity much earlier but it would 'hardly have been fair'. His double in black seizes it feverishly. But it is the young telepath who puts the finishing touch to the defeat of the man in black. The real Prisoner, according to Alison, has a little mole on his left wrist. There is a mole on the wrist of the man in white.

While the incontestable winner accompanies Alison out of the room with a casual 'Be seeing you!' Number 2 turns to the man in black, evidently peeved:

*NUMBER 2: What in heaven's name made you do a stupid thing like that ... Surely you must realise that Number 6 and that girl have got a genuine rapport. Someone's going to have to pay dearly for this ... Number 118. Why was there no mole on Number 12's left wrist? I said why was there no mole? Don't you realise you've jeopardised the whole operation ... report to me first thing in the morning. First thing...*

The next scene shows us the Prisoner lying fully dressed in his dark jacket on the bed where he woke up that same morning with dark hair and a moustache, in House Number 12. He seems to be in a deep but troubled, almost delirious sleep. In the nightmarish kaleidoscope of his mind, we see the distorted faces of Number 2, of Alison, of his double ... Amid their jeers, the

same phrases re-echo, like some litany, revealing his mental disintegration: 'Who are you?' 'Who are you?' 'He's the one! He's Number 6!' His hands are strangely clenched, one clutching the other, his arms move as though to defend himself. His body, seized with spasms and fitful shivering, has obviously retained the memory of the monstrous electric-shock conditioning he has undergone.

'He's cracking, Number 12, it won't be long now,' remarks Number 2, watching on the screen in the Control Room, to the man in the white jacket standing beside him.

The viewer suddenly feels completely reassured. The man in the dark jacket is indeed, and always has been, the only real Prisoner. But does the Prisoner himself know this?

After darkness has fallen, we see him emerging painfully from his hallucinated sleep, then sitting on his bed looking dazed. There seems little doubt that the Masters of the Village have won.

But suddenly his eyes happen to fall on the small bruise under his left index fingernail. The sight of this tiny dark-blue mark acts on his mind like a saving trigger. He feverishly searches his pocket for the photo taken by Alison at the end of their mind-reading session and compares his injury with the one in the picture. On his finger the bruise is now in the middle of his nail, which is proof in itself that several days have passed. So the date 10th February is bogus, so...

This tiny grain of reality is sufficient to thwart Number 2's incredible ploy. The spark of awareness that it ignites casts an enduring light in the Prisoner's mind, which had been invaded by the shadows of madness.

He stands in front of a mirror searching his face; the memory of the intervening days since the evening he spent with Alison resurface. Scenes of the cruel mental conditioning he has suffered superimpose themselves on his image in the glass as if in some incredible film, strangely reminiscent of the experience of the dying man who sees his whole life flash before him. The Prisoner relives at accelerated speed every stage of his 'mental death', before being reborn as a fully conscious individual – conscious in particular of having fallen into another of Number 2's traps.

Back to his old self, he will immediately try to extricate himself. He finds in the apartment material evidence of what his memories have revealed to him: doctored cigarettes, for instance, intended to reinforce the new likes and dislikes 'suggested' by the electric shock treatment. Then by subjecting himself, voluntarily this time, to a powerful electric shock, he contrives to cancel out the left-handed reflexes instilled by the treatment.

The Prisoner who leaves House Number 12 is once again a man in possession of all his physical and mental faculties; he is determined to track down his double.

He certainly seems to be causing Number 2 a lot of concern. Worried at not being able to get him to appear on the control screen, Number 2 raises the alarm. The Prisoner is waylaid by two guards who emerge from the shadows and challenge him to give the password. The Prisoner very quickly finds out that the one given to him by Number 2 – Gemini – is not the right one, and has to take on the two thugs.

His right-handed boxing skills work wonders this time, and he has no trouble in dealing with them. The Village streets seem very empty at night, but a little further on he has to hide behind a flowering shrub to escape the sinister Rover.

Having reached 'home' he finds his double lying on the bed in his bedroom, the sneer on his face momentarily wiping out all resemblance between them, the nerve-gas pistol that he trains on his visitor making it quite clear which side he is on.

The Prisoner then puts on a remarkable act, simulating the state he actually almost succumbed to just a little while before.

PRISONER: *I couldn't sleep, I came here ... who am I?*
DOUBLE: *You know who you are. You're Number 12.*
PRISONER: *Yes I'm Number 12. But sometimes in my dreams I'm, I'm somebody else.*
DOUBLE: *Who?*
PRISONER: *I don't know ... Sometimes in my dreams I resign my job.*
DOUBLE: *Why did you resign your job in your dream?*

The only response he receives is more incoherent remarks. Totally convinced of the success of the enterprise, he decides to inform Number 2. But just as he turns his head towards the telephone, the Prisoner jumps on him. To the effect of surprise is now added his adversary's perfect physical control, and after a short struggle he is rendered powerless. The Prisoner then forces him to reveal his name – Curtis – and, more important, the real password: *Schizoid Man.*

The double manages to break free, but on the threshold of the cottage these remarkable twins find themselves together once more in the path of Rover. They both give the password, fearfully repeating, 'Schizoid Man! Schizoid Man!' But the Prisoner's double, whose nerves seem less strong than his alter ego's, makes as if to run for it – a fatal move. Whether for this reason, or for some other reason that will remain unknown to us, Rover pounces on him and suffocates him to death.

While his terrified screams die out, the Prisoner, decides on the spur of the moment to take advantage of the situation. Imitating Curtis' voice, he telephones Number 2 and informs him of the death of Number 6. Putting on the now deceased Number 12's white jacket with the black trim, and the badge with the number 6 on it – he makes his way to the Green Dome.

He meets up with Number 2, who is shattered by the death of Number 6, a 'failure' that will now have to be reported. Despite one slight gaffe, the Prisoner manages, during their brief exchange, to allay his suspicion and he learns of Curtis's imminent departure – and therefore of his own. But first he is instructed to talk to Alison, since the mysterious Masters of the Village think she might have some insight into Number 6's motivation.

At Alison's house, he continues to play the role of Curtis, who is about to leave the Village. But their meeting is rather strained. Alison tries to explain to him that her relationship with Number 6 did not really allow her to read his mind, but nevertheless, she stares thoughtfully at him. The act put on by the bogus Number 12 evidently fails to dupe her intuitive spirit.

A little later we see the Prisoner packing his case or rather Curtis', whose civilian suit and tie he is now wearing, an outfit that makes him look slightly uncomfortable.

Number 2 personally drives the mini-moke that takes the Prisoner to the helicopter. The conversation on the way is very awkward for the Prisoner. Evasively he answers Number 2's questions about 'the job'; the embarrassed tone of his voice arouses the latter's mistrust and he too begins to look at the Prisoner thoughtfully:

NUMBER 2: *You are edgy. I've never know you quite so strung up.*
PRISONER: *You mean I'm not as I was.*
NUMBER 2: *Yes. I remember Susan saying only a month ago, that you were genuinely quite unflappable. You have changed ...*
PRISONER: *We all change. The job, it changes us.*

Number 2 does not seem very convinced by this generalisation. Finally they reach the helicopter that will fly the Prisoner to the landing strip where a jet will be waiting to pick him up.

At this point it seems reasonably certain that the Prisoner has succeeded in escaping; but given the knowledge we now have of the Village world, we are aware that nothing is certain.

Just as he is about to climb into the helicopter, the Prisoner catches sight of

Alison. The young girl, who has obviously been waiting for him, comes over. She looks him in the eye, and with a serious face says:

ALISON: *I'm ashamed of what I did to Number 6 yesterday.*
PRISONER: *Why are you telling me?*
ALISON: *Everyone has to tell someone.*
PRISONER: *It was your job.*
ALISON: *It was a betrayal.*
PRISONER: *Isn't everything we do here a betrayal?*
ALISON: *It's not often one gets a second chance.*
PRISONER: *There are no second chances.*
ALISON: *There are sometimes. For the lucky ones. If I had a second chance I want you to know that I wouldn't do it again...*

It becomes clear that Alison knows perfectly well who he is, but also that she will take this opportunity to remain silent.

Ready to leave, the Prisoner climbs into the helicopter, a black blindfold over his eyes in compliance with 'security regulations'. Just before take-off, Number 2 says with a smile:

NUMBER 2: *You won't forget to give Susan my regards, will you?*
PRISONER: *I won't, goodbye.*

The helicopter now flies over the Village. The Prisoner still blindfolded, his face turned to the sky, his whole being reaching out towards freedom, does not see it, any more than he sees the tall green trees turning as the helicopter wheels round, then returns to land exactly where it started. When he climbs out of the machine, two men grab him and tear off his blindfold. Number 2's smiling face greets his eyes:

NUMBER 2: *Susan died a year ago, Number 6.*

In this episode, the Prisoner is defeated but not crushed. He has failed in his escape-plan, but he has retained his integrity.

The Village's pseudo-scientists treat him like Pavlov's dog, planning his mental disintegration, and attempting to break his spirit; miraculously he remains himself.

The story itself is a maze which leads not only the Prisoner, but also the viewer into ever more convoluted traps, ensnaring both protagonist and audience.

# Episode Six:
# The General

On a beautiful summer's day a helicopter circles above the flowering gardens, the fountains, statues, ponds, and picturesque villas that make up the Village. With the exception of the Prisoner, not one of the Villagers sitting on the café terrace takes the slightest notice of the surveillance machine.

But he suddenly sees that he is *not* the only one taking an interest in it. His eyes meet those of a dark-haired, serious young man sitting alone at a nearby table. His eyes, oddly expressive for an inhabitant of the Village, are fixed on the Prisoner's; then suddenly he looks away.

On a poster stuck up on the wall, the honest and persuasive face of a middle-aged man with a penetrating gaze endorses a rather enigmatic statement: 'It can be done. Trust me.'

An announcement comes over the loud-speaker and suddenly the terrace, then the streets of the Village, empty of people.

*LOUDSPEAKER: Attention, ladies and gentlemen, attention. This is an announcement from the General's department. Will all students taking the Three Part History Course please return to their dwellings immediately. The Professor will be lecturing in approximately thirty minutes. I will repeat that . . . this is a special announcement . . . from the general's department. Repeat from the General. Will all students taking the Three Part History Course return to their dwellings immediately.*

On the terrace only a single customer now remains: the Prisoner. He orders another coffee from the white-haired old waiter:

*WAITER: Sorry sir we're closing. You did hear the announcement sir about the Professor?*
*PRISONER: I'm not one of his students.*
*WAITER: One coffee sir. Two credit units if you please. You're never too old to learn sir.*
*PRISONER: Who told you that? The Professor?*
*WAITER: No Sir. The General. Good luck with your exams sir.*

While the loud-speakers repeat the mysterious General's announcement, the Prisoner is rejoined by the serious young man whose badge reveals that he is Number 12. He stands in front of a far more explicit poster on which the same persuasive looking man this time asserts: '100% entry – 100% pass – Speedlearn: A 3-year course in 3 minutes. It can be done!'

*NUMBER 12: You don't believe it. A university level degree in three minutes.*
*PRISONER: It's improbable.*
*NUMBER 12: But not impossible.*

*PRISONER: Nothing's impossible in this place.*
*NUMBER 12: You should enrol Number 6. You'll find the Professor most interesting.*
*PRISONER: Really?*
*NUMBER 12: With an extraordinary range of knowledge.*
*PRISONER: The only subject I'm interested in is getting away from this place.*
*NUMBER 12: Exactly.*
*PRISONER: Who are you?*
*NUMBER 12: A cog in the machine.*
*PRISONER: Who's the General?*

They are interrupted by the more and more intrusive drone of the helicopter, to which is now added the familiar siren of a Village ambulance. We then discover the object of so much 'solicitude': on the beach a horde of Villagers are setting off in pursuit of an old man:

*PRISONER: Who are they after?*
*NUMBER 12: The Professor I think.*
*PRISONER: Why?*
*NUMBER 12: You know Professors. Absent-minded. Best of luck with your exams.*

Number 12 walks away and the Prisoner goes down to the beach. Meanwhile, in the Control Room, the disquieting bald-headed Supervisor – who, together with the butler, seems to be one of the Village's few regular main characters – follows the man-hunt on the giant screen. The orange alert is sounded.

On the beach the Prisoner suddenly trips on a half-buried object. Having picked it up and brushed the sand off, he realises that it is a small tape-recorder in perfect working order. The voice that emerges from it is none other than that of the mysterious Professor, sending out a solemn appeal to 'ladies and gentlemen, fellow Villagers, students'. But the Prisoner has no time to learn more; on the arrival of a security mini-moke, he switches off the machine and hastily hides it in the sand.

The two brawny guards in the mini-moke have not noticed his sleight of hand, but his presence in this lonely place, away from the crowd, arouses their suspicions. They do not greatly appreciate the sarcasm of his responses to their questioning, and when he tells them that he is 'playing truant' they firmly suggest taking him home so as not to 'start' the term with a black mark'. The muscles rippling under their striped shirts lend particular emphasis to their words.

Meanwhile, the pack of Villagers has caught up with the breathless Professor; unceremoniously they drag the old man back to the Village.

On returning home, the Prisoner finds his television set already switched on; on the screen an enthusiastic advertisement sings the praises of Speedlearn. The Prisoner settles down in front of the set with a tomato juice. The presenter is succeeded by a middle-aged woman. On behalf of her husband, the Professor, she apologises for delaying matters – he is just completing his lecture notes. She starts to give details of 'our future programme', but is rather breezily cut short by the presenter, who announces, after we have heard him answering the phone in an obsequious tone of voice, that the Professor is now ready to deliver his lecture. The kindly face of a middle-aged intellectual with a receding hairline appears on the screen. Having apologised for being late, he introduces Speedlearn:

*PROFESSOR: It is quite simply the most important most far-reaching, most beneficial development in mass education since the beginning of time. A marriage of Science and Mass Communication which results in the abolition of tedious and wasteful schooling.*

*A three years' course indelibly impressed on the mind in three minutes.
Impossible. That's what I said until I was introduced to the General. And
then I realised that not only was it possible but that Education was ready
for a giant leap forward from the Dark Ages into the twentieth and
twenty-first centuries. Ladies and gentlemen, I have been a teacher for
thirty years. Speedlearn has made me as obsolete as the Dodo.*

The presenter replaces the Professor on the screen and announces the
subject of the lecture: 'Europe since Napoleon', 'a hard, complicated six
months' study'. Students are then invited to relax and to watch the screen for
fifteen seconds. The Professor himself does not appear on the screen but a
picture of his face with the same sharp and penetrating look that is repro-
duced on the posters. The Prisoner, his half-full glass in his hand, appears to
be following this new kind of television programme with some interest. But
suddenly his gaze becomes oddly fixed. Without blinking, his eyes remain
riveted to the Professor's which seem to come nearer and from which there
now shines a strange, dilating dot of green light. The Prisoner drops his glass,
which rolls on the floor. The moment the jingle that precedes the official
announcements in the Village is broadcast he snaps out of this curious state
of hypnosis. On his television screen the presenter informs 'students' that the
fifteen seconds are over. The dazed Prisoner is wiping the carpet on which
the contents of his glass have spilled, when the door opens automatically and
he sees Number 2 enter, followed by one of his henchmen brandishing some
kind of metal detector. While the latter runs the detector over the walls of
every room, Number 2 – the neurotic milk-drinking apparatchik whom we
saw in the episode 'A, B and C' – explains to the Prisoner that he is looking for
a tape-recorder the Professor has 'lost'. He even goes so far as to offer the
Prisoner a deal: his freedom in exchange for the tape-recorder. All he gets is
an ironic reply, but just as he is about to leave he suddenly changes his mind
and starts firing questions at the Prisoner testing his knowledge of history.
Although the Prisoner tells him that history has never been his strong
subject, he responds instantly and mechanically to the questions put to him
equally mechanically by his strange examiner. He gives one date after
another: the Treaty of Adrianople, September 1829; the recognition of Greek
independence, 1830, and launches into an extraordinary patter about Bis-
marck, the Prince of Denmark, and Frederick of Austenburg, which he
delivers without drawing breath.

*PRISONER: . . . He realised that a successful war against the Danes in
1864 would serve the same purpose as Cavour of Italy's entrance into the
Crimean War.*

The test at this point becomes quite mad, with the Prisoner and Number 2,
apparently in a kind of trance, now chanting *in chorus*. When their reservoir
of 'knowledge' runs out, Number 2, concludes, as naturally as you please:

*NUMBER 2: Very good. Ten out of ten. Don't underestimate yourself,
Number 6, and don't underestimate me.*

As soon as he has gone, the Prisoner, aghast at what has happened, rushes
to the phone. Increasingly suspicious, he then asks the operator, *in exactly
the same order*, the questions that Number 2 has just put to him. And in the
same order come the same mechanical responses. Without waiting to get to

'Cavour of Italy's entrance into the Crimean War', he replaces the receiver in a fury, just as the loud-speakers announce fifteen minutes to curfew, and paces the room in that typical caged-animal manner of his, impatiently snapping his fingers. But a sudden inspiration seems to cross his mind. He dashes for the door, and heads for the beach, now in darkness. He scrabbles in the sand to no avail, but just as he realises that the tape-recorder has vanished from its hiding-place, he hears something that tells him he is not alone. He plunges into the bushes and hauls out the mysterious Number 12.

*PRISONER: Anything I can do for you?*
*NUMBER 12: You want to get out of this place don't you?*
*PRISONER: So?*
*NUMBER 12: Here's your passport. Number 2 offered you a deal, didn't he? Don't you trust him?*
*PRISONER: I don't trust Number 2, I don't trust you and I don't trust your tame professor.*
*NUMBER 12: Who do you trust, Number 6?*
*PRISONER: I trust me.*
*NUMBER 12: Join the club... Oh, what was the Treaty of Adrianople?*
*PRISONER: September 1829.*
*NUMBER 12: Wrong. I said what, not when. You need some special coaching.*

Alone on the beach once more, the Prisoner now listens to the Professor's voice on the tape-recorder Number 12 has given him.

*PROFESSOR: ... is the Professor speaking. I have an urgent message for you. You are being tricked. Speedlearn is an abomination. It is slavery. If you wish to be free there is only one way. Destroy the General. Learn this and learn it well. The General must be destroyed.*

The morning of the following day – a day just as sunny as the one before – finds the Villagers in a state of great excitement, busy checking each other's newly acquired knowledge of history as they drink their coffee on the terrace. Stereotyped questions, dates of battles and treaties are gaily exchanged to the accompaniment of a particularly lively tune played by the brass band. It seems as though every event in the Village turns into a festive occasion.

In the decidedly less convivial setting of the underground 'Board Room' with the disquieting pyramid structure and its luminous eye, a decidedly less jovial Number 2 is drinking milk and talking on the red telephone. He assures his mysterious interlocutor of the anticipated success of the experiment under way and of the total co-operation of the Professor once a couple of days' rest and 'adjustment' have helped him recover from his 'mild aberration'. In the next scene we see Number 2 in the Control Room watching the Professor on the screen absorbed in his work at his typewriter. The academic is suddenly interrupted by a doctor and a nurse in white coats, who come bursting in. Despite his protests, the nurse leads him away for some mild therapy. After his departure the doctor introduces the sheets of paper covered with the poor overworked Professor's notes into a machine, in which they are converted into a metallic-looking strip of perforated tape.

Number 2 then asks to be put through to the 'seminar', an art lesson conducted by the Professor's wife, which is taking place in the romantic setting of the gardens of the private residence where this apparently particularly privileged couple live. Among the art students he is surprised to see the Prisoner, who is applying himself to his drawing.

WIFE: *Can I help you?*
PRISONER: *I don't know. Can you?*
WIFE: *Finding things a bit strange?*
PRISONER: *That is the trouble. I can't find anything at all.*
WIFE: *What exactly are you looking for?*
PRISONER: *What are we all looking for?*
WIFE: *Well, let's see. That gentleman over there. What do you think he's doing?*
PRISONER: *Tearing up a book.*
WIFE: *He's creating a fresh concept. Construction arises out of the ashes of destruction. And that woman?*
PRISONER: *Standing on her head?*
WIFE: *She's developing new perspectives.*
PRISONER: *Really. Him?*
WIFE: *He's asleep. One learns only when the mind wants to. Not at set times.*
PRISONER: *Is that what your husband believes?*
WIFE: *It's self-evident, surely? What's your subject?*
PRISONER: *What's yours?*
WIFE: *Modern art.*
PRISONER: *Really? What do you think of this?*

He then turns his drawing round, to reveal a portrait of herself, the self-styled specialist in modern art. In this work, executed in an unabashedly realist style, her face is perfectly recognisable, despite the harsh expression and rather masculine features. She is dressed in a military uniform that looks remarkably like that of a general.

WIFE: *Not altogether flattering. So art's your subject too?*
PRISONER: *No, no ... Military history ... Generals and that kind of thing.*
WIFE: *I'm afraid you may be wasting your time.*
PRISONER: *What a pity ... I understood that your husband was quite an authority on the subject.*
WIFE: *He may be ...*

Then she tears up her 'portrait' in a fury:

WIFE: *... but I'm not.*
PRISONER: *Oh, creation out of destruction?*

The Prisoner leaves the garden and the Control Room's field of vision; the Supervisor's cameras are unable to follow him inside the Professor's sumptuous residence. Whilst he gazes with some perplexity at the disconcerting spectacle of statues veiled in white sheets standing in a huge and luxuriously furnished reception room, the far from friendly voice of the Professor's wife suddenly rings out, telling him that this is a private room. But the Prisoner seems much more concerned with his investigation and his attempt to discover the identity of the mysterious 'General' than with observing social graces. With scant courtesy he subjects his unwilling hostess to a real interrogation:

PRISONER: *The whole house is most elegant. Books, paintings and a very elegant garden.*
WIFE: *The Professor and I have certain privileges.*

*PRISONER: As prisoners? Or as warders?*
*WIFE: We came here voluntarily. We have everything we need. We're perfectly happy.*
*PRISONER: Doing what?*
*WIFE: My husband is a teacher. He teaches.*
*PRISONER: I see ... and you are the artist.*

While she reiterates, to no effect, her wish that he should leave the house, he starts to unveil one of the statutes.

The busts of some major historical characters are revealed. But if the Prisoner was hoping to uncover that of the mysterious 'General', he is greatly disappointed: one bust represents a former Number 2, the next, himself! Just as he is uncovering that of the present Number 2, the flesh-and-blood model for the study emerges from an adjoining room, in which we can see someone in a white coat.

*NUMBER 2: Really not a bad likeness is it? Are you playing truant?*
*PRISONER: Doing a little homework.*

The Professor's wife then tries to explain to Number 2 that she is in no way responsible for the presence of this undesirable visitor. Number 2 reassures her, with heavy irony directed at the Prisoner.

*NUMBER 2: You don't have to explain, my dear. Number 6 and I are old friends. I can recommend him as a thoroughly zealous student. With a tendency to overdo it.*

A doctor in a white coat enters from the Professor's bedroom, in which we see a nurse bustling round. The Prisoner grabs a heavy walking-stick which he holds in a strangely threatening manner, apparently at odds with his question:

*PRISONER: How's the Professor? Co-operating?*
*DOCTOR: I've given him some sedation.*
*PRISONER: Has he been overdoing it too?*
*DOCTOR: Probably a bit excited ... You know your husband, my dear. This Speedlearn. He's as enthusiastic as a child.*
*PRISONER: And sleeping like a babe.*
*DOCTOR: He's not to be disturbed.*
*PRISONER: I wouldn't dream of it.*

The Professor's wife begins to panic, then suddenly utters a cry of horror as the Prisoner, now standing by the bed in the Professor's room, raises the heavy cane and brings it down violently on her husband's face – which shatters into bits of plastic.

*PRISONER: You should take greater care of him Ma'am ... he's gone to pieces.*

As he walks off, Number 2 suddenly announces that he is withdrawing the offer he made with regard to the tape-recorder, since the Professor doesn't need it now. The Prisoner then retraces his steps, takes it out of his pocket and throws it at Number 2, saying that he doesn't either. Number 2, at a loss for words, catches it in the air, and the Prisoner makes for the door, not without scoring the final points in a 'game' that has gone entirely his way:

*PRISONER: Best of luck with your exams. Why don't you open the blinds and let in some daylight? You've got nothing to hide, have you?*

After his departure Number 2 deters the Doctor from alerting the Control Room.


*NUMBER 2: You do your job, I'll do mine. My dear, I'm afraid he's made a bit of a mess of your masterpiece.*
*WIFE: What does he want?*
*NUMBER 2: What some of us want ultimately. To escape.*
*WIFE: He persists about the General.*
*NUMBER 2: I shouldn't worry too much my dear. I have an obsession about him myself.*


These exchanges take place to the sound of one of the strangest musical themes in the series. The clay face of the Prisoner's bust fills the screen; we realise that the artist has given him a curiously tormented expression.

But we have no time to reflect on this; the scene is succeeded immediately by images of the jubilant Villagers celebrating the success of Speedlearn. It is after dark and the air is filled with the frenzied rhythms of syncopated music. The results – if we were to believe the television presenter, whom we see, microphone in hand, forcing his way through the riotous crowd waving placards in praise of Speedlearn – far exceed expectations. He quizzes some of the happy crowd, who remove their carnival masks for a moment to give one hundred percent correct answers to the presenter's questions. The Prisoner does not escape being interviewed on his way home and we hear him give the correct dates of the Boer War without a moments thought. But in the thick of the crowd his eyes meet again the serious and enigmatic gaze of young Number 12, the only other inhabitant of the Village who appears to have escaped this collective madness.

A little while later Number 12 joins the Prisoner at home. A power failure, which he claims as his work, puts them beyond the reach of the Control Room's surveillance for a brief moment. Number 12 makes a particularly interesting proposition: that of substituting for the Professor's next televised lecture the solemn and subversive warning on the tape-recorder. He gives the Prisoner a miniaturised version inside a cylinder like the barrel of a pen and a security pass that will allow him to get into the Board Room the following evening, when the next lecture is due to be broadcast.

Dawn comes, and the usual lovely day promises to be a big one, not only for Number 2 and his exciting experiment in mass education, but also for the Village's eternal spoilsport. This is to be one of the most outlandishly futuristic shows of the whole series.

But first, a short scene shows the Professor, this time the flesh-and-blood version, lying in bed with his wife. The Doctor is leaning over him with solicitude. According to the Doctor, the patient is now able and more importantly willing to complete his lectures.

While a particularly rousing march, a real parody of all the military music in the world, is played, the metal doors to the Control Room slide open to reveal a strange group of men, all dressed in black suits, long coats, top hats and sunglasses. Each of them has, tucked under his arm, a black briefcase. One after the other, at the command of a voice from a loud-speaker, they each state their position: 'Board Member, Lecture Approval Session. Education.' One after the other, they each introduce into a slot a pass disc on which is engraved the emblematic penny-farthing. An ingenious miniature hand in plastic then seizes it.

Then we see one of these men in black pass to Number 2, whom we recognise immediately despite his big dark glasses, a briefcase whose contents seem particularly precious: a few sheets of paper, which he glances through with an air of satisfaction, and a small cylinder containing the Professor's new lecture, miniaturised by means of some unknown technology.

Whilst preparations are made for the grandiose event and checks worthy of a space-launch from Cap Canaveral are carried out, one last man in black presents himself at the checkpoint. Beneath the top hat and behind the dark glasses, we recognise the impassive features of the Prisoner. Thanks to the pass disc supplied by Number 12, he manages to get through the electronic barrier and ends up alone in one of the many metal corridors of the Village's underground installations. This one is guarded by two men in the uniform of the Military Police. The series is rich in variations on the theme of security. Having neutralised the guards in a farcical scene which once again makes the henchmen of the Village Authority seem ridiculous, the Prisoner gets into the Projection Room. The projectionist is a little more difficult to overpower and the Prisoner's arm is slightly wounded in the fight. He quickly slips on the white coat of the technician lying unconscious on the floor, just in time for the control sceen to find him, in one of its final checks, at the controls of the projector. He then sets about replacing the miniaturised lecture with the alternative version, taken from his pocket. In the Council Room, Number 12 comments on the operation in progress:

NUMBER 12: ... thus the miniaturised course can be projected through the Sublimator at speeds thousands of times faster than the eye can record. It is imposed directly onto the cortex of the brain and is with occasional boosts virtually indelible. Tonight's lecture, for instance ...

But during a final check, Number 2 notices the blood running down the projectionist's arm. And a close-up on him enables Number 2, despite the dark glasses, to recognise the face of his eternal opponent. It is not long before two MPs, holding coshes, loom up behind him.

The Prisoner's failure is total; it is the Professor's 'official' lecture that is broadcast to the Village's 'students'. But though he may have lost a battle against the General, he has not yet lost the war ...

A little later we see him, still dressed in his white coat but with his left arm now in a sling, surrounded by Security guards, responding in his own fashion to interrogation by Number 2, who is assisted by Number 12:

NUMBER 12: Who were they, Number 6? Who let you in? What are their names? There's an organisation, isn't there? Dissidents. Who's the head man?
PRISONER: Santa Claus.
NUMBER 12: Who's the head of the organisation? You'd be wise to tell us.
NUMBER 2: He won't tell you anything. He's a trained conspirator. Very hard man. This reactionary drivel, which you were on the point of sending out to our conscientious students. The freedom to learn. The liberty of rare mistakes ... Old-fashioned slogans. You are an odd fellow, Number 6. Full of surprises.

But Number 2 is interrupted by the telephone and we hear him reassuring the Professor's wife. Having put down the receiver, he makes a few rather cynical remarks about that 'lovely woman ... She'd talk him into anything to keep him alive. Such is the course of true love.' Then he returns to the problem in hand.

NUMBER 2: I'm sure that a man of your calibre will appreciate that rebels ... that rebels must be kept under the closest possible surveillance with a view to their extinction if the rebellion is absolute.

But in order to eliminate them, you still have to know who they are. Unable to rely on the Prisoner's confession, Number 2 falls back on the mysterious General.

Some time later an odd group of men in disparate clothing (Number 2 and Number 12 in black suits, the Prisoner wearing a white coat and a sling, the others in MP uniform) come to a door on the other side of which we are at last going to find the famous General. But it opens to reveal the Professor in his study, working at his typewriter.

*NUMBER 2: Plato, Aristotle, Voltaire, Rousseau ... and the rest. They're all here. All available to the General. There is no question, no question from advanced mathematics to molecular structure ... from philosophy to crop spraying, which the General cannot answer.*

At this point some heavy curtains draw back automatically to reveal an astounding spectacle: a room in which a gigantic computer sits enthroned, at the end of an access ramp. With a theatrical gesture, Number 2 introduces this as the General, and launches into an enthusiastic paean of praise for this colossal invention:

*NUMBER 2: All the Professor's own work. He gave birth to it and loves it with a passionate love ... but probably hates it even more. That mass of circuits, my dear fellow, is as revolutionary as nuclear fission. No more wastage in schools. No more tedious learning by rote ... a brilliantly devised course, given by a leading teacher, subliminally learned and checked and corrected by an infallible authority and what have we got?*
*PRISONER: A row of cabbages.*
*NUMBER 2: Indeed. Knowledgeable cabbages.*
*PRISONER: What sort of knowledge?*
*NUMBER 2: For the time being past history will have to do ... but shortly we shall be making our own.*
*PRISONER: Napoleon could have used it ...*

But Number 2 forsakes the exciting prospects opened up to the human spirit by the General's existence in order to put to the giant computer a security question:

*NUMBER 2: Point one: a traitor in the Village. Point two: security pass discs were issued to Number 6. Point three: access to these is through ... through where? Through where?*
*NUMBER 12: Administration sir.*

The Prisoner suddenly claims to have a question that the General will be incapable of answering. Confident of the prodigious machine's infallibility, Number 2 takes up the challenge. The Prisoner then types out, with his good hand, the letters of his question. This is then transcribed onto a perforated strip of tape, which the Professor introduces into the computer, which starts to process the question, then the inconceivable happens!

The needle on one dial suddenly swings out of the 'Normal' zone and creep inexorably towards the 'Danger' zone, where it remains stuck. Alarming crackling sounds are heard and smoke starts to escape from the machine. Despite Number 2's shouted orders, the Professor fails to halt the malfunction. The smoke becomes blacker and blacker, and the poor scientist receives a lethal electric shock. Number 12, who rushes to his aid, is also killed. Finally, a terrific explosion signals the death of the General as well.

In a state of shock, a white-faced Number 2 pulls out of the charred and smoking wreckage the perforated tape, now all twisted and blackened, which carried the fatal question.

*NUMBER 2: What was your question?*
*PRISONER: W.H.Y. Question mark.*
*NUMBER 2: Why?*
*PRISONER: Why?*

Before the bars, the ritual signal marking the end of each episode, close on the Prisoner's face, a final scene shows him in the Professor's garden, going up to the grieving widow . . .

With his iconoclastic question, the Prisoner has not only destroyed the monstrous computer of the Masters of the Village, but like David, armed only with the sling and a single brilliant idea, he has also defeated the Goliath of the supposed omnipotence of computer technology.

But despite his resounding victory over the General, he is still a prisoner in the Village.

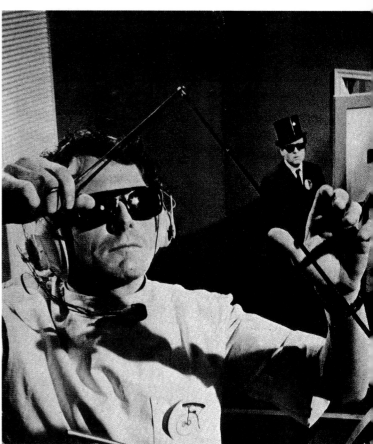

# Episode Seven:
## Many Happy Returns

On the morning of a day unlike any we have ever seen in the Village, no rousing music, no cheery voice comes over the loud-speakers to waken the Prisoner. In his bed, he looks at his watch in disbelief.

A few moments later, in his bathroom, he discovers that there is not the slightest trickle of water coming from the tap in the sink, or from the shower. He tries in vain to switch on his electric coffee-pot. The radio, like the telephone, remains persistently silent. And when he manually opens the door onto the street, the only sound he hears is that of the wind and of dead leaves swirling on the ground. The Village seems as deserted as it was on the morning of his arrival. But this time the bell that the Prisoner rings at the top of the tower awakens no one, and when he rushes to the café terrace it is only to find that no waitress has cleared the tables from the day before.

The raucous cry of the seagulls and the flapping of a coloured parasol, overturned by the wind, rolling on the ground make the silence and the still-ness reigning over the deserted village even more oppressive. A black cat with yellow eyes seems to be the only other inhabitant...

The Prisoner, now wide awake, soon realises what this apparent aban-donment means for him. Wisely, he first checks that the Green Dome is as empty as all the other buildings. Having with great difficulty prised open the metal doors that only the day before slid open automatically, he finds in Number 2's spherical chair nothing but a folding stick, an absurd relic of a formidable vanished power.

The Prisoner is in no position to linger at the scene and at once takes advantage of this gift of fate.

But when he tries first to leave the Village by road, the rutty dirt track that his mini-moke follows does not take him far: just to the end of a promontory, encircled by high mountains whose craggy peaks are lost in the clouds, sug-gesting that the Village is, perhaps, on an island. From this point he is able to survey the whole deserted settlement.

Axe in hand, the Prisoner, is already busy cutting down trees, the trunks of which he will use to build a raft.

The strange, often discordant music of the series has given way to smooth 'exotic' rhythms, evocative of the South Seas, of adventure, and escape which accompany all the Prisoner's strenuous preparations. After some time he is at last ready to leave. He has changed Number 6's jacket for a thick pullover and loaded the raft, rigged up with a rudimentary sail, with all the provisions and equipment necessary for his survival at sea – provisions and equipment 'borrowed' from the Village shop. With scrupulous honesty, and not without some irony, he leaves an IOU for 96 work units written in chalk on the counter, and signed *Number 6?*

Suddenly, just as he is on the point of setting sail, an alarming noise right behind him breaks the silence. He jumps but when he turns round, it is with relief that he sees the black cat staring at him with its yellow eyes from a garden table on which it is settled next to some bits of broken crockery.

Among the objects obtained 'on credit' is a camera, and before his depar-ture he records on film several souvenir snapshots of this amazing holiday resort.

Although no cheery voice announces it, the weather is fine. A breeze fills the black sail on the Prisoner's raft, which slowly heads for the open sea. But its occupant wastes no time watching the place where he has lived through so many nightmares disappear behind him. With elements taken from a radio he immediately sets about making the compass that will guide his voyage, apparently northwards. Then he carefully wraps up in a plastic bag the precious roll of film, now the only proof of the Village's existence. Finally, on the blank verso of a page from the *Tally Ho*, which he will use as a logbook, we see him write, not without some degree of emotion, 'Day 1'.

The beginning of the voyage is uneventful. The log gradually fills up: Day 5, 7 ... We are not surprised to note that the Prisoner is psychologically remarkably well-equipped to face situations of adversity: alone on the high seas, on his precarious raft, he takes the trouble to shave. The sea remains calm, but as the days go by fatigue proves itself his main enemy; more and more frequently he drops off to sleep only to awaken with a start a few seconds later. On the eighteenth day the solitary navigator's face is covered with an straggly beard, his features are drawn, his eyes unable to focus ... Finally he collapses.

Stretched out on his back, completely unconscious, he is unaware of the sound of an engine that comes up beside him at nightfall. When he manages weakly to open his eyes, he sees two men busy transferring his provisions onto a boat, to which they have fastened his raft. But he is too exhausted to react, even when the sinister sailors throw him into the water! We see his inert body floating face down, then disappearing as the boat leaves him behind. But it is difficult to believe that the man we have so often seen resisting the inhuman treatment doled out by the Masters of the Village is dead; we are not surprised to see him recover, surface, swim a few strokes and catch up with the boat. He manages to clamber aboard without attracting the attention of its dangerous crew, who are wordlessly sharing a stolen snack in the pilot's cabin, a predictably loutish look on their faces. An incessant stream of incomprehensible words from the ship's radio is drowned out by the noise of the engine. Then we see the stowaway, now in the hold, opening a box whose contents reveal to him that his looters are gunrunners.

His strength depleted, his clothes soaking wet, his hair dishevelled and plastered down with sea water, his face now bearded, the escaped Prisoner seems to have lost none of his reflexes of a trained combatant, nor, above all, any of the shrewdness of Number 6. Luring the pirates into a trap, by creating a cabin fire, he succeeds in taking control of the boat.

The few exclamations shouted in German by the two men in the course of these latter scenes suddenly make us realise that not a single word has been uttered since the beginning of the episode. This impresses upon us once again to what extent the incidental music – the beauty and effectiveness of which is brought out particularly strongly by the silence of the characters – is as much an essential element of the series as the images and the script.

Captained by the Prisoner, who changes its original course, the boat now forges ahead at full speed into the night. Suddenly, ahead of him, the beam from a lighthouse signals that the coast is near.

But, meanwhile, the pair of gunrunners have regained consciousness and succeed in freeing themselves. Now himself the victim of a surprise attack in the pilot's cabin, he has to confront them in a violent brawl. His attackers turn out to be formidable adversaries, yet he manages to keep them at bay, until one of the gangsters draws a gun on him. He is left with no alternative but to jump in the water, and we see him desperately swimming to escape the shots fired from the pirate boat. But no doubt unwilling to come any closer into shore, the boat eventually turns around and the fugitive finally reaches land unharmed.

Once again the Prisoner wakes up in strange surroundings. It is daylight, and he is stretched out on the pebbles of a deserted beach, waking from a deep sleep and opening his eyes to see screeching gulls circling in the sky above him. Obviously aching all over he stands up to find himself looking at the sheer cliffs of a wild coastline.

He takes care to check that his log and his roll of film, wrapped in plastic, have not suffered from being in the sea. Putting them back in his trouser pocket with an air of satisfaction, he starts to climb the sheer face of the cliff. From the top he can see a lighthouse from which he learns that the coast is not uninhabited. Indeed, it is not long before he meets someone: a swarthy man with a moustache and dark hair, leaning on a stick and holding a dog on a leash. For the first time since the beginning of the episode we hear the Prisoner's voice. He asks a simple question: 'Where is this?'

But he gets no response from the man with the fierce face, who rapidly walks off, looking back over his shoulder. The Prisoner, following him from a distance, sees him join a small gypsy encampment; an age-old distrust seems to be in the air. But it has to be admitted that the Prisoner, in his dirty clothes made shapeless by the sea water, with his beard and dishevelled hair, resembles a disreputable tramp more than the well-groomed agent who resigned from some British secret security or scientific service.

The gypsy camp is poverty-stricken. Beside a rusty caravan and a rather emaciated horse, three people – two men, including the one the Prisoner has followed here, and a woman – are gathered round a fire with a pot hanging over it. The woman proves to be a lot more hospitable than her companions. Warily keeping his distance, the Prisoner witnesses a brief but violent altercation between her and the man with the dog. Although we understand no more than the Prisoner of the guttural language in which she shouts, it is clear that she is reproaching him for his unfeeling attitude towards a man so obviously exhausted and hungry. Suddenly she goes over to the Prisoner holding a cup in her hand. He hesitates to accept it at first, but when she has added an explicit gesture to her words, raising her hand to her mouth, he grabs it and starts to drink the proffered brew.

This is one of the most overwhelming moments in the series, primarily because of the beauty of the images and the strange poetry of the scene, in which we see the silhouettes of the Prisoner, the emaciated horse and the gypsy woman outlined against the sky. But also because for the first time since his abduction, the fugitive from the Village experiences a genuinely human relationship. Perhaps too because the young gypsy woman has demonstrated, by standing up to her group, the same determination shown by Number 6.

Having thanked the young woman, the Prisoner asks her where the nearest road is. He does not understand her reply, but her extended arm seems to point him in the right direction. Later, some way on, the fugitive, now lost after crossing a deserted moor, cuts through a thicket in the hope of finding some landmark. A few metres ahead of him, outlined against the spring-green foliage, appears the amazing figure of a wonderful uniformed English bobby. Then we see a road with cars driving past on it. The escapee from the Village has succeeded: he is back in his own country!

But his troubles are not yet over and he quickly realises that there is a police roadblock below his vantage point. The voice coming over the radio in one of the police cars seems to be talking – this time in English – about a fugitive. Overcome with fear, he manages, after having rejoined the road a little way ahead, to jump onto the back of a moving lorry that has just been checked through the roadblock. With the aim of getting some sorely-needed sleep, he makes himself as comfortable as possible under some sacking in the otherwise empty trailer.

Some time later, he is suddenly jolted awake by the sound of a police siren. In a panic, he jumps out of the lorry and lands heavily on the ground. When he gets to his feet, he finds himself, dazed, in the thick of traffic in some big city. A red doubledecker bus just misses him. He is in London!

All he has to do now to get to his house at last is to walk across town. When we see him lifting the knocker of 1 Buckingham Place, having taken the precaution of checking out the vicinity, it seems like centuries ago that we saw the sinister undertaker climbing the steps behind him.

An elderly maid in uniform opens the door to him, regarding with an air of disapproval the far from smart clothes of the tramp standing on the doorstep.

*PRISONER: Who owns this house?*
*MAID: I beg your pardon?*
*PRISONER: I'm sorry. What I meant was, I'd like to see your master.*
*MAID: My mistress is not at home.*

He asks if he can wait inside, but her only response is to close the door in his face. Suddenly a familiar noise announces the arrival of his Lotus 7, which stops just outside his door. We recognise the licence number KAR 120C. A middle-aged woman with a slender sporty figure, dressed in an elegant trouser-suit and with her short hair under a cap, gets out of the car and goes into the house. Just as she is about to close the door, the Prisoner rushes up to her.

*PRISONER: What's the number of that car?*
*MRS BUTTERWORTH: Terribly interesting.*
*PRISONER: KAR 120C. What's the engine number?*
*MRS BUTTERWORTH: Do tell me.*
*PRISONER: 461034 TZ.*
*MRS BUTTERWORTH: Marvellous.*
*PRISONER: I know every nut and bolt and cog. I built it with my own hands.*
*MRS BUTTERWORTH: Then you're just the man I want to see. I'm having a good deal of overheating in traffic. Perhaps you'd care to advise me. Come in...*

Inside, the Prisoner finds himself in a very familiar setting – that in which we first saw him, a very long time ago now, packing his bags, but also that in which we have often see him pacing up and down, like a caged animal, in the Village house identified as number 6.

His hostess having left him alone for a few moments in the drawing room, the exile, home at last, examines all the familiar objects – objects doubly familiar in fact, since they are in every detail identical to those he has left behind in the Village with the exception of a wedding photograph of his hostess. When he picks up the telephone receiver, an exact replica of that in the Village, no operator asks him for his number, and when he draws back the curtains, what he sees are apartment and office blocks whose reassuring ugliness certainly do not belong in the harmonious, pretty landscape of the Village.

The new occupant of these premises pretends not to notice that her strange visitor is dressed like a tramp, and behaves like a perfect lady of the house. Having invited him to 'make yourself at home', she offers him a cup of tea, and she introduces herself as Mrs Butterworth. The Prisoner claims his name is Smith, Peter Smith. His hostess's warm welcome seems to have restored his equanimity somewhat, and it is in a much calmer tone of voice that he now tries to find out what exactly has happened.

*PRISONER: What's the date?*
*MRS BUTTERWORTH: Saturday, March the eighteenth.*
*PRISONER: Tomorrow's my birthday.*
*MRS BUTTERWORTH: You're an odd fellow.*
*PRISONER: Yes... you, er... must think I'm crazy.*
*MRS BUTTERWORTH: Who isn't these days?*
*PRISONER: You know, this er, was my house.*
*MRS BUTTERWORTH: Really... in better days.*
*PRISONER: Yes. Before I went away.*
*MRS BUTTERWORTH: You must miss it.*

All the agression has drained from 'Peter Smith', whose confusion Mrs Butterworth seems to find touching. A very natural confusion, considering that his home has for him become doubly synonomous with exile. The new occupant of the house readily answers his questions and tells him that she has signed a new ten-year lease on his former home, 'fully furnished'. Their conversation is interrupted by the arrival of the maid – the one we saw slamming the door in the 'tramp's' face – carrying a tea-tray. Mrs Butterworth kindly offers her guest a plate full of appetizing little sandwiches. Almost shyly, the Prisoner takes one and raises it to his mouth; the whole world fades away around the starving fugitive. A little later there is nothing but a few crumbs left on the plates. His hostess sits smiling at him, with a look of astonishment tinged with a certain tenderness, while he wipes his mouth, a little embarrassed, and tells her with genuine gratitude that it was 'the best fruit cake I ever tasted'.

His stomach assuaged, he is now able to return to his main preoccupation. Mrs Butterworth, who is more and more understanding, kindly agrees to show him the lease and the documents relating to the sale of the car. Although she has acquired the premises through an agency that he does not know of, everything seems to be in order. Apparently convinced of his hostess's good faith, the Prisoner apologises for his rudeness, thanks her and, not wanting to trouble her any more, is about to leave.

But the lonely widow – in the course of their conversation she reveals that her husband, Arthur, a Navy man, is now deceased – seems to have become attached to the man who has arrived on her doorstep from nowhere and in whom she now shows an obviously feminine interest. She offers not only to lend him some of her husband's clothes but also some money. Then, despite his polite protests, she invites her guest to use the bathroom on the first floor.

A little while later the Prisoner, not very elegant in the late Arthur's clothes, but clean and shaven at last, climbs behind the wheel of the Lotus 7 – his hostess has even lent him her own car. She wishes him luck, and as he switches on the ignition, cuts short his thanks.

*MRS BUTTERWORTH: No speeches... off you go. Don't forget to come back.*
*PRISONER: I'll be back.*
*MRS BUTTERWORTH: I might even bake you a birthday cake.*

We watch with some emotion as the Lotus, to the accompaniment of the programme's introductory theme music, follows a route that already seems almost mythical: the same one taken at the very beginning of the story by the main character on his way to resigning, the route the viewer ritually takes with him at the beginning of each new episode.

But, for now it is not the resolute man who comes through the door of his boss's office, where we have seen him so many times before furiously throwing down his letter of resignation. It is the weary survivor of an interminable nightmare whom we see contemplating with visible emotion the room where time seems to have stopped and where the same bald bespectacled official sits in front of the same map of the world pouring himself a cup of tea.

Later, elsewhere, in a comfortably furnished office with a balcony over-looking a garden, we find the Prisoner in the company of two men busy examining prints of his photographs of the Village.

The one called 'the Colonel' has a robust physique, a forceful face, and wears the casual clothes of a golfing type. The other one, by contrast, with thinning hair, in a suit and tie, looks like a self-important bureaucrat, almost as unpleasant as a Number 2.

They do not seem to take very seriously the account the Prisoner has just given them.

COLONEL: *Pretty spot . . . mixture of architecture. Italianate . . . Difficult. Certainly has a Mediterranean flavour. What do you think Thorpe?*
THORPE: *I think I wouldn't mind a fortnight's leave there. Prison for life, eh? It's a far cry from Sing Sing.*
PRISONER: *I'm sorry to interrupt a fortnight's golf, Colonel, but this is not a joking matter.*
COLONEL: *My dear fellow, you really mustn't blame Thorpe. After all, you yourself on occasion could be a little sceptical. That's why you were such a good man. Why we were so sorry to lose you.*
PRISONER: *The evidence is there.*
COLONEL: *A set of photographs from ground level of a holiday resort. And a school boy navigational log on the back of what you call the Village newspaper.*
PRISONER: *I'm sorry, it was the best I could do in the circumstances. You'd hardly expect the village store to issue sextants, would you?*
COLONEL: *Indeed, indeed. If the place is as you say it was. The* Tally Ho.
PRISONER: *A daily issue.*
COLONEL: *Morning or evening?*
PRISONER: *Daily at noon.*
COLONEL: *'What are the facts behind the Town Hall?' Town Hall?*
PRISONER: *That's right.*
COLONEL: *Town Council?*
PRISONER: *That's correct.*
COLONEL: *Were you a member?*
PRISONER: *I could have been. It's democratically elected once a year.*
COLONEL: *Democratically.*
PRISONER: *That's what they claim.*
COLONEL: *And they're all numbers. No names. No names at all?*
PRISONER: *Just numbers.*
COLONEL: *I see.*
PRISONER: *Numbers in a village that's a complete unit of our own society. A place to put people who can't be left around. People who know too much or too little. A place with many ways of breaking a man.*
THORPE: *Intriguing.*
PRISONER: *They have their own cinema, their own newspaper, their own television station. A credit card system, and if you're a good boy and cough up the secrets you are gracefully retired to the old people's home.*
COLONEL: *But no escape?*
PRISONER: *They also have a very impressive graveyard.*
THORPE: *Which you avoided.*
PRISONER: *The Village was deserted.*
THORPE: *Perhaps they were on the democratic annual outing.*

*PRISONER: The Town Hall. Number 2's residence. My house. The old people's home.*
*COLONEL: My dear fellow, you really mustn't get excited. You must forgive us. You see, we have a problem. Tell him our problem, Thorpe.*
*THORPE: You resign. You disappear. You return. You spin a yarn that Hans Christian Andersen would reject for a fairytale.*
*COLONEL: And we must be sure. People defect. An unhappy thought, but a fact of life. They defect, from one side to the other...*
*PRISONER: I also have a problem... I'm not sure which side runs this Village.*
*COLONEL: A mutual problem.*
*PRISONER: Which I'm going to solve.*
*COLONEL: Quite.*
*PRISONER: If not here, then elsewhere.*

Though the Prisoner's determination does not totally overcome the mistrust of his former colleagues, it does at least persuade the Colonel to check out his story. We see, in succession a plainclothes policeman sitting, notebook in hand, on Mrs Butterworth's sofa; then a bobby on a bicycle, prodding with his foot the embers of a fire at the gypsy encampment. In the end, apart from the pirate boat, which proves untraceable, all the facts confirm what the Prisoner has said. Incidentally, in the course of the enquiry, the Prisoner finds out that the roadblock on the way into London that caused him so much anxiety had been set up to catch an escaped convict.

His ex-colleagues, who are joined by two uniformed military officers, a Marine commander and an RAF Group Captain, are now seriously engaged in trying to locate the Village. While poring over maps, the commander questions the Prisoner on his sea voyage. Finally, thanks to his log, the information he is able to provide on the probable speed of his raft, wind direction, and the time he slept, and taking into account the position of the lighthouse (on the south coast of England), an area to be explored is demarcated on the map: the Village, perhaps situated on an island, ought to lie somewhere between the Moroccan coast and southern Portugal and Spain.

The next day, Sunday 19th March, is the Prisoner's birthday. It is also the first day of his exploration mission, in the company of the RAF Group Captain. We see him at dawn (a milkman is unloading a crate of bottles) at the airfield where a small two-seater reconnaissance plane awaits them, ready to take off. His ex-colleagues, Thorpe and the Colonel, have accompanied him.

*RAF GROUP CAPT: The clearance has just come through for refuelling in Gibraltar...*
*PRISONER: Good ... then we'll sweep as far as we can today, and again tomorrow...*
*COLONEL: ... and tomorrow and tomorrow ... you're a stubborn fellow, Number 6.*
*PRISONER: James, you call me that once again, and you're liable for a bout in hospital.*

The Prisoner, who is ready first, goes out to the plane, dressed in a flying suit, his flying helmet under his arm, obviously impatient to leave. Meanwhile we see the milkman enter the cloakroom where the RAF Colonel has almost finished changing. Then the Prisoner climbs into the plane, and the pilot, also in a flying suit, his flying helmet on, his oxygen mask already over his face, soon comes running out to join him.

Thorpe and the Colonel, standing by a hanger, follow the plane with their eyes.

*THORPE: Interesting fellow...*
*COLONEL: He's an old, old friend ... who never gives up...*

The two senior officials get into their car: a superb shiny black Rolls-Royce.

Later, much further away, the plane, which has been flying at low altitude for quite some time, follows a jagged coastline – edged by a deep-green sea – which could very well be that of an island. The Prisoner, who is acting as navigator, suddenly asks the pilot to fly a little lower. Like him, we would recognise the tiny built-up area they are flying over, anywhere. 'That's it, we've found it!' exclaims the Prisoner. At that very moment the pilot removes his oxygen mask. We discover with amazement that the face which turns to the navigator is not that of the RAF Group Captain but of the milkman! But we are given no time for further reflection. He suddenly pulls a lever and with a nasty smile on his lips shouts at the Prisoner: 'BE SEEING YOU!' We then realise that the lever controls an ejector seat.

While we watch his parachute open and come down, we too feel as though we have been brutally ejected from reality.

The reality the Prisoner finds, after a hard landing on the sand, is that of the Village, which is just as deserted as on the long-ago day of his departure on the raft, and where time seems strangely to have stood still. The black cat, which watches him with its yellow eyes while he crosses the beach after casting off his parachute, is in exactly the same spot, on the same garden table, beside the same pieces of broken crockery.

With steps made even heavier by his flying boots, the Prisoner walks up a street paved with grey stones at the end of which stands the Green Dome. We see him looking down with a gloomy face from the terrace of his residence onto the vexing spectacle of the abandoned Village's completely empty central square. Then he goes back inside his house. Instantaneously, inexplicably, everything starts working again all around him, as though a magic wand has been waved. A powerful jet of water runs in the shower, a light comes on, and the contents of the coffee-pot start to boil.

The woman whom we then see walk into the house, preceded by the black cat, is a real wicked fairy. She is Mrs Butterworth, wearing the same dress as when she was interviewed in London by the plainclothes policeman, and bringing him the birthday cake she promised him. But there is nothing friendly about her heavily ironic smile. There are six candles stuck into the cake. And most importantly, there is now pinned to her neat blue-and-white dress a badge against whose black background a penny-farthing and the figure 2 stand out in white.

*NUMBER 2: Many happy returns!*

While she puts down the cake, the Prisoner goes to the window and draws back the curtains. This time it is definitely the Village that he sees out there – the Village with all its insane gaiety restored, where coloured umbrellas twirl around the pond in the central square to the accompaniment of a joyful brass band. Prominent in the foreground is a huge black-and-white parasol under which stands the enigmatic butler.

The Prisoner's odyssey, so rich in imagery and adventure, has twisted round into a nightmarish Möbius strip: on one side the Village, and on the other side . . . the Village!

The malevolent omnipotence of its rulers has swept aside the Prisoner's new hope of escape, and at the same time scattered the jigsaw pieces which enabled the viewer to try and fit together some spatio-temporal landmarks. But the viewer's need for some logical thread to the series is eclipsed as he is drawn deeper into the web of the story, and into the Prisoner's nightmare.

# Episode Eight:
# Dance of the Dead

Once again, people in white coats come into the Prisoner's bedroom during the night. Once again, when he wakes up the next day, he will have no memory of this nightmare. For our part, we are not likely to forget the angular face and paranoid eyes of the 'doctor' who masterminds from the Control Room the 'scientific' experiment intended to break the resistance of the Prisoner. Nor are we likely to forget the physique – like that of a concentration-camp guard – of the nurse, bent over the unconscious man. Now he has a headband on his forehead, instead of electrodes...

We see him under the effect of a powerful electric shock suddenly sit bolt upright in bed, reacting to some powerful current or transmitted wave, and half-open his expressionless eyes. Then, with twitching lips, he is made to answer the telephone. A middle-aged man with a tired face, wearing the sailor-shirt 'uniform', is calling him from the Control Room. This man, who has evidently turned into a 'vegetable', obedient to the doctor's orders, introduces himself as Dutton, one of the Prisoner's former colleagues, and asks him, on behalf of some mysterious Committee, to disclose information about certain files.

But like all previous ploys, this one comes up against the impregnable mental barrier that protects the Prisoner's vital secret. His body convulsed by increasingly violent spasms, his face quivering, he suddenly shouts: 'Who is that? Who is that?' Then he falls back unconscious.

At this precise moment the experiment is interrupted by the unexpected arrival of Number 2: a small thin woman, no longer young, wearing trousers and a cap, whose bony face and dessicated body have lost all femininity. She seems to be the most sinister Number 2 yet seen in charge of the Village. More intelligent than most of her predecessors, she will also prove to be more authoritarian and above all more cruel.

*NUMBER 2: Stop ... get that man back to the hospital.*
*DOCTOR: Number 6 was about to talk.*
*NUMBER 2: Don't you believe it. He'd have died first. You'll never force it out of this man ... he's not like the others ...*
*DOCTOR: I would have made him talk. Every man has his breaking point.*
*NUMBER 2: I don't want him broken. He must be won over. It may seem a long process to your practical mind, but this man has a future with us ... There are other ways.*

Another day dawns on the Village; painfully the Prisoner emerges from his disturbed sleep. Never has the music issuing from the loudspeakers sounded so syrupy. And when he opens the door of his villa, the Village seems never to have looked more lovely in the sunshine ...

*SPEAKER: Good morning. It's another lovely day, so rise and shine. Life's for living.*

It is not the sun that appears on the Prisoner's television screen but the face of Number 2, installed in her spherical swivel-chair, sipping her morning coffee.

*PRISONER: How did I sleep?*
*MAID: Sound as a bell. Have a nice day. Feel free.*

The Prisoner exits without replying, closing the bathroom door behind him; she spins round in her chair. We then hear her, like all her predecessors, telling some mysterious person on the other end of the phone that there will be no trouble and that it is 'just a question of time'. She ends by saying that preparations are being made for the following evening.

The day promises to be even more glorious than usual. The new maid who brings the Prisoner his breakfast tray is wearing a magnificent low-cut dress that makes her look as though she has just stepped out of a Watteau painting.

Then the postman – an old man wearing a uniform cap whose antiquated penny-farthing we see outside the door – delivers some mail.

*OLD MAN: Special delivery . . . sign your number here, Number 6.*

We are not surprised to see the said Number 6 grab the letter and shut the door, completely ignoring his request. The letter is an invitation: 'The Village requests No. 6 to attend the Carnival and Dance.'

A little later we see the Prisoner observing, from the height of the imposing balcony overlooking the central square, the jubilant citizens on this, the eve of their Village Carnival. Loud brass band music fills the air and for once he is not alone: as he watches the colourful noisy spectacle he strokes a black cat. But suddenly another hand is laid on the cat's back. It belongs to Number 2.

*NUMBER 2: I see you've made a friend. You've got your invitation for the carnival tomorrow. It's one of our little traditions. Each year there's a fancy dress and a ball in the evening. We've promised a cabaret this year. You'll come.*
*PRISONER: I have a choice?*
*NUMBER 2: You do as you want.*
*PRISONER: As long as it's what you want.*
*NUMBER 2: As long as it's what the majority wants. We're democratic. In some ways.*

The Prisoner is urged by Number 2 to enjoy some female company for the Carnival. Called upon to choose from a trio of pretty girls sitting on the café terrace, he is clearly not attracted by their stereotyped beauty, or their forced gaiety, and he selects a young girl with a serious face, sitting apart on her own, whose beauty is more unconventional. But she seems nervous when he comes over to her.

*PRISONER: Don't go.*
*GIRL: I must.*
*PRISONER: There's a reason?*
*GIRL: Reason?*
*PRISONER: Number 2 wants you to go. Or does she? Am I playing her game or yours?*
*GIRL: Not mine.*
*PRISONER: Don't mind me. Go if you like. How long have you been here?*
*GIRL: Questions are a burden to others . . . answers a prison for oneself.*
*PRISONER: What did you do to have yourself brought here?*
*GIRL: Questions are a burden.*
*PRISONER: And answers are a prison to oneself.*

The young girl, who looks scared, stands up and brings their conversation to an abrupt end. The Prisoner tries to follow her through the Village's labyrinth of flower-lined paths, but he is deterred from doing so by Rover, who gently bounces along, exuding menace. A little way on, he rather violently comes up against the invisible force field preventing access to the Town Hall.

It is not very surprising to see the Prisoner's 'nice young lady' – who wears the number 240 – now in the position of Supervisor, in front of the screen in the Control Room with another woman. It is noticeable that in this episode the Village seems to have mobilised a predominantly female team against the Prisoner. We will even discover, some time later, that his only companion, the black cat, is in fact a she-cat.

The Prisoner gets home to find the animal outside his door. Inside, the maid, still in eighteenth-century costume, is dusting the furniture.

MAID: *Have a good walk? Where did you find it?*
PRISONER: *It found me.*
MAID: *You're not allowed animals. It's a rule.*
PRISONER: *Rules, to which I am not subject.*
MAID: *I'll take it with me.*
PRISONER: *You might get scratched. Where does it come from? How did it get here? The milk, the ice-cream. Potatoes and aspirins? At night? I've never seen a night ... I just sleep.*

Rebellion, which is always simmering in the Prisoner's mind, seems suddenly to flare up inside him. He puts a cushion against the television screen, which he knows is an observation monitor for the Green Dome. But an intolerable screeching sound reveals the pointlessness of his action. Then he explodes on seeing through the window some unwanted flowers that hide the stupid face of a delivery man.

PRISONER: *Supposing I don't want any flowers.*
FLOWER MAN: *Everybody has flowers. For carnival tomorrow. Be seeing you.*

At ten-thirty that evening, when curfew has passed, the presence of the cat seems to give him the idea of finally seeing nighttime in the Village. He does not have the hot, drugged drink brought to him by an elderly maid with a motherly voice, and he does not stay long beneath the lamp over his armchair, which intermittently lights up his face, while a soft distant voice murmurs:

VOICE: *Sleep, sleep, sleep ... that's it ... sleep softly until tomorrow ... lovely gentle sleep ... and a lovely tomorrow.*

Having realised that the door to his house is locked, no doubt for the whole night, he jumps from a window and lands, as agile as a cat. But he is not as free: in fact none of his movements has escaped the control screen of the 'nice young lady' he picked out for himself for the Carnival – the very young woman assigned by Number 2 to watch him night and day as his observer.

Immediately informed of the Prisoner's escape, Number 2 seems to attach very little importance to it. Having located him without any difficulty, as he runs headlong for the sea, she sends the Village 'guardian' after him. In a scene of strange beauty, we follow the parallel progress of the Prisoner and the monstrous white ball, the former running on the wet sand gleaming in the moonlight, the latter keeping up with him by rolling along the surface of the water. Their progress is accompanied by one of the finest and most characteristic pieces of theme music, into which Rover's equally characteristic whistling sound blends.

When the fugitive finally collapses, out of breath, we see the ball retreating away, recalled by Number 2, who now watches the Prisoner as he settles himself in the shelter of a cave.

*NUMBER 2: He'll eventually go back to his room. It's the only place he can ever go.*

She does not know the Prisoner; in fact it is not the syrupy Village voice that wakes him next morning in his room, but the raucous cry of the gulls on the beach.

When he gets up, rather dazed, he discovers a body washed up by the sea during the night. In the pockets of the deceased, a dark-haired man, he finds a wallet from which he extracts the photograph of an unknown man and woman and a small case containing an unusual miniature radio receiver which seems to be working.

The atmosphere meanwhile reigning in the Village is in striking contrast with the sombre scene of the deserted beach and the dark cave into which the Prisoner has dragged his macabre find. From the balcony overlooking the square, a town crier wearing a stock and a tricorn hat rings a bell, unrolls a parchment and addresses the crowd of Villagers:

*CRIER: A proclamation! All citizens take notice that Carnival is decreed for tonight. Turn back the clock. There will be music, dancing, happiness, all at the Carnival. By order.*

Never has the Villagers' explosion of joy been so noisy, never has the brass band music been so deafening, the enthusiasm so unbridled. But despite the noise, the exotic costumes, the lively music, the dancing, the faces glimpsed beneath the twirling coloured umbrellas remain oddly expressionless.

On his return home the Prisoner finds his maid waiting for him; she tells him that his outfit has arrived.

*PRISONER: Don't I get a choice?*
*MAID: Other people choose. It's a game.*
*PRISONER: I expected something exotic.*
*MAID: What is it?*
*PRISONER: My own suit. Specially delivered for the occasion.*
*MAID: What does that mean?*
*PRISONER: That I'm still myself.*
*MAID: Lucky you.*

As soon as she has gone away, the Prisoner examines the contents of the dead man's wallet, then tries to listen to the radio – unaware that he is being observed by Number 2 and the 'Doctor'.

*DOCTOR: What are we going to do with him?*
*NUMBER 2: There you go again. You mustn't be so eager, Doctor. Your techniques are efficient but not always beneficial. Number 6 will yet be of great value.*
*DOCTOR: He can't do as he likes.*
*NUMBER 2: He's an individual, and they're always trying. His observer will ring me the moment he puts a bomb in your lovely hospital. Incidentally, how's progress with Dutton?*
*DOCTOR: Well, he's given us quite a lot of information, but he's reluctant to go any further. I'm afraid I'll have to be extreme. Of course, I'll win in the end. I always do.*
*NUMBER 2: Rather a small fish, you know. Still, it'll give you an opportunity to experiment. After all, he is expendable.*

Meanwhile, the Prisoner leaves his house and finds an elevated look-out platform away from prying cameras. Sitting on a low wall overlooking the Village, he tries to pick up a transmission on the radio receiver. After a burst of static an enigmatic message comes across the airwaves.

*RADIO: Nowhere in the world is there more beauty than here. Tonight when the moon rises the whole world will turn to silver. Do you understand? It is important that you understand. I have a message for you. You must listen. The appointment cannot be fulfilled. Other things must be done tonight. If our torment is to end, if liberty is to be restored, we must grasp the nettle even thought it makes our hands bleed. Only through pain can tomorrow be assured.*

But the Prisoner's refuge turns out to be as illusory as all the others. He is suddenly obliged to change frequency as Number 2 comes onto the platform accompanied by his Observer, the young Number 240.

*NUMBER 2; Where did you get it?*
*RADIO: That practise dictation was at sixty words a minute.*
*NUMBER 2: Hardly useful. The view's lovely from here. I'm sad, Number 6. I thought you were beginning to . . .*
*PRISONER: Give in?*
*NUMBER 2: Be happy. Everything you want is here.*
*PRISONER: Everything's elsewhere.*
*NUMBER 2: Don't force me to take steps. We indulge any member of our community for a time. After that . . .*
*PRISONER: Yes I know. I've been to the hospital. I've seen.*
*NUMBER 2: You've only seen a fraction.*
*PRISONER: I know where you stand, don't I?*
*NUMBER 2: She's one of our best observers.*
*PRISONER: We have one each?*
*NUMBER 2: Only our more fractious children. Shall we go down? You're not thinking of jumping?*
*PRISONER: Never.*

The Prisoner, now standing on the wall looking out, does not move. As Number 2 goes off, taking the radio with her, the Prisoner approaches his 'guardian angel.'

*GIRL: I have my duty.*
*PRISONER: To whom?*
*GIRL: To everyone. It's the Rules. Of the people, by the people, for the people.*
*PRISONER: It takes on a new meaning.*
*GIRL: You're a wicked man.*
*PRISONER: Wicked?*
*GIRL: You have no values.*
*PRISONER: Different values.*
*GIRL: . . . You won't be helped.*
*PRISONER: Destroyed.*
*GIRL: You want to spoil things.*
*PRISONER: I won't be a goldfish in a bowl.*
*GIRL: I must go. I may see you later?*
*PRISONER: Can you avoid it?*

After this revealing exchange, the Prisoner returns his attention to his own affairs. He has succeeded in smuggling a lifebelt and a rope from the stone boat, and by cutting through the wood manages to get into the cave where he has hidden the body of the stranger. Meanwhile, in the Control Room, young Number 240 searches for him in vain on her screen. A little later the tide gently takes the corpse, tied to the life belt, out to sea. This macabre substitute for a bottle is carrying to the outside world the wallet, well protected in a plastic bag, into which the Prisoner has slipped a note and the photograph from his own identity card.

When he turns to face inland, he discovers that a man standing at the entrance to the cave has been watching the entire scene! The man is wearing the same striped shirt as on the night we first saw him, like a zombie, calling the Prisoner on the phone from the Control Room. In the light of day his tired face looks chalky, and there seems to be no strength left in his emaciated body.

DUTTON: You. You of all people. I'd never have believed it.
PRISONER: Roland Walter Dutton.
DUTTON: Who was he?
PRISONER: A body, it was washed up on the shore. How long have you been here?
DUTTON: You don't know?
PRISONER: Would I ask?
DUTTON: It's difficult to say. A couple of months. And you?
PRISONER: Quite recently.
DUTTON: How's London?
PRISONER: About the same.
DUTTON: Yes. Places don't change. Only people.
PRISONER: Some people.

The two men decide to continue their conversation inside the cave, where Dutton confesses to his ex-colleague that, under the pressure of the Village authorities, he has cracked and revealed all his secrets.

DUTTON: Everything I know. The irony of it is, they don't believe me. You know I didn't have access to the vital stuff. They'll take me back to hospital. And by the time they realise I'm telling the truth, it'll be too late.
PRISONER: When?
DUTTON: They released me for seventy-two hours. So that I can reconsider in the peaceful atmosphere of the Village.
PRISONER: There's still hope.
DUTTON: No, my friend. Not for me. Such noble thoughts are long dead. Soon Roland Walter Dutton will cease to exist.

It is nightfall, the wonderful night of Carnival. As a curtain-raiser to the festivities we see next one of the most beautiful and poetic scenes of the whole series.

At the far end of the vast beach stretching out at low tide before the Village, the dark silhouette of the Prisoner looking out to sea stands out against the sky in which a fading light still lingers. When he turns round, his contemplation disturbed by the sound of an all too familiar voice, we discover that he is in evening dress. The voice is that of Number 2, the figure the Prisoner walks towards is dressed as Peter Pan:

NUMBER 2: You're waiting for someone, Mr Tuxedo? Or expecting someone?
PRISONER: Mr Peter Pan.
NUMBER 2: So it seems.
PRISONER: With his shadow.
NUMBER 2: You're being hostile again. What were you looking at?
PRISONER: A light.
NUMBER 2: A star.
PRISONER: A boat.
NUMBER 2: An insect.
PRISONER: A plane.
NUMBER 2: A flying fish.

The Prisoner walks across the expanse of sand, which seems like the stage of some unearthly theatre. The two adversaries, now very close to each other, continue their strange conversation, their faces bathed in the peculiar light of the sunset.

PRISONER: *Somebody who belongs to my world.*
NUMBER 2: *This is your world. I am your world. If you insist on living a dream, you may be taken for mad.*
PRISONER: *I like my dream.*
NUMBER 2: *Then you are mad. Now go on up to the Town Hall.*
PRISONER: *May I...*
NUMBER 2: *You may enter tonight. It's Carnival.*

The Town Hall offers a dream-like spectacle on their arrival. But we are in the Village and the nightmare is never far away. The decorations are magical, the fancy dress costumes a dazzling sight, but a deathly silence reigns over the whole assembly and the guests turn their frozen faces and expressionless eyes towards Number 2 and the Prisoner.

But as soon as Number 2, her eyes gleaming with unnatural enthusiasm, gives the order, the celebrations begin. A hubbub of conversation rises from the now animated crowd, then an orchestra of musicians wearing stocks and powdered wigs starts to play a piece of baroque music. Number 2 offers the Prisoner a glass of champagne.

PRISONER: *I rarely drink.*
NUMBER 2: *Then you'll enjoy it all the more. Self-denial's a great sweetener of pleasure... Undoctored.*
PRISONER: *Why haven't I a costume?*
NUMBER 2: *Perhaps because you don't exist.*

At this point the Prisoner is joined by his Observer. Number 240 is dressed as Little Bo-Peep, an entirely suitable costume for someone whose role is not to let a single sheep escape. At Number 2's suggestion she leads the Prisoner onto the dance floor. We see the Doctor circulating among the guests, and his costume seems an equally apt choice: he is dressed as Napoleon.

Whilst they rather perfunctorily dance to the oddly syncopated rhythms of the eighteenth-century music, the Prisoner tries again to obtain some information from his lady companion.

PRISONER: *How many of these have you been to? This is my first and last.*
GIRL: *Don't be silly.*
PRISONER: *Who's saying that, you or the computer?*
GIRL: *Me.*
SUPERVISOR: *Don't stop... Dance.*
PRISONER: *Don't behave like a human being, it might just confuse people.*
GIRL: *Only you are confused. Though not for long. There are treatments for people like you.*
PRISONER: *She, she must get instructions. Who do they come from? Is he here tonight, the man behind the big door?*
GIRL: *There's no need to know. This place has been going for a long time.*
PRISONER: *Since the war? Before the war? Which war?*
GIRL: *A long time.*

At the end of the dance the Prisoner manages to leave the ballroom, apparently without attracting attention. In the cloakroom he grabs a white coat hanging on a hook and puts it on over his dinner jacket, with the obvious intention of taking advantage of the opportunity to explore the premises normally out of bounds.

He has just tried to open a few doors, without success, when a woman in a white coat, obviously mistaking him for a technician, hands him an urgent message for Number 2. He opens what looks very much like an invitation card to find three words written in white letters on a black background, sinister and enigmatic: *Roland Walter Dutton.*

But a door beside him suddenly opens automatically. He then walks through some imposing empty offices, whose lamps – which come on by themselves as soon as he enters the room – reveal functional furniture and rows of Village Administration filing cabinets. The graceful baroque strains from the ballroom have by now given way to the grating chords of some resolutely contemporary music.

The last room that he visits is different. When he unlocks the door with a key which he finds hanging up outside, he finds himself in a mortuary. In one of the drawers, he is amazed to discover the body from the beach – the one to whom he had given the job of delivering his message and his photograph to the outside world.

He has not got over his surprise when a voice at his elbow speaks. It is Number 2, still dressed as Peter Pan and accompanied by the black cat, which goes up to the Prisoner.

*NUMBER 2: She's taken to you. I'm jealous. Oh, she's mine. She works here too … She's very efficient. Almost ruthless.*
*PRISONER: Never trust a woman. Even the four-legged variety.*

Number 2 confirms the total failure of his attempt to communicate with the outside world. The contents of the wallet in the dead man's pocket have been amended slightly; it is now news of the Prisoner's death that he will carry. 'A small confirmation of a known fact,' concludes the malevolent Peter Pan, before inviting him to rejoin the festivities, where a cabaret awaits them – a cabaret in which the Prisoner is to take part.

It is in fact a staged trial in which he is to play the principal role, that of the accused, brought before an extraordinary court presided over by three 'judges' already familiar to us: the paranoid Doctor, the Village town crier, and the maid assigned to the Prisoner. Their costumes are variations on the theme of absolute power through the ages: Napoleon, Nero and Queen Elizabeth I. The absence of a jury suggests that this is a kind of revolutionary tribunal, reminiscent of the Reign of Terror. Number 2, as Peter Pan, and young Number 240, as Little Bo-Peep, are appointed Defender and Prosecutor respectively, the accused's crime being the possession and unlawful use of a radio set.

Behind the façade of this grotesque theatrical parody of a trial played out before the Village people, one of the most ruthless battles in the war between the Village and its sole opponent is to be waged. Behind the trivial crime for which he is being prosecuted lies another, infinitely more serious.

Towards the end, after young Bo-Peep has asked the Court to pass the severest possible sentence, the Defender, in her Peter Pan outfit, launches into a particularly ominous speech. Strange lights start to wheel around her …

*NUMBER 2: I would beg the court to remember that beneath its panoply of splendour, beneath the awful majesty of the Rules, beat human hearts. This is a human being, with weaknesses and failings of his kind. That he had a radio and has broken Rule after Rule cannot be denied.*
*PRISONER: Has anyone ever seen these Rules?*

*NUMBER 2: I plead, your Lordships, for clemency. He is new, and guilty of folly. No more. We can treat folly with kindness, knowing that soon his wild spirit will quieten and the foolishness will fall away to reveal a model citizen.*
*PRISONER: That day you'll never see.*

A few moments later, just as the 'judges' begin to confer before returning their verdict, the 'accused' plays what he thinks is an unexpected trump card. He asks the Court to allow him to call a character witness: Roland Walter Dutton.

*TOWN CRIER: No names are used here.*
*PRISONER: He's a man I think I knew. A man who is scheduled to die, and therefore better fitted than I to say the things that need to be said.*

Permission is granted. But the arrival of the 'witness', whom Number 2 leads in by the hand like a child, clinches the victory of the Prisoner's implacable enemy. The man, who wears a grotesque jester's costume, is living proof that Roland Walter Dutton has actually ceased to exist. With a stupid leer on his lips, he stares with vacant eyes at his ex-colleague and waves a stick at the end of which is attached a ridiculous white balloon, which cannot help but remind us of another . . .

Finally, the 'accused' is found guilty and the town crier, dressed as Caesar, delivers the sentence: death. The sentence is to be carried out 'in the name of the People, in the name of Justice'.

At this point, as often in the series, everything suddenly topples into madness, on this occasion a particularly grandiose form of madness. The Prisoner tries to run away. We see him first of all slowly moving through the crowd of silent spectators, frozen in total immobility. But suddenly the brightly coloured horde of Villagers in fancy dress go chasing after him with high-pitched squeals.

As though he is caught in some diabolical game of Snakes and Ladders, the Prisoner's flight will take him back to the morgue. But this place of death is no refuge, and in order to escape his pack of pursuers, whose cries are getting nearer, he drops through a trap door into the Village's secret underworld. A few seconds later he emerges in a strange corridor that gives the impression of being outside time: spaced at intervals along an amazing red carpet are rows of enigmatic busts. Finally a pair of double doors open onto a vast office, whose incongrously antique furniture seems to belong to a long-distant past. This extraordinary room could well be the headquarters of the Power ruling the Village.

Intrigued by a strange mechanised sound, the Prisoner discovers a very modern teleprinter in operation behind an antique screen. Just as he has managed to stop this crazy machine by furiously pulling out electric wires, people in shimmering costumes appear on the other side of a glass panel and through the door comes the ubiquitious Number 2, her inseparable shepherdess at her side.

*NUMBER 2: It's a one way mirror. They can't see you. They've never been in here and they never will. They lack your initiative. Deal with them . . .*
*PRISONER: Why are they trying to kill me?*
*NUMBER 2: They don't know you're already dead . . . locked up in the long box . . . in that little room . . .*

Then, as we see the young shepherdess walking away with a group of Villagers on the other side of the one-way mirror, she spitefully adds:

*NUMBER 2: She's no longer your observer. Observers of life should never get involved.*
*PRISONER: You'll never win.*
*NUMBER 2: Then how very uncomfortable for you, old chap.*

At this point inexplicably, insanely, the teleprinter, whose torn-out wires we see lying tangled on the floor, starts working again. Number 2 laughs dementedly as the strip of paper on which mysterious messages are printed out in short bursts starts feeding through.

When the ritual bars close on the Prisoner's face at the end of this predominantly noctural, subterranean and female episode, it is as though the gates of Hell have closed on him.

In fact never has his situation seemed so hopeless. He has not only been defeated by the ruthless power of the Masters of the Village, but, cut off from his own world, he has also been rejected by the entire community which for him now constitutes the world.

The main theme of this complex and enigmatic episode is death: the physical death of the man lying in the drawer in the morgue; the mental death of Roland Walter Dutton; the symbolic death of the Prisoner; but above all the death of desire, of love, of any joy in life.

# Episode Nine:
# Checkmate

If we were not already familiar with the world of the Village, the aerial view we get in the first shots of this episode would put us in mind of beauty, harmony, peace and happiness. But when the camera closes in on its narrow flower-lined streets, what we see is Rover on one of its sinister rounds. The sight of the enormous white ball bouncing silently on the ground, its whine replacing birdsong, is one which arouses nightmare associations.

As usual everything falls quiet and comes to a standstill as it passes: the quaint mini-mokes, the curious cyclists and the carefree strollers beneath their coloured umbrellas. The latter fearfully huddle together on the pavement in order to let the beast pass; they remain frozen in total immobility . . . with the exception, however, of two men.

The first, naturally, is the Prisoner, observing the scene from an elevated balcony. The second, who is much older and wears a blue jacket with white trim and the statutory boater, continues walking determinedly.

As the monstrous 'guard dog' moves away, the Prisoner, intrigued, sets off in pursuit of the man, who leads him to the central lawn where white boards are laid to create a magnificent giant chessboard, each alternate green 'square' being grass.

The old man with a stick then turns round to the Prisoner and asks him whether he plays chess. When the Prisoner says yes, the man, without any further explanation, leads him over to the game that is just about to begin. We then discover, along with the Prisoner, that the chess pieces are the Villagers themselves, who all wear multicoloured striped capes for the occasion. Moreover, each of them holds in his hand a wooden pole topped with the emblem corresponding to his position on the board. At this point a dark-haired young woman with a thin face and big expressive eyes, holding a crook with a crown on the top of it, comes over and tells him that she is the Queen and that he will be the Queen's Pawn. A few seconds later, each of the human chessmen having taking up position, the game begins before a crowd impatient to watch this new entertainment.

The living pieces have no more autonomy than they do in their everyday lives. The real players are two men perched on elevated platforms on either side of the board from where, with the aid of megaphones, they direct the movements of their respective pieces. One of them is the new Number 14 – the man with a stick whom the Prisoner followed; the other, a venerable old gentleman. The butler, dressed in a cape, bowler hat and black gloves, standing under his huge black-and-white umbrella, watches the game from the pavilion overlooking the lawn. He copies all the moves on a normal-sized chessboard set out on a table in front of him. The whole spectacle is followed on the control screen of the Supervisor, this time a grey-haired man in his fifties.

The gentleman playing against Number 14 seems to intrigue the Prisoner – now wearing the same multicoloured cape as the others, and holding a pawn's crook – and he asks his 'Queen', standing in an adjacent square, who he is. The Queen turns out to be more talkative than most of the Village inhabitants, and above all, favourably disposed towards him.

*QUEEN: I've heard rumours.*
*PRISONER: Such as?*
*QUEEN: That he's an ex-Count.*

*PRISONER: From?*
*QUEEN: Who knows? His ancestors are supposed to have played chess using their retainers. They say they were beheaded as they were wiped off the board.*
*PRISONER: Charming.*
*QUEEN: Don't worry ... it's not allowed here.*

But the Prisoner, taking advantage of the friendliness she shows towards him, quickly returns to his eternal preoccupation.

*PRISONER: Who is Number One?*
*QUEEN: It doesn't do to ask questions.*

The Queen's Pawn is undaunted, and while orders continue to issue from the megaphones and the human pieces pursue their colourful ballet on the chessboard, he returns to the attack:

*PRISONER: Why were you brought here?*
*QUEEN: That was a good move, wasn't it?*
*PRISONER: I know a better one.*
*QUEEN: Oh?*
*PRISONER: Away from this place.*
*QUEEN: That's impossible.*
*PRISONER: For chessmen ... not for me.*
*QUEEN: They told me there wasn't a hope.*
*PRISONER: I don't believe what they tell me ... you surprised?*
*QUEEN: Maybe I could help.*
*PRISONER: How?*

The Prisoner fails to hear the instruction that comes over the megaphone for the Queen's Pawn to move. The order is tirelessly repeated, then re-echoed in an ever more imperious tone by all the loud-speakers in the square, until the Prisoner is forced to comply and move to the new square assigned to him by the chessplayer. The Supervisor and Number 2 – a slim young man with dark hair, whose face with its charcoal eyes is that of the villain in a melo-drama – have been following the scene on the screen in the Control Room, but without hearing what is said.

*SUPERVISOR: Number 6 looks very placid.*
*NUMBER 2: He's just a pawn. One false move and he'll be wiped out.*
*SUPERVISOR: Not while the Queen's protecting him.*
*NUMBER 2: The Queen. She'll take no risks to help him.*

A little later an unexpected incident of scandalous proportions disrupts the smooth progress of the game. The Villager playing Queen's Rook – a middle-aged man with a receding hairline, whose striped shirt emphasises his plumpness – suddenly moves without being instructed to do so, and triumphantly places the King in check. His triumph is short-lived; the reaction from the Control Room is sharp:

*SUPERVISOR: Control room to hospital, control room to hospital, report to chessboard ... Call substitute, call the substitute, the substitute, the substitute, the substitute ... Remove White Queen's rook to hospital ...*

The arrival of the ambulance is as usual almost instantaneous, and it is not long before the rebellious chessman has left the game – on a stretcher. The Prisoner is concerned about what will happen to him, but the Queen tells him that 'he'll be well looked after' and that 'they'll get the best specialists to treat him'.
Shortly after, the game having resumed, the Queen suddenly finds herself on a square very close to that of the opposing King. From Number 14's

megaphone comes the ritual word announcing the end of the game: 'Checkmate!'

Having congratulated his pawn, the winning player then suggests that the Prisoner joins him in a stroll. The Prisoner accepts and the two men walk off together, one leaning on his stick, the other with his hands in his pockets.

*PRISONER: Sir, why do you use people?*
*CHESSPLAYER: The psychiatrists say it satisfies the desire for power. It's the only opportunity one gets here.*
*PRISONER: Depends which side you're on.*
*CHESSPLAYER: I'm on my side.*
*PRISONER: Aren't we all?*
*CHESSPLAYER: You must be new here. In time most of us join the enemy against ourselves.*
*PRISONER: Have you?*
*CHESSPLAYER: Let's talk about the game.*
*PRISONER: Alright, why do both sides look alike?*
*CHESSPLAYER: You mean, how do I know black from white? New men always ask that . . .*
*PRISONER: Well?*
*CHESSPLAYER: By their dispositions. By the moves they make. You soon know who's for or against you.*
*PRISONER: I don't follow you.*
*CHESSPLAYER: It's simply psychology, the way it is in life. You judge by attitude . . . people don't need uniforms.*
*PRISONER: Why complicate it?*
*CHESSPLAYER: It keeps the mind alert.*
*PRISONER: What use is that to you here?*

Were their conversation not so interesting their walk through the Village would be a distraction, for no other episode allows us to 'visit' to quite the same extent. Still talking, they find themselves outside the main shop, the kind of souvenir shop where you can find everything – except the really important things, such as a proper map . . .

*CHESSPLAYER: You were asking?*
*PRISONER: Yes, why you bother to keep your mind alert.*
*CHESSPLAYER: Now, through habit . . . just to defy them . . . I'm too old.*
*PRISONER: For what?*
*CHESSPLAYER: Escape.*
*PRISONER: You had a plan.*
*CHESSPLAYER: Everybody has a plan but they all fail.*
*PRISONER: Why?*
*CHESSPLAYER: It's like the game. You have to learn to distinguish the blacks from the whites.*

At that precise moment, marking a pause in their conversation, the metallic notes of a music-box drop into the silence, and we see a hand place a quaint little marionette made of varnished wood in the shop-window.

A little later the Prisoner, on his way home, notices that he is being followed by the Queen. When he turns and confronts her, she tells him that she is prepared to help him escape because 'I like you'. But he rather churlishly declines what is in any case a somewhat vague and unconvincing offer.

As the Prisoner leaves his villa the next morning, Number 2's mini-moke pulls up alongside him. He accepts the offer of a lift to the hospital to see the rebel Rook from the previous day's game undergoing a 'rehabilitation course'.

We then witness in their company one of the new experiments in mental therapy devised by the Village scientists, for whom Pavlov is evidently one of their main intellectual gurus.

123

Under the supervision of a psychiatrist in a white coat, a dessicated woman with an angular face, we see the 'patient', who, she explains, has been dehydrated. On waking up from an induced sleep he makes straight for a row of different coloured drink-dispensers. Crazed with thirst, he ignores the order not to touch them. When he presses the button on the yellow dispenser not a single drop comes out, and when he presses the button on the blue one he receives a powerful electric shock that hurls him to the ground.

PRISONER: *Don't tell me. It hurts you more than it hurts him.*
NUMBER 2: *In a society one must learn to conform.*

Meanwhile the experiment continues. The parched man must press the button on the blue dispenser if he wants to have a drink. We see him trembling, his whole body wavering between two tortures. Finally he overcomes his fear of the electric current and quenches his thirst, watched triumphantly by the psychiatrist.

PRISONER: *You must be proud of yourself.*
NUMBER 2: *We're proud of him. It's been a long struggle. From now on he'll be fully co-operative.*
PSYCHIATRIST: *I'm glad ... he's given me a lot of trouble.*

Clearly disgusted, the Prisoner obviously has no intention of listening to, or of watching, any more, and he heads for the door. But on his way he cannot help retorting:

PRISONER: *Your troubles are only just beginning.*
PSYCHIATRIST: *Is he in for treatment?*
NUMBER 2: *Not yet.*
PSYCHIATRIST: *Pity. I should like to know his breaking point.*
PRISONER: *Well, you could make that your life's ambition.*

As for the Prisoner, he has found an immediate objective in life! Profiting from what the man with the stick has told him, he undertakes to classify the inhabitants of the Village into two categories, the Whites and the Blacks – in other words, the Prisoners and the Guardians, with the more distant objective of placing in check those tirelessly attempting to transform him into a compliant 'pawn' on the squares of the diabolical chessboard to which they have confined his life. His technique is simple but effective: the Guardians arrogantly hold his gaze, whereas the Prisoners look away and lower their eyes – as does the rehabilitated Rook, on his release from hospital. The man, who wears a badge with the number 58 on it, initially runs away, scared at the Prisoner's approach. But the Prisoner runs after him, and eventually catches up with him on a terrace set high on the sheer rockface outside the Village. Prey at first to terror resulting from his recent conditioning, Number 58 gradually reveals his secrets, having already 'confessed it all before'. He is unable to tell the Prisoner whether he has been there a month, or a year, but what he does tell him is that he invented a new electronic defence system: 'I thought all nations should have it. It would have assured peace.' The Prisoner in turn confides that he needs someone who still has an independent mind.

Some time after, the two men resume their conversation on the sidelines of the giant chessboard, on which a game is in progress. The Prisoner then explains his tactics.

PRISONER: *You were intimidated without force ... by my manner you assumed I was a guardian.*
ROOK: *That's true.*
PRISONER: *By your manner I knew you were a prisoner ... subservient.*

Their sudden alliance does not fail to arouse the suspicions, first of the Supervisor, then of Number 2 who asks the Control Room to add sound to the picture on the screen. But the movement of a statue head swivelling round on its stone shoulders alerts the two men and Number 2 only hears them exchanging harmless comments on the chessgame. Nevertheless Number 2 takes the trouble to phone the psychiatrist to check that the rehabilitation treatment the Rook has undergone is totally reliable and decides there is no need to have them kept under surveillance. The stone face now pointing away from them once more, the two conspirators continue their conversation.

PRISONER: *The guardians pose as prisoners but non of them has been intimidated by me.*
ROOK: *They know you're a prisoner.*
PRISONER: *Yes. Only other prisoners would obey me.*
ROOK: *So you've found a way to identify them. So where does it get you?*
PRISONER: *It's the first step. No escape plan can succeed without knowing who we can rely on.*
ROOK: *What is the plan?*
PRISONER: *First things first ... let's find our reliable man.*

To the accompaniment of some jauntily ironic music, the two men then start combing the Village in search of real prisoners. The test based on the theory put forward by the man with the stick continues to work wonders. Those who respond arrogantly to their questions or orders reveal themselves unmistakeably, despite their appearance or their jobs, to be guardians, and therefore on the side of the Authorities: for instance, the gardener who tells them rudely that 'you'll have to wait a minute'. On the other hand, the house painter who at once offers to do the job again 'if it's not satisfactory' is a prisoner like them. So too is the shopkeeper who obsequiously agrees to an inspection of his books.

The meetings of the newly formed small group of conspirators attract the distrustful attentions of the Supervisor and Number 2 who, to be on the safe side, decides to bring the Prisoner in for psychiatric tests. But the patient's association of ideas, although they might in some instances be considered curious (for instance, the word 'free' prompts the response 'for all') gives, in the opinion of the psychiatrist, no cause for alarm. Other tests reveal 'positive signs of abnormality' – such as 'a total disregard for personal safety and a negative reaction to pain'.

NUMBER 2: *He wouldn't be able to fake that?*
PSYCHIATRIST: *I've never met a man who could. It would require super-human will-power.*

This brilliant scientist, Number 23, will soon show further evidence of creative thinking. We are familiar with the patient in the striped shirt who is now brought in in a wheelchair. But beneath her funny sunhat, the Queen's face is expressionless, her big black eyes strangely fixed. The psychiatrist then explains to Number 2 that in research carried out on dolphins, transistors were planted in their brains. Without going quite that far, the same principle may prove effective for their purposes. The patient is given an injection and placed in front of a screen on which the Prisoner's face appears.

PSYCHIATRIST: *You see the gentleman on the screen ... isn't he handsome? Isn't he manly? You love him passionately, devotedly. You would do anything for him, anything ... you would even betray him to save him from his own folly ... He loves you too. He has sent you this locket; you will wear it always, next to your heart ... you understand me?*

Then addressing herself to Number 2, she continues her description of her new experiment. The Queen will seek out the object of her manufactured passion, and if the Prisoner attempts to escape she will be frantic at the idea of losing him. The acceleration in her heart-beat, picked up by the transmitter hidden in the locket, will then alert the Control Room.

A little while later the young woman appears on the Supervisor's screen and demonstrates the effectiveness of this remarkable surveillance technique, reliant simply upon love! Beneath the badge pinned to her striped shirt, the Queen's heart does indeed begin to beat faster as soon as she sets eyes on her hero in the dark jacket with white trim. And when the Prisoner drives away from the Village in a buggy, she cannot help but follow him in another.

But at a crossroads she suddenly loses sight of the object of her love, who takes a sharp left turn, much to the annoyance of the Control Room, where the bleep transmitted by the Queen's lovesick heart slows down. To cap it all, the Rook, Number 58, with whom the Prisoner meets up, dismantles the external camera that the Supervisor is just about to employ to find the missing 'Prince Charming'. While a certain degree of panic reigns in front of the darkened sceen, and the Supervisor alerts the maintenance department, the real prisoners' conspiracy moves into a critical stage. Having made off with the camera, the Rook helps himself to a cordless telephone from a public kiosk, then steals some things from the toolbox of the engineer who turns up to replace the missing camera.

The two men take the precaution of splitting up before reaching the Village centre. Having advised his accomplice to 'get that stuff hidden' the Prisoner jumps out of the car just as his doting lover appears in her buggy – to the great relief of the Control Room, where images once again flash up on the giant screen.

In the car the Prisoner, who is obviously being given a lift by the romantically stricken driver, greets with coldness and above all with scepticism her passionate declaration of love.


PRISONER: *Love . . . you're crazy.*
QUEEN: *Yes – about you.*
PRISONER: *You don't even know me.*
QUEEN: *I know how I feel.*
PRISONER: *Who put you up to this?*
QUEEN: *Nobody . . . how can you doubt me?*
PRISONER: *It's easy . . . and I'm waterproof. A slight drizzle won't wash away my doubts. So don't try.*
QUEEN: *I only want to be near you.*
PRISONER: *Everybody's near in this place. Far too near.*


That evening, just before curfew, the hypnotised young woman's renewed charm offensive proves even less successful. On this occasion the Prisoner, at home in his dressing gown busy brushing his teeth, is surprised to hear the sound of someone cheerfully singing to herself in his kitchen, where he finds the Queen lovingly making him hot chocolate. Slightly amused, he initially accepts a cup, but quickly becomes irritated, and then downright angry.

The next day is a particularly glorious day in the Village, and a great many inhabitants go down to the beach to take advantage of the sunshine or to indulge in their usual childish seaside games – with the exception however of three, whose pursuits are decidedly more serious. The first is Number 2, who carries out his eternal round of inspection among the coloured tents pitched on the sand, his only concession to his surroundings being an impressive pair of dark glasses which give his face a distinctly sinister look. The second person is Number 58, who is wearing a bathrobe; Number 2 enquires after his health as he passes by, and advises him not to forget to take his pills and above all to go back to hospital immediately if he gets 'another attack of egotism'. The third is the Prisoner; his sombre dark jacket with white edging looks as out of place as his determined step among all the carefree bathers in swimming costumes.

For the conspirators this lovely sunny day is D Day, or rather E – Escape – Day. Well-concealed under one of the tents, the Prisoner and Number 58 are now busy checking an assortment of electrical equipment. But they still need a transistor for the radio the Rook is assembling, and his accomplice decides to go in search of one.

An opportunity presents itself to turn his admirer's crush on him to his advantage, and at the same time to 'disconnect' the Control Room. While climbing the rocky path from the beach, he literally stumbles upon his starry-eyed lover sitting nearby in a bathing costume, with a towel over her shoulders. With rather bad grace he agrees to sit down on a rock beside her for a moment. The Queen's sentiments remain unchanged, but too do the Prisoner's. But suddenly one sentence in her tedious amorous chatter catches his attention, and he becomes keenly interested in the locket with his photograph in it, which he supposedly gave her. When he opens it, sure enough he finds his portrait, but also some electronic micro-circuitry connected to a transistor. Having pocketed the locket with an air of satisfaction, he hastily abandons his besotted admirer, promising with a hypocritically charming smile to get her a much better picture of himself.

Meanwhile, in the Control Room, where the bleep has stopped, a certain anxiety reigns again. The Supervisor and the psychiatrist soon see the Queen on their screen without her locket, but they assume that she lost it in the water. Then a few seconds later they are reassured to see the Prisoner reappear, striding across the beach with his usual determination.

They are unaware that he is on his way to warn the others. Shortly afterwards, the message begins to circulate in some quarters of the Village: 'Tonight at moonset. Rook to Queen's Pawn six. Check.'

After nightfall the two conspirators, hidden in their tent on the deserted beach, finally manage to get an answer to the mayday call they have been sending out for some time on their makeshift transmitter. A ship, the *MS Polotska*, now seems to be heading towards what it believes to be an aeroplane in distress, its right engine in flames. Its task is complicated by the fact that its would-be occupants are obviously unable to give their position. The Prisoner conceals their ignorance by faking, with the help of some crumpled paper, the crackling sound of a fire that intermittently drowns out their message.

A little later the Prisoner leaves his accomplice, installed with his transmitter on an inflatable raft, to await the ship while he goes back to join the small group of other fugitives in the stone boat. Among them we recognise the man with the stick, the shopkeeper, the house painter . . .

The Prisoner and Number 58 are not the only ones to have received the *Polotska*'s response to their mayday call, and in the Control Room the Supervisor and his assistant try to locate the origin of the distress signal. It is not long before a searchlight sweeps across the stone boat. The Prisoner at once realises the danger, and orders his team to attack the watchtower. After a short but violent struggle, effectively scored with the dramatic music that accompanies most action scenes in the series, the coast is once more plunged into darkness.

In the Control Room the Supervisor judges the situation to be sufficiently alarming to disturb Number 2 in the middle of the night. Number 2 is not actually asleep. When the telephone rings, he is deep in meditation, wearing the white tunic of a judoka and sitting in the lotus position on the floor of his amazing circular office. Having given vent to his understandable annoyance, he resolves to take the situation in hand. But first of all this spectacular martial arts expert slices through a plank set up in front of him with a single chop, accompanied by the ritual karate cry.

Yet despite remarkable training, he will not be able to resist the small group of determined men, led by the Prisoner, who come bursting into the room. Number 2 is easily overpowered, but the fugitives' plot does not seem to be going according to plan. For some unknown reason the distress signal suddenly stops, and the Prisoner has to leave his companions in order to go and see what is happening on the beach. He finds the raft abandoned and the transmitter inexplicably silent. But just at that moment he notices the dark mass of a boat coming towards the coast.

A little later, having been taken on board, he asks to see the captain. But in the captain's cabin, a television screen suddenly comes on and the triumphant face of Number 2 appears!

*NUMBER 2: I hate to disappoint you, but the* Polotska *is our ship. The weather forecast is very bad, you wouldn't have stood a chance in that toy boat.*

At that moment the face of Number 58, who disappeared so mysteriously from the raft, appears on the screen next to Number 2.

*PRISONER: You're one of them.*
*ROOK: I'm not. You are.*
*PRISONER: As I was saying ... a slight misunderstanding.*
*ROOK: You deliberately tried to trap me.*
*PRISONER: I did what?*
*NUMBER 2: The mistake was yours. We can't have you maligning Number 6.*
*ROOK: You mean he really is a prisoner?*
*PRISONER: He released you.*
*NUMBER 2: You only have yourself to blame.*
*PRISONER: How'd you make that out?*
*NUMBER 2: I gather you avoided selecting guardians by detecting their subconscious arrogance. There was one thing you overlooked.*
*PRISONER: What was that?*
*NUMBER 2: Rook applied to you your own tests. When you took command of this little venture your air of authority convinced him that you were one of us.*
*PRISONER: And he convinced the others. What's happened to them?*
*NUMBER 2: They'll be back tomorrow on the chessboard ... as pawns ...*

The Prisoner's last-ditch stand will not get him far. Although he manages, after smashing the television in a fury, to gain control of the boat thanks to his fists, he quickly discovers that the controls are jammed and in any case an enormous white ball is rolling on the surface of the water towards him ...

The final shot shows us the black-gloved hand of the butler moving the White Queen's pawn into the square on his chessboard intended for the Prisoner.

This episode, in which for the first time the Prisoner does not appear as the only rebel, gives us a less pessimistic vision of the world of the Village.

His ultimate defeat seems all the more fraught with political significance for his world, the Village chessboard, but also for ours. His failure – a symbolic one – is that of all bids for collective freedom.

There remains to the Prisoner the individual course. But the episode also shows just how efficient the Authority's surveillance systems (technical and human) are and therefore how unlikely his escape. But perhaps the most vivid image in this episode is that of the human chess game.

# Episode Ten:
# Hammer into Anvil

It is not the harmonious baroque setting of the Village centre that appears at the beginning of this episode but the imposing medieval-style fortress containing the medical authorities' ultramodern, even futuristic, installations.

The new Number 2, wearing a dark blazer, is standing at the foot of a bed where a dark-haired young woman with bandaged wrists is lying. His interrogation does not only concern her health.

*NUMBER 2: Why did you slash your wrists 73? Aren't you happy here? You aren't being very co-operative, my dear...*
*NUMBER 73: There's nothing I can tell you.*
*NUMBER 2: Oh, come now... you must know where your husband is...*
*NUMBER 73: He's still over there.*
*NUMBER 2: Where?*
*NUMBER 73: Oh, somewhere there. He had work to finish.*
*NUMBER 2: Was he devoted to you?*
*NUMBER 73: He is devoted to me.*
*NUMBER 2: Oh, so you don't mind about him and the woman Maryka?*
*NUMBER 73: That's a lie.*

As he speaks, Number 2, a middle-aged man with thinning hair and every inch the bureaucrat – by far the most loathsome apparatchik we have so far seen in this position – takes a bundle of photographs from a briefcase held under his arm, and examines them with a sadistic smile.

*NUMBER 2: Stop protecting your husband's memory, 73. He went to her hotel several times... then there was the villa of course. Let me show you just how loyal your dear husband is to you. They look quite at home together... would you like to know the date, place, look...*

Holding back the tears with difficulty, the young woman turns her head away, her eyes closed, while Number 2 makes for the door:

*NUMBER 2: I've wasted enough time...*

But exasperated by her silence, he changes his mind and, his face full of menace, looks back at his victim, now staring at him in horror.

However absolute their power, the Village Authorities have at least one opponent: happening to pass beneath the hospital windows, the Prisoner hears young Number 73's screams of distress and barely seconds later he comes bursting into her room, not without having bumped into several individuals in white coats on the way. But he is too late to prevent the terrified woman from throwing herself out of the window.

The Prisoner observes for a moment in silence the body of the woman, finally free of her tormentors, lying on the ground, then he turns to Number 2.

*NUMBER 2: You shouldn't have interfered. Number 6. You'll pay for this.*

Never has the Prisoner's determination been so great as at this moment, as he looks into the eyes of the craven torturer standing before him.

*PRISONER: No, you will.*

Although by the very nature of their position rather despicable creatures, the previous Number 2s have often retained in the course of their duelling with the eternal Village rebel, some of the social graces from their previous life. A few have shown a certain sense of humour, even a touch of elegance. This is evidently not the case with the present occupant of the spherical chair, who has absolutely nothing of the gentleman about him. So in order to get the Prisoner to accept one of his 'invitations' to the Green Dome, he can think of no other means than sending four thugs after him in a buggy.

They catch up with him on a dirt track outside the Village and Number 2's 'guest', being so heavily outnumbered, is eventually overpowered. But he puts up a good fight and makes his aggressors pay dearly for their victory. At the end of a spectacular punch-up, he is unceremoniously thrown into the car, and a little while later literally dragged to a chair facing Number 2.

*NUMBER 2: You defied my instructions to come here! We have things to discuss.*
*PRISONER: About the girl you murdered.*
*NUMBER 2: Never mind the girl. I want to talk about you.*
*PRISONER: You're wasting your time. Many have tried.*
*NUMBER 2: Amateurs.*
*PRISONER: You're a professional. A professional sadist.*

Number 2's only response is to draw slowly from his swordstick a very fine blade, and with a smile that is indeed sadistic he brings the tip of it close to the Prisoner's eyes. Number 6 holds his gaze.

*NUMBER 2: Light blue, fearless … or are you? Each man has his breaking point you know. And you are no exception. Ah you react… Are you afraid of me? What is going on up there?*
*PRISONER: Disgust…*

Unable to contain himself, the disappointed sadist then violently strikes his adversary, then sits down in his chair, replacing the blade in its sheath.

*NUMBER 2: You think you're strong. Hmm, we'll see.* Du musst Ambose oder Hammer sein.
*PRISONER: You must be anvil or hammer.*
*NUMBER 2: I see you know your Goethe.*
*PRISONER: And you see me as the anvil.*
*NUMBER 2: Precisely. I am going to hammer you.*

It is in quite a different tone of voice that this unsavoury bureaucrat answers the telephone – the red one – which then rings.

*NUMBER 2: Number 2. Yes sir. Yes sir, everything's under control. No sir. No problems. Assistance? No no sir, I can manage. Yes sir, of course... be seeing you.*
*PRISONER: You were saying? Something about a hammer.*
*NUMBER 2: Get out.*
*PRISONER: Thank you very much.*
*NUMBER 2: I'll break you, Number 6.*
*PRISONER: Yes...*

After he has left Number 2 picks up the phone, a yellow one this time.

*NUMBER 2: Get me the Supervisor ... Supervisor, Number 2. Alert all posts. Special surveillance on Number 6. Report any unusual activity to me personally.*

Number 2 has every reason to be worried about the Prisoner, whom we now see walking away through the Village streets, thoughtfully rubbing his fists, bruised in the recent fight. It is not long before reports on his 'unusual activity' are flooding into the circular office in the Green Dome.

The first comes from the assistant in the Village shop, where the Prisoner listens to the six absolutely identical recordings in stock of Bizet's *L'Arlésienne* (none of which he buys), looking at his watch throughout, apparently in order to time something. But what? The zealous sales assistant wastes no time in taking the records to Number 2, who listens to the famous suite, six times over. But he is unable to answer this disturbing question.

To crown it all, the assistant produces a copy of the *Tally Ho* which the Prisoner apparently left behind in the shop, and on which he has circled the word 'security' in the headline, and drawn an enigmatic question mark over it.

The minute he is alone, Number 2 presses a button. His control screen then shows him the Prisoner sitting at his desk at home, writing. Then he sees the former secret agent fold a sheet of paper and put it in his blazer pocket, taking care to remove the second page from his writing pad, on which he knows that an imprint of his message might be visible to a professional eye.

A little later the Prisoner is sitting on the terrace of the nearby café. He has not long to wait before seeing a young man in a grey blazer slip into his house. His badge reveals his 'identity' to be that of (the new) Number 14, whom we have already seen driving the buggy full of Number 2's henchmen.

Deciphering the traces, imperceptible to the naked eye, left on the next sheet of paper in the writing pad stolen from Number 6's house is child's play for Number 2, who has some very refined equipment at his disposal. But the enigmatic message that he projects onto a screen – TO XO4 REF YOUR QUERY VIA BIZET RECORD. NO. 2'S INSTABILITY CONFIRMED. DETAILED REPORT FOLLOWS. D.6. – awakens his worst fears. Number 6 could very well be a plant detailed to spy on him.

Surveillance of Number 6, night and day, becomes Number 2's sole pre-occupation. Just after curfew that evening the supposed double agent leaves his house, carrying the envelope that Number 2, sitting in front of the control screen with his sidekick Number 14, has seen him pull out from under his bed where he had obviously hidden it.

Following him down the dark Village streets, the two men see the suspect enter the stone boat, only to emerge shortly afterwards without his envelope.

Back in his office, having rather abruptly dismissed his trusty assistant, Number 2 feverishly opens it. But the sheets of white paper that he takes out seem hopelessly blank, with no trace of any message. A man wearing badge number 263 on his white coat comes running in answer to his call, and is told to drop everything in order to examine the sheets in his laboratory. But the result the poor technician brings is not one designed to please his irascible superior.

*TECHNICIAN: I'm sorry sir but there's nothing.*
*NUMBER 2: Nothing? Nothing at all?*
*TECHNICIAN: No sir. They're just blank sheets of paper.*
*NUMBER 2: They can't be. Why should he hide blank sheets of paper in the stone boat? Or are you hiding something?*
*TECHNICIAN: What do you mean sir?*
*NUMBER 2: I mean, was there a message there and you're not telling me?*
*TECHNICIAN: Why should I do that sir?*
*NUMBER 2: Perhaps you're in with him.*
*TECHNICIAN: In with whom?*
*NUMBER 2: 6. Number 6. You don't know what I'm talking about. Get out.*

Without waiting to be told twice, the man in the white coat rushes for the sliding metal doors.

The next morning finds the Prisoner apparently in a very good mood placing an ad due to appear in the following day's issue of the *Tally Ho*. But the young newspaper employee seems to be having some difficulty in deciphering the text.

*GIRL:* Hay mas mal . . .
*PRISONER:* Hay mas mal en el aldea que se sueña.
*GIRL: Nine words. That'll be three units please sir.*
*PRISONER: Good.*
*GIRL: Spanish, isn't it?*
*PRISONER: Yes. Cervantes* – Don Quixote.
*GIRL: Oh yes.*
*PRISONER: Sort of a personal joke between myself and a certain friend.*
*GIRL: I see. That word* aldea. *Doesn't it mean village?*
*PRISONER: Yes.*

The Prisoner's days seem decidedly full. A moment later he is on the phone in a public callbox talking to the Director of the hospital's Psychiatrics Department. In a secretive tone of voice, he asks this important person about his report on Number 2! When the Doctor expresses total bafflement, he tells him that he is right not to want to talk about it on the telephone, and alluding to some future meeting, hangs up.

Shortly afterwards, the same eminent Doctor is expressing equal bafflement, but this time in the presence of Number 2, with whom he has to listen to a tape-recording of his conversation with his mysterious caller.

But the identity of the caller is no mystery to Number 2, who then wildly undertakes to prove to the bewildered psychiatrist – using an oscilloscope to identify the voice pattern, which, like fingerprints, cannot be disguised – that it was none other than Number 6. But as the demonstration goes on and he feverishly projects voice curves onto a screen, the doctor in the white coat starts to study him with increasingly professional interest.

*NUMBER 2: You aren't preparing a report on my ... mental health?*
*DIRECTOR: Of course not.*
*NUMBER 2: And Number 6 didn't see you later?*
*DIRECTOR: No.*
*NUMBER 2: Then why did he ring you?*
*DIRECTOR: I told you I don't know.*
*NUMBER 2: You're a psychiatrist, aren't you? Would you say that Number 6 was mad?*
*DIRECTOR: Not according to our records.*
*NUMBER 2: Then he had a reason for telephoning you, didn't he? What was it?*
*DIRECTOR: Why don't you ask him?*
*NUMBER 2: Would you like to sit in this chair?*
*DIRECTOR: I was merely suggesting...*
*NUMBER 2: Don't tell me what to do. You can go.*
*DIRECTOR: Thank you.*

The next Villager to be subjected to interrogation is the leader of the band, who has received a request from the Prisoner to play the Farandole from the *L'Arlésienne*. Number 2 does not understand why the man he is ever more convinced is a double agent determined to bring about his downfall simply walked away without listening to a single note. Of course the unfortunate musician cannot explain this either, least of all to his inquisitor, whose questions become heavier and heavier with menace. The interview ends with an explosion of paranoia far greater than previous instances.

The person responsible for all this ranting and raving is in the cemetry, standing at a grave bearing the number 73, where someone has laid a bunch of daffodils. As he leaves, the Prisoner notices another freshly dug grave, in which a former Number 113 lies.

A little later the Supervisor delivers a 'personal message' broadcast with scant discretion over all the loud-speakers, from Number 113 to Number 6.

*SUPERVISOR: Warmest greetings on your birthday. May the sun shine on you today and every day. And that concludes the personal messages. We continue with music...*

These posthumous good wishes do not pass unnoticed. Whilst we see Number 6 listening to the announcement with an air of satisfaction, Number 2 is enraged by it. In no time he comes bursting into the Control Room. Called upon to explain the broadcasting of an obviously coded message – the old lady who was Number 113 died a month ago, and it is not Number 6's birthday – the Supervisor is as powerless as his colleagues to calm his superior. Number 2, now screaming like a madman from the metal gallery that looks down on the impressive surveillance installations, relieves the bald-headed man of his duties. Then as the sacked Supervisor's replacement takes over and the cameramen look round in alarm, Number 2 exits still making further threats.

*NUMBER 2: And steer clear of Number 6. Or you'll lose more than your job, understand?*
*ASSISTANT: Yes, Number 2.*
*NUMBER 2: And that goes for all of you. I'll break this conspiracy.*

Reading the *Tally Ho* soon gives him further proof of the conspiracy. Together with his devoted right-hand man, he translates Cervantes' enigmatic words:

*NUMBER 2: 'There is more harm in the village than is dreamt of.'*

Number 14 advises his superior to let him deal with Number 6, who is undermining his authority and poisoning the whole Village. So as not to displease the 'masters', if he is indeed their agent, he will arrange an accident. But just as the two men are about to go and put their sinister plan into effect, the troublemaker himself makes an unexpected entrance in the hall adjoining the circular office.

He tells the dumbfounded Number 2 that it was he who summoned him. Then when he denies this, the Prisoner suggests that 'someone in this village is impersonating you'.

Number 2 turns on his heel and locks himself in his office. The Prisoner finds himself alone with Number 14.

*NUMBER 14: You're a troublemaker, Number 6. D'you know what I'd like? Really like? To dust you down. I'd really enjoy that.*
*PRISONER: What's stopping you?*

The Prisoner then suggests to Number 2's stooge that they settle the matter with a game of kosho. The two men confront each other in this very peculiar combat sport, an eccentric combination of traditional wrestling and the martial arts.

The game takes place in a huge room containing two trampolines separated by a tank full of water, the whole area being surrounded by a narrow ledge. The winner is the first one to succeed in throwing his opponent into the water. As is often the case in the series, their costumes are a strange mixture of tradition and modernity: a long red tunic worn with a belt round the waist, a motorcyclist's helmet, ankle-high rubber-soled lace-ups, and odd gloves, one brown, the other white. The music to which their bounding around and grappling takes place is decidedly oriental. In the end the Prisoner (in the white helmet) succeeds in getting Number 14 (in the black helmet) in a very bad position over the water tank, and the game ends to his advantage, without his having to throw his adversary in. They ceremoniously bow to each other before going their separate ways.

After this bizarre interlude the infernal machine that, as far as Number 2 is concerned is the Prisoner's imagination, restarts.

In the Village shop he buys a small notebook and, improbably, a cuckoo clock, obviously chosen for the large wooden box in which it is contained. After his departure the shopkeeper rushes off to tell Number 2 of this surprising purchase.

In fact, his purchase proves to be extremely practical. The huge box, in which the Prisoner places the crumbs from a sandwich, turns into a trap into which he lures a pigeon. Afterwards, he conspicuously places what is left of the clock at the foot of the Green Dome – and before long two bomb disposal experts turn up at the spot in a buggy.

A little later, inside a bunker lined with sandbags, Number 2 finds one of the explosives experts standing at a table covered with cogs, producing a ridiculous 'Cuckoo' sound by activating the absurd mechanism of the dismantled clock.

Meanwhile the Prisoner is busy with a completely different bird. Tracked by the Supervisor's battery of cameras, he climbs a hill in the 'restricted area' outside the Village, from where he releases the pigeon, now carrying a message written on a page torn out of the little notebook. A flag with the emblematic penny-farthing in black on a white background flaps in the wind, whilst the Village's impressive military resources are deployed against the winged creature.

The message the bird was carrying – 20 60 40 47 67 81 91 80 – is decoded by the encryption experts to read: 'Vital message tomorrow 06.00 hours by visual signal.'

Sure enough, the next morning the Prisoner is on the beach at six o'clock precisely, and starts sending signals with the aid of a pocket mirror which he uses to reflect the sun's rays. But to whom? This is precisely what Number 2, directing the Control Room's team of cameramen himself, tries to discover. But neither Camera 5 nor Camera 13, nor radar, nor sonar, succeed in locating a plane, helicopter, boat, or submarine to which they could be addressed. In desperation Number 2 has the Morse message decoded. But this time the cryptology department is incapable of making sense of its crazy contents: 'Pat a cake, pat a cake, baker's man/Bake me a cake as fast as you can.'

By the end of this sequence Number 2 seems very close to breaking point.

The Prisoner meanwhile continues to carry out his programme of destabilisation. On the café terrace he suddenly leans over Number 14, who is eating his breakfast, and starts whispering conspiratorially.

*PRISONER: Morning. Did you sleep well? I didn't – I'd a terrible night. Insomnia, couldn't sleep. So restless … and there's no point in lying in bed when you're awake, is there?*
*NUMBER 14: What are you talking about?*
*PRISONER: So I got up and went out, had a long walk on the beach … marvellous at that time of day, invigorating. The air, it's brisk and clear.*
*NUMBER 14: You must be out of your mind.*
*PRISONER: The rain on your face, the wind on your cheeks … don't look now, the waiters are watching. Yes, it's the only way, I'm so glad you agree with me …*

As soon as the Prisoner left the terrace the waiter rushes to the phone.

At the end of a particularly hysterical scene Number 2 turns on his most loyal collaborator, now suspected of working with Number 6. Beside himself with rage, he ends up by striking Number 14 violently and shouting at him:

*NUMBER 2: Traitor! Traitor! Traitor! You've lost, you and your friends. I'll break the lot of you. You too. You're in this plot, aren't you? Oh yes. Get out. Get out of this house.*

In Villa Number 6, where the Prisoner is comfortably installed in an armchair, listening to some music, the atmosphere is decidedly more serene. But Number 14's eruption is scarcely in keeping with the sedate rhythms of the Vivaldi music which fills the room.

*NUMBER 14: Turn that thing off.*
*PRISONER: I beg your pardon?*
*NUMBER 14: Turn it off I said.*
*PRISONER: I'm listening … music makes for a quiet mind … I'd rather you didn't. What's your problem?*
*NUMBER 14: You put the poison in.*
*PRISONER: I did?*
*NUMBER 14: With Number 2. I'm finished.*
*PRISONER: I'm sorry to hear that.*
*NUMBER 14: I'll kill you …*

The fight that then takes place is one of the most spectacular but also one of the most unusual of the series. While the two men tussle, wrestle, roll on the ground, throw punches of incredible violence at each other, not for one moment does the Venetian composer's majestically slow movement cease to play. The brutality of the two fighting men has very little to do with the formality of kosho, and after a while the Prisoner's comfortable room looks like a saloon bar after a drunken brawl. But in the midst of all the broken furniture and objects hurled to the ground the turntable on which the record continues to play remains miraculously unharmed. Suddenly the harmonious sound is punctuated by the din of shattering glass: the Prisoner has just thrown Number 2's henchman through the french window.

For Number 2 the time has now come to pay for the suicide of the young girl, and it is the Prisoner himself who calls in the debt.

The Village boss is alone. The last person to walk out on him is the butler, whom we see leaving in a city suit, wearing a bowler hat and carrying a suitcase.

As the metal doors to the huge circular office open, the Supreme Authorities' representative is huddled behind the large penny-farthing that together with the spherical chair and the control desk constitute the room's permanent fixtures. He clutches the handlebars in a convulsive grip and stares wildly at the man in the dark blazer with white trim who comes in and walks determinedly down the access ramp.

*PRISONER: I've come to keep you company. I hear all your friends have deserted you. You can't trust anyone anymore ... pity. It's odd, isn't it? All this power at your disposal and yet, you're alone. You do feel alone, don't you?*
*NUMBER 2: What do you want?*
*PRISONER: To talk and to listen.*
*NUMBER 2: I've nothing to say.*
*PRISONER: That's not like the old Number 2. Where is the strong man, the hammer? You have to be hammer or anvil, remember?*
*NUMBER 2: I know who you are.*
*PRISONER: I'm Number 6.*
*NUMBER 2: No. D6.*
*PRISONER: D6?*
*NUMBER 2: Yes ... sent here by our masters. To spy on me.*
*PRISONER: Sorry, I'm not quite with you.*
*NUMBER 2: Oh yes, oh yes, you can stop acting now, you know. I was on to you from the beginning. I knew what you were doing.*
*PRISONER: Tell me.*
*NUMBER 2: All those messages you sent. And all the people you recruited. I knew you were a plant. You didn't fool me.*
*PRISONER: Maybe you fooled yourself.*
*NUMBER 2: What does that mean?*
*PRISONER: Let us suppose for argument's sake that what you say is true. That I was planted here...*
*NUMBER 2: By XO4.*
*PRISONER: XO4?*
*NUMBER 2: Hmmm...*
*PRISONER: Oh very well then, by XO4. To check on Village security. To check on you.*
*NUMBER 2: You were.*
*PRISONER: What would have been your first duty as a loyal citizen? Not to interfere. But you did interfere. You have admitted it yourself. There is a name for that – sabotage.*
*NUMBER 2: No.*
*PRISONER: Who are you working for, Number 2?*
*NUMBER 2: For us. For us.*
*PRISONER: That is not the way it is going to sound to XO4.*
*NUMBER 2: I swear to you...*

*PRISONER: You could be working for the enemy. Or you could be a blunderer who's lost his head. Either way you've failed. And they do not like failures here.*
*NUMBER 2: You've destroyed me.*
*PRISONER: No. You destroyed yourself. A character flaw ... you're afraid of your masters. A weak link in the chain of command, waiting to be broken.*
*NUMBER 2: Don't tell them. Don't report me.*
*PRISONER: I don't intend to. You are going to report yourself.*
*NUMBER 2: I have to report a breakdown in control. Number 2 needs to be replaced ... Yes, this is Number 2 reporting ...*

While the metal door opens automatically behind him, the Prisoner looks down from the top of the access ramp and with an air of satisfaction considers for a moment the former Number 2, slumped in his spherical chair in the middle of that huge circular office.

At the end of this episode, the most positive of the series, the Prisoner's victory seems complete.

Yet whilst his perfect knowledge of the field enables him to turn his adversaries' weapons against them and win a battle, he is still in the dark about the war in which he has come to be involved. He has not yet unmasked his real enemy.

# Episode Eleven:
# It's Your Funeral

It is the morning of another day, and a pretty, slender young blonde in a red-and-white sailor shirt and white canvas cap enters House Number 6. The door opens automatically to let her in.

In the Control Room the bald-headed Supervisor is watching the scene with Number 2, a fair-haired young man with agreeable features but with a supercilious expression on his face, who wears big horned rimmed-glasses and for the time being is still in his dressing gown.

The young girl, goes over to the bed where the Prisoner is apparently still sleeping, and gets as hostile a welcome as the previous lady ambassadors sent by the Village to charm him. Woken by a slight noise, the ex-secret agent, alert as ever, roughly grabs her arm just as she bends over him.

*PRISONER: What are you doing here?*
*GIRL: I was just going to wake you up.*
*PRISONER: You have ... who are you?*
*GIRL: I'm a number. Just like you. Does it matter which?*
*PRISONER: How did you get in?*
*GIRL: The door was open.*
*PRISONER: Always is, to them, isn't it?*
*GIRL: I'm not one of them.*
*PRISONER: No ... what do you want?*
*GIRL: Help.*
*PRISONER: Go to the Town Hall. Your Citizens' Council promises help and advice to everyone.*
*GIRL: Their Citizens' Council.*
*PRISONER: As far as I'm concerned, what's theirs is yours.*
*GIRL: I am not one of them.*
*PRISONER: No. No one is. Go back and tell them I was not interested. That I wouldn't even listen. What's the good. They know already. I won't go for it. Whatever it is. So you may as well stop trying.*

The message is received by those to whom it is addressed.

*NUMBER 2: We never stop. Number 6. Now we'll see how accurately they've timed it. She was given a drug yesterday. One of the super-strength meprobromates we've developed. She doesn't know anything about it, of course.*

On the screen, the young girl collapses by the door.

*SUPERVISOR: Yesterday?*
*NUMBER 2: Hmm, well the drug remains dormant until triggered by the nervous system ... and then it releases itself to the desired quantities to produce instant tranquility, or temporary oblivion.*

*SUPERVISOR: But why?*
*NUMBER 2: Well, in anticipation of Number 6 throwing her out. Which he was about to do.*
*SUPERVISOR: And will, when she revives.*
*NUMBER 2: Oh, no, no, you see, she's become a lady in distress. He's going to be all good deeds and sympathy.*

After a while – as Number 2 notes, 'exactly the time the chemists anticipated' – the young girl comes round.

*GIRL: Sorry. Exhaustion.*
*PRISONER: No. Drugs. Your pupils are contracted.*
*GIRL: I don't take drugs.*
*PRISONER: Forced feeding, then.*
*GIRL: Why would they?*
*PRISONER: You tell me.*
*GIRL: You mean you'll condescend to listen?*
*PRISONER: I'll listen. As long as what you're saying doesn't become too obviously phoney, yes.*
*GIRL: I'll find help somewhere else.*
*PRISONER: They told you to find it here, didn't they?*
*GIRL: Believe what you like, it doesn't matter anymore. No . . . no, it does matter. This concerns the welfare of everybody in this village.*
*PRISONER: And welfare is our biggest consumer item. Yes.*
*GIRL: Joke about this if you can. Assassination.*
*PRISONER: Are you trying to organise one or prevent one?*
*GIRL: Prevent . . . They would have to take reprisals, everybody would suffer.*
*PRISONER: What can I do for you?*
*GIRL: I've just told you I need your help in preventing an assassination.*
*PRISONER: They've heard, they're aware and they don't need anyone's help.*
*GIRL: They don't believe me.*
*PRISONER: No comment.*
*GIRL: So much caution. In a man like you it seems so wrong.*
*PRISONER: Many times bitten, forever shy. But they are not shy. They love to listen.*
*GIRL: You don't understand. My name, my number, is on a list.*
*PRISONER: Honours or deportation?*
*GIRL: Jamming.*
*PRISONER: Jamming . . . oh, domestic science.*
*GIRL: You learn about jamming one of these days . . . it's our most important means of fighting back.*
*PRISONER: Alright, enlighten me now.*
*GIRL: No. I tell lies, remember? I'm sorry I ever bothered you.*
*PRISONER: Call in anytime you like.*

Meanwhile, Number 2 is engaged in the most routine of activities: he is speaking on the phone with the mysterious agent of the Village's authorities. He tells them that everything will be all right but that there has been a delay. From his conversation – in the course of which we see him, like so many others before him, lose his arrogance and become obsequious in his manner – it emerges that Number 6 is being called upon to play an important part in some plan of which he is unaware.

In the context of this devious plan the Supervisor issues the order for Number 2 to be supplied as quickly as possible with the day's 'Activity Prognosis' on Number 6.

A little later in the Village's imposing Computer Room, where a feverish bustle now reigns, a young woman, wearing the striped shirt, cape and little beach hat worn by the Village's female population, is busy viewing images that appear, accompanied by a commentary, on a screen.

*VOICE: Today's Activity Prognosis on Number 6. Number 2 requires it ... 6.30 a.m. Subject exercises daily with a walk around the Village... Daily, subject climbs the bell tower... reason unknown... subject eccentric... certainly watching, waiting, constantly aggressive... is possible that the subject likes the view ... 7.30 a.m. Physical workout with subject's home-made apparatus. 8.15 a.m. The subject cooling off. 9 o'clock a.m. Coffee at café and buys newspaper. 9.20 a.m. Subject will proceed on foot to Old People's Home for a game of chess, ending with an eleven-move checkmate win by subject... Subject honours other eccentric resident, by sitting for portrait, or perhaps subject has ulterior motive.*

Meanwhile, Number 2 is listening to a dark-haired young man, whose badge identifies him as Number 100. They are talking about a plan for which Number 100's division will be 'operational exactly on time'.

In the Old People's Home, the artist, an old man wearing a sailor shirt and canvas beach hat is conversing with Number 6, his model. But the subject of their conversation is something quite other than art.

*ARTIST: What they do, these jammers, is talk. They talk about the plots they're hatching.*
*PRISONER: Plots?*
*ARTIST: Well, escapes mostly. But plans and developments for all kinds of mischief. They do it to confuse the observers. Still ... please!*
*PRISONER: So sorry...*
*ARTIST: The plots they talk about are always make-believe. Non-existent. But control can't know that until they've checked them out. Used to run themselves ragged investigating the schemes of jammers.*
*PRISONER: Used to?*
*ARTIST: They don't bother much anymore. Now they keep a list of all known jammers. Anything control picks up from these, they just let ride.*

The Prisoner learns nothing more about this previously unsuspected aspect of Village life. The artist proudly reveals his completed work. His model congratulates him on the portrait – an uncompromisingly non-figurative daub – which he describes as 'a perfect likeness'.

Meanwhile in the Green Dome's circular office, the assistant detailed to provide the Activities Prognosis on Number 6 presents the results of her department's work to Number 2.

*NUMBER 2: Good. How accurate are these? What is the percentage of right and wrong?*
*ASSISTANT: I'm afraid we don't know that.*
*NUMBER 2: Why not?*
*ASSISTANT: Twice we programmed our machines for percental appraisals of their own efficiencies. Each time they've refused to give back the requisite information.*

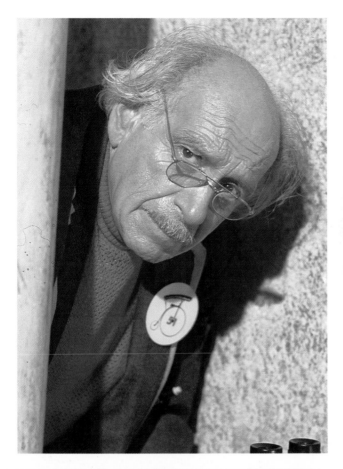

*NUMBER 2: Refused? How?*
*ASSISTANT: Simply by not returning the data to us.*
*NUMBER 2: They'll be wanting their own trade union next.*

The young woman then gives an account of the Prisoner's immediately anticipated activities, checked on a screen against what he is actually doing. It is now 10.19. At 10.20, having bought a newspaper, he should, according to the Prognosis also buy a bar of soap and a bag of sweets. Number 2 protests. Since the Prisoner never eats candy, the prognosis must be wrong. But a moment later an old woman is refused a bag of sweets because her credit allowance is all used up. The Prisoner then very kindly buys a bag for her, thereby conforming, even in this 'spontaneous' gesture, to the faultless programming of his use of time. But Number 2 soon puts a stop to the sequence of pictures. He has just learned that at 11.50 the Prisoner has his twice-weekly kosho practice.

While the Prisoner and his opponent bounce on the trampolines in the gymnasium, Number 2's assistant finds his way into the changing room and replaces the watch left in Number 6's blazer pocket with another absolutely identical watch.

Once again the fight ends in victory for the Prisoner, who bows formally to his sweat-soaked adversary. But when he gets back to the changing room it comes as a unwelcome surprise to discover that his watch is not working.

When he comes into a shop, filled with clocks, pendulums, watches, alarm clocks, clockfaces of every style and period, and where, paradoxically, time seems to have stood still, the Village watchmaker, a white-haired old man, greets him suspiciously.

But the device that the Prisoner finds there, in the absence of the craftsman, busy in his workshop mending his watch, is very much up to date: a detonator that can be activated from a distance. His curiosity aroused, he asks the watchmaker about it, but the old man replies evasively that it is just a toy.

Evidently not very convinced by this explanation, the Prisoner leaves, and Number 100 emerges from a hiding-place from which he has watched the whole scene. Whilst he looks satisfied, the white-haired old man on the other hand looks rather confused and asks him what they have to gain by letting 'Them' see what they're up to. Having told him that 'it will all be explained to you in time', Number 2's man then says that it is a way of adding to 'Their' confusion.

On leaving the watchmaker, the Prisoner bumps into his pretty morning visitor, who tells him that the old man is her father. Having seen the detonator, her irascible host is now thoroughly disposed to believe her. A little later, on the café terrace, she tells him that her father, with a fellow conspirator she knows nothing about, its plotting an assassination attempt against Number 2. The Prisoner then agrees to help her try to prevent an irresponsible act which would attract terrible reprisals against the whole Village population.

From the conversation between Number 2, who is following the scene on his screen, and one of his assistants we learn that his plan involves both an assassination attempt and at the same time an attempt by Number 6 to prevent it.

*ASSISTANT: Whatever you like to call it. Plan Division Q is still murder.*
*NUMBER 2: You have your specific duties, stick to them. Leave the rest to one double zero.*
*ASSISTANT: You think Number 6 has fallen for it?*
*NUMBER 2: No, no, not yet. But he will, he will...*
*ASSISTANT: And after it's all over you'll be showered with official congratulations.*
*NUMBER 2: Yes ... well after he's been here to warn me that an assassination is being plotted, and that I am the intended victim.*

A little later, when he goes into the watchmaker's shop with the young blonde girl, the Prisoner is unaware that his actions are programmed for him by the very people now watching: Number 2 and Number 100, who in response to a question from his superior, tells him that he is confident of the subject's indoctrination.

The said indoctrinated subject, the father of the pretty blonde girl – her badge tells us that she is Number 50, but he calls her Monique – cannot be persuaded to give up his plan and begins to get angry.

WATCHMAKER: *You refuse to understand. What I am doing is for a principle. We are in this prison for life. All of us. But I have met no-one here who has committed a crime. I will protest in a manner they cannot ignore.*
PRISONER: *Some other way, then. Not by an act of murder.*
WATCHMAKER: *Assassination.*
PRISONER: *Call it what you like, the important matter is that the entire Village will be punished.*
WATCHMAKER: *Maybe it's what they need to wake them up. To shake them out of their lethargy. To make them angry enough to fight.*
PRISONER: *Assuming they survive the punishment.*

On leaving the shop, the Prisoner reaches the next stage of what he still does not know is a course signposted by Number 2. Nor is he aware that the Supervisor's cameras are tracking him as he walks through the blooming Village square on his way to the Green Dome.

When he enters the circular office Number 2, obviously deeply engrossed in a file he has been reading, breaks off and leaves his spherical chair, coming towards him with his hand outstretched.

NUMBER 2: *Ah, Number 6 my dear fellow, do come in. Do come in. Hmm, shall I order coffee or would you prefer some tea?*
PRISONER: *You can forego the amenities. This is not a social call.*

It is with perfectly feigned surprise that Number 2 learns that a plot to assassinate him is being hatched.

NUMBER 2: *I don't believe it.*
PRISONER: *They should have told you. There are some unhappy people here.*
NUMBER 2: *Yes, well I have seen the list of malcontents . . . it might interest you to know that you happen to be top of the bill.*
PRISONER: *I'll do my best to live up to it.*
NUMBER 2: *Yeah. What, by saving my miserable life?*

Their conversation continues for a while in the same tone: with the Prisoner becoming more and more vehement as he tries vainly to convince the potential victim who becomes increasingly ironic.

When the Prisoner broaches the subject of jamming, the man sitting in the spherical chair is openly derisive:

NUMBER 2: *Oh, don't tell me, it's the little watchmaker that concerns you. Yes, well, we expected something like this . . . that they'd try to get to us*

*through a dupe. Hmm, so they chose you to lead us into believing their
fantasy eh ...? Tell me, how did they sell you the idea, Number 6? Did
they show you the gun?*
PRISONER: *They're not going to shoot you. They're going to blow you up.
You may find out yourself. Quite suddenly. In which case you won't be
laughing.*

As soon as the sliding door has closed behind his visit, Number 2 checks
that their conversation has been tape-recorded and filmed.

Later in the day the constant brass band music breaks off for a moment to
give way to an official announcement.

VOICE: *Good afternoon everyone, good afternoon. I've some exciting
news for you. Your Citizens' Council officially proclaims Thursday, the
day after tomorrow, as Appreciation Day. The day when we pay due
honour to those brave and noble men who govern us so wisely. You will
all be delighted to hear that the proceedings will be opened with an
address from Number 2 himself, and concluded by the unveiling of our
new appreciation monument. There'll be speeches, thrills and
excitement.*

'Maybe more excitement than planned,' comments the Prisoner, who is sitting on the café terrace with the watchmaker's daughter.

After nightfall they both slip into the shop, which is in total darkness and
where the silence is broken only by a strange concert of ticking sounds of
every kind.

There the Prisoner discovers inside a red velvet case a copy of some kind of
large gold medallion with the emblematic penny-farthing stamped on it, the
'Great Seal of Office' that Number 2 wears at all ceremonies. When he opens
it, he finds some plastic explosive that can be detonated by radio.

The next day, when he bursts into the circular office in the Green Dome,
there is an elderly man, with balding white hair and a tired face, sitting in the
spherical chair.

OLD NUMBER 2: *Number 6, isn't it? I've been expecting you.*
PRISONER: *I want to see Number 2.*
OLD NUMBER 2: *I am Number 2. You've come to tell me there's a plot
against my life, haven't you? You know my colleague is very concerned
about these imminent death by violence projects that you've been report-
ing during my absence.*
PRISONER: *Plots? I've reported one only.*
OLD NUMBER 2: *Not so. My very efficient colleagues, should I say my
heir presumptive, has been collecting evidence that every interim
Number 2 who has served here while I've been on leave has been
cautioned by you. About some improbable conspiracy to murder him.*
PRISONER: *Really.*
OLD NUMBER 2: *You obviously don't believe me. Well, the psychiatrist
warned me that that might be the case. Shall I show you proof?*

With the tip of his multicoloured umbrella he presses a button which
summons up on the screen the scene in which the Prisoner tells the young
fair-haired Number 2 about his imminent assassination.

The same scene is projected twice more – but while the Prisoner's warning
remains the same, the occupant of the spherical chair is different each time:
first a bearded man, then a dark-haired woman ...

The Prisoner refuses to watch any more.

*OLD NUMBER 2: So you're convinced?*
*PRISONER: I'm convinced that those excerpts were fakes.*
*OLD NUMBER 2: You think they were doctored. For what purpose? Why should we want to convince you that you're not well?*
*PRISONER: Perhaps it's you they want to convince.*
*OLD NUMBER 2: Me? Tomorrow I hand over to my successor. I retire.*
*PRISONER: Perhaps they're trying to save a pension.*

As the sliding metal doors close behind his visitor, the face of the old Number 2 suddenly turns thoughtful. And when he finds out a moment later from one of his assistants that it is not possible for him to review the film he has just had sceened for the Prisoner's benefit, the doubt planted in his mind by Number 6 grows into a very alarming certainty.

For the Prisoner too some things have become perfectly clear: not only the planned assassination of the old Number 2 by his successor, but also the fact that an attempt has been made to discredit him precisely because he was the only person likely to be believed if he divulged the existence of the assassination plot to its intended victim. But the watchmaker's daughter, with whom he is seen having coffee, finds it hard to believe him:

*GIRL: If they're going to do away with the man, why all the rigmarole? Why don't they just go ahead and do it?*
*PRISONER: What would the rank and file think? They'll be due for retirement themselves one day.*
*GIRL: They brainwashed my father into doing their dirty work. What will happen to him? What will they do? Please, we must prevent this thing. For my father's sake.*
*PRISONER: For everybody's sake.*

While the young Number 2, his face beaming, tells his mysterious interlocutor on the phone that everything is working out beautifully, thanking him in a particularly obsequious manner at the end of their conversation, a further intrusion by the Prisoner into the old Number 2's office proves unwelcome. The old man seems resigned to the fate his people have in store for him:

*OLD NUMBER 2: Preventing is only postponing. You never understand us, Number 6. We never fail.*

Yet he turns rather pale on learning the selected mode of 'execution':

*OLD NUMBER 2: I can think of better ways to die.*
*PRISONER: And better causes to die for.*

The big day arrives. For the amorphous crowd of Villagers in their brightly coloured clothes whom we see converging on the central square to the sound of the brass band, this is just yet another 'spontaneous' celebration. The same cannot be said of the two Number 2s, standing on the balcony next to the full complement of Council Members: the outgoing Number 2's haggard face is at odds with the emotive tribute paid to him by a speaker in tails and a top hat. Despite assurances from the trusty Number 100, Number 2's young successor looks rather tense; he communicates with his accomplice by whispering into the miniaturised transmitter-receiver concealed in the arm of his large-framed glasses. As for the Prisoner and the watchmaker's daughter, they are downright worried: the old man has disappeared, not having come home the night before.

We suddenly catch sight of the watchmaker on top of the bell-tower, from where he observes the progress of the ceremony with the aid of a powerful pair of binoculars. But a second later the sun is reflected on the glass; the flash of light reveals his position to the Prisoner. Without wasting a minute, the Prisoner, followed by young Monique, rushes to the tower.

At the top of the tower he easily overpowers the old man and seizes the detonator. But Number 100, who bars his way at the foot of the tower, proves much more difficult to neutralise. After a violent struggle the Prisoner wins by a knock-out, then races to the official platform, arriving just as the ceremony is ending. With a relief easy to imagine, the old Number 2 has placed a gold seal round his successor's neck. The younger man, his face rather drawn, is now receiving the congratulations of the Council Members.

The Prisoner then gives the detonator to the retired official:

*PRISONER: It's your passport. No one will question its authority. The helicopter's waiting.*
*OLD NUMBER 2: They will get me eventually.*
*PRISONER: Fly now, pay later.*
*OLD NUMBER 2: They'll find me wherever I am.*
*PRISONER: As long as it's not here. Take it and go.*

The new Number 2, staring terrified at the detonator that controls the device hidden inside 'his' medallion, does not lift a finger to stop his predecessor from going. But the next moment, just as he is about to remove his dangerous badge of office, the Prisoner energetically seizes his hand, crushing it in his own. Vigorously shaking his arm, the Prisoner addresses him in a loud, ostensibly friendly voice.

*PRISONER: Yes and so the great day is nearly over. Came off rather well, I thought. Better than planned. And now you can even look forward to your own retirement and I'm sure they'll arrange something equally suitable for you when the day comes . . . Be seeing you . . . won't I?*

*

The Prisoner is the great victor of this episode, when once again he turns the Village Authorities' machinations – in which they believe they have trapped him – against the authors of the plot.

But this time it is not a question of single combat. On the one hand, the Authorities are seeking not so much to break him as to use him for their own ends. The Prisoner, for his part, has not only his own safety in mind but also that of the community to which, reluctantly, he seems to belong more and more. The episode is a strong demonstration of the impasse that violent bids for freedom can lead to when manipulated by the oppressor.

# Episode Twelve:
## A Change of Mind

If the Activities Prognosis on Number 6 supplied by the computer is to be believed, it is a little after 7.30. The Prisoner, dressed in a tracksuit, is working out on a fixed bar in the small private gymnasium he has set up for himself on the outskirts of the Village. He vigorously punches a sandbag. It is the start of another fine day for him.

A rather bad start; two thugs in striped shirts who emerge from the undergrowth and come towards him with an air of menace do not seem to appreciate such individual activity. The Prisoner's daily workout and above all his natural fighting spirit stand him in good stead, securing him victory in a particularly brutal brawl. But before running away, his aggressors threaten him with having to face the 'Committee', and he is next seen in the waiting room of the Council Chamber, summoned to appear before the Council on account of his 'anti-social' behaviour. On one of the walls an Orwellian poster proclaims in large letters: 'The Community needs you!'

The Prisoner is not the only one to have attracted the attentions of the Citizens' Council. The young girl in blue sitting next to him is shaken by violent sobs, but for the time being the Court is concerned with Number 93:

*VOICE: The Council Chamber have considered your case, Number 93, and already there are signs of disharmony in your behaviour. You appear to be a reasonable man, but there is plenty of evidence showing your unwillingness to work for the community. The court has a busy morning, and there are several cases waiting to be dealt with. Number 6 is seriously in need of help, and we want to do something for 42. She appears to be in a permanent state of depression, always in tears ... it is your duty Number 93 to prove that you are once again a suitable member of our society. The only way now to regain the respect of your fellows is to publicly acknowledge your shortcomings. Go to the rostrum and confess. We will tell you what to say ... They're right of course.*

Number 93 is a bearded fellow in a red jumper; his high-pitched voice is in stark contrast with his imposing build.

*NUMBER 93: They're right of course.*
*VOICE: Quite right.*
*NUMBER 93: Quite right.*

In the same little quavering voice he mechanically repeats the phrases dictated over the loud-speaker and admits to being 'inadequate', 'disharmonious', and that he is 'truly grateful'. The rhythm of his 'spontaneous' confessions gradually speeds up, so that by the end the words are coming faster and faster and he is shouting louder and louder: 'Believe me, believe me, believe me!'

The voice now calls upon Number 6 to enter the Council Chamber. The Council members wear the standard striped sailor shirt, but superb black toppers replace the usual boaters and canvas beach-hats for the occasion. In the role of master of ceremonies we find the uniquitous butler.

CHAIRMAN: *I take it you have completed the written questionnaire of confession.*
PRISONER: *Yes . . . naturally.*
CHAIRMAN: *Please do not be hostile to the Committee. We are here to help you.*

The Prisoner's chair is suddenly raised, then starts to spin round. The faces of his alarming 'benefactors' pass before him. But he does not seem very impressed, either by the assembly's overweening solemnity, or by the seriousness of the charges brought against him, in particular that of his non-cooperation; he retains the same provocative attitude. A little later, the Chairman announces a tea break and the session is adjourned without the assembly having heard the smallest confession from the Prisoner. It is decided that the next hearing will consider medical reports on Number 6's state of health.

Out in the hall the Prisoner stops for a moment to listen to the 'spontaneous' confessions bleated out by Number 93 still coming over the loudspeaker, then leaves, sarcastically approving.

Once outside, he is surprised to find that the other inhabitants turn their backs on him. Number 61 does not even take the trouble to respond to his ritual greeting. Then in the square one of them wordlessly holds out to him a copy of the latest edition of the *Tally Ho*, in which appears an article announcing the continuation of hearings investigating complaints against Number 6, as well as the already printed confession of Number 93.

He gets home to find Number 2 in his kitchen, eating a biscuit. Judging by his portliness, this must be the last of many. With his flabby body, his flat pear-shaped face, his thinning plastered-back hair and his little eyes gleaming with malice, this Number 2 is not one of the most sympathetic that we have seen taking on the Prisoner.

PRISONER: *I might have guessed. Did you enjoy the show?*
NUMBER 2: *There is a saying: the slowest mule is nearest to the whip.*
PRISONER: *And another: he who digs a pit will one day lie in it. Or is Number 2 above investigation?*
NUMBER 2: *Nobody is above investigation. And failure to co-operate makes one an outcast.*
PRISONER: *No more taxis, no more credit . . .*
NUMBER 2: *Believe me, it could be only the beginning.*
PRISONER: *You should know.*
NUMBER 2: *I hope that you do not think that I am a member of this committee.*
PRISONER: *Oh, of course not. Never.*
NUMBER 2: *I assure you, no matter what significance you may hold for me, to the Village and its Committee, you are merely Citizen Number 6, who has to be tolerated and if necessary shaped to fit.*
PRISONER: *Public Enemy Number 6.*
NUMBER 2: *If you insist. But public enemies cannot be tolerated indefinitely. Be careful. Do not defy this committee. If the hearings go against you, I am powerless to help.*

They are interrupted by the arrival of an attractive young blonde wearing the coloured cape favoured by the Village women. She walks in with a determined step and is introduced by Number 2: she is Number 86, someone who has 'valuable experience with the Committee'. In response to an ironic question from the Prisoner, who has returned to making the tea with his back to her, she tells him in an aggressive voice that she once suffered the shame of having to answer for being 'disharmonious'. But now she seems to have been given the task of dealing with the Prisoner, and after Number 2 has gone she starts lecturing her protégé – with predictable results.

*NUMBER 86: First your frivolous attitude towards the committee. Most dangerous. The hearings are televised. That is why your behaviour is so important. You stand before the entire community. The Social Group is your one hope . . . fortunately I too have been attached to the Group.*

This scene is watched by Number 2 who is standing in front of his control screen with the bald-headed Supervisor:

*NUMBER 2: Females. If that woman makes one mistake we could lose him. D'you hear that. Lose him.*

The dynamic Number 86 has dragged the Prisoner to a meeting of the Social Group held in one of the Village gardens. The case of Number 42 – the young girl who was in tears in the hall outside the Council Chamber – is under discussion:

*1ST MEMBER: There can be no mitigation. We all have a social obliga-tion to stand together.*
*GIRL: I don't contest the validity of the complaint. My point is . . .*
*2ND MEMBER: No exceptions. All right, so you say you're a poet. You were composing when you failed to hear Number 10's greeting.*
*1ST MEMBER: Neglect of a social principle.*
*PRISONER: Poetry has a social value . . .*
*1ST MEMBER: He is trying to divide us . . .*
*2ND MEMBER: His intentions are obvious. To stop us from helping this unfortunate girl.*
*GIRL: You're trying to undermine my rehabilitation, disrupt my social progress . . .*
*PRISONER: Strange talk for a poet . . .*

The members of the Group go on to prove that they are totally united. They all turn on the troublemaker with the same hate in their faces, the same insults on their lips: 'Rebel!' 'Reactionary!' 'Disharmonious!' – before walking off in a fury.

Left alone, the Prisoner too turns to go. He makes his way through a wood and finds himself face to face with three men in white coats. 'Just in time for your medical, Number 6,' one of them says. Having with a quick glance assessed their strength, the Prisoner agrees to get into their buggy.

At the hospital the Doctor congratulates him on his fitness and remarks that 'the life here suits you'. He concludes his examination by testing the Prisoner's reflexes:

*DOCTOR: Excellent, fit for any contingency.*
*PRISONER: Anything specific in mind?*
*DOCTOR: My dear chap, how suspicious you are of us all. Be seeing you. Next . . .*

The health of some of the Villagers seems decidedly less good than that of the Prisoner. For instance, the patient he sees through the red glass of a small window off a corridor; a young man in a striped shirt, strapped into a kind of electric chair. He has electrodes attached to his temples, and writhing and groaning, stares in terror at the screen in front of him on which is seen an enormous white ball softly bouncing. Suddenly, his expression changes into ecstatic laughter when the menacing image of the Village guardian gives way to the smiling face of Number 2. When the latter in turn gives way to the word 'Individualist', the man again starts writhing in terror, his whole body seized with violent spasms. The strains of some particularly discordant music underline the horror of the scene. The Prisoner then tries to open the door from the corridor into the room, above which we read the notice 'Aversion Therapy' – but to no avail. His efforts seem to upset another patient in a striped shirt, who is quietly sitting on a bench.

*LOBO'MAN: Relax, fellow, relax...*
*PRISONER: You his keeper?*
*LOBO'MAN: So excited all of you. Rushing and shouting...*
*PRISONER: You ever been in there?*
*LOBO'MAN: Not in there...*
*PRISONER: That's odd...*
*LOBO'MAN: Not odd, please. Different maybe.*
*PRISONER: Different?*
*LOBO'MAN: I'm one of the lucky ones, the happy ones, I was..*
*PRISONER: Yes.*
*LOBO'MAN: I was Unmutual.*

It is not long before the Prisoner comes across this infamous term again, used this time by the Council Chairman, dressed in a striped black-and-white shirt and top hat.

*CHAIRMAN: The Fellow Analysis Report submitted by the Social Group leaves us no choice ... we are bound to classify you as Unmutual. We must warn you that if any further complaint is lodged against you, it will be necessary to propose you for the treatment known as Instant Social Conversion.*

When his seat stops turning, the Prisoner, apparently in some kind of trance, finds himself alone in the room, facing the enigmatic and silent Butler.

He goes outside to find the flower-lined streets of the Village strangely empty. And when he takes a copy of the *Tally Ho* from a dispenser in the square, a man hurriedly moves away, avoiding him like the plague. Inside the paper is an article illustrated with his photograph telling the Villagers the big news of the day: Number 6 has been declared 'Unmutual' – information that is later blared over the loud-speakers.

*LOUDSPEAKER: Your attention please. Here is an important announcement. Number 6 has been declared Unmutual until further notice. Any unsocial incident involving Number 6 should be reported immediately to the Appeals sub-committee. Thank you for your attention.*

This issue of the *Tally Ho* is treated by the Prisoner in the same way as the earlier one. But this time when he gets home, having rolled the paper into a ball and thrown it angrily into the gutter, he notices that his phone line has been cut. Just as he slams down the receiver, the door opens automatically to reveal four Village women in multicoloured capes, striped shirts and canvas hats. To the fore is an imposing matron identified as Number 48 and the young depressive poet, Number 42.

*NUMBER 48: We represent the Appeals sub-committee.*
*PRISONER: Quick off the mark Number 42. Appeals sub-committee already? You certainly get around.*
*NUMBER 48: Do not sneer at Number 42. To volunteer for social work of this nature requires considerable moral courage.*
*PRISONER: Risk of infection from the Untouchables.*
*GIRL: Bitterness will not help you, Number 6. You have brought your misfortunes on yourself.*
*PRISONER: Nevertheless, you ladies, I'm sure out of the goodness of your hearts, are going to help me.*
*NUMBER 48: It is clearly premature to look for contrition in the poor creature.*

With these words the right-thinking ladies of the Appeals Sub-Committee turn on their heels and walk off, leaving the Prisoner to his solitude. While he prepares himself a meal in his kitchen his comings and goings are observed by Number 2 and the Supervisor:

*NUMBER 2: Now let's see how the loner withstands real loneliness. And for his sake I hope it will not be for long. Did you hear, for his own sake.*

The Prisoner is without any doubt an individualist and a person whose single combat to regain his freedom isolates him from the rest of the Village herd. But he is none the less a social creature and he soon begins to miss the company even of those so unlike him. We find him in the woods on the out-skirts of the Village angrily tearing off bits of branches, totally powerless to defend himself against this new and faceless enemy. A little later, we see him on the deserted beach watching a flight of migratory birds passing overhead, their cries filling the air. The expression in his eyes is not that of a man envious of their freedom but of an animal deprived of the company of others of his species. Defeated, he prefers to risk what the Council Chamber might throw at him and to go and sit on the café terrace, rejoining the apparently carefree life of the Village and its familiar announcements:

*LOUDSPEAKER: Your attention please ... Weather, the day will conti-nue warn and sunny, with a danger of sudden storms ...*

But when he orders a coffee the waiter turns his back on him without answering, and the next announcement reminds him of his pariah status:

*LOUDSPEAKER: Incidents regarding Unmutuals should be reported to the Appeals sub-committee. Thank you for your attention.*

Meanwhile the customers get up and, one after the other, leave the terrace. It is not long before the Prisoner finds himself alone, confronted by a group of Villagers who stare at him in silence, then suddenly come towards him with a menacing look. Back in his villa the Village pariah finds company: the militant ladies of the sub-committee. But the quality of human contact he has just experienced among his fellow citizens has put the fight back in him, and he sarcastically rejects the help of these clucking 'charitable' women who now go off in anger.

After their departure he has the chance of some more human contact with Number 2, who calls him on the phone.

*NUMBER 2: I warned you. The community will not tolerate you indefi-*
*nitely.*
*PRISONER: You need a scapegoat. Citizens unite to denounce this*
*menace in our prescence.*
*NUMBER 2: A scapegoat. Is that what you think it is? Allow me to reassure*
*you that after conversion you won't care what it is ... you just won't*
*care.*
*PRISONER: Oh yes, the ordeal of social conversion.*
*NUMBER 2: You'll soon have lasting peace of mind and adjustment to the*
*social system here ...*
*PRISONER: Drugs?*
*NUMBER 2: Would drugs be lasting? What would be lasting ... is isola-*
*tion of the aggressive frontal lobes of the brain.*

Just as the Prisoner hangs up, an announcement comes over the loud-speaker, confirming the Village's monstrous plan:

*VOICE: Your attention please. Here is an announcement for all staff*
*psychologists and psychiatrists. Those wishing to study the conversion*
*of Number 6 on Hospital's closed circuit television please report*
*immediately to the hospital common room.*

When the Prisoner leaves his house, rather anxious, he hears a commotion coming dangerously near. And it is not long before a baying mob of Villagers, led by the two most active militants of the Appeals sub-committee, comes bearing down on him. It is the shrewish Number 48 who gives the signal for attack:

*NUMBER 48: Splendid, Number 6. Just in time for the procession!*

The 'procession' is all too reminiscent of a lynching. The pretty multi-coloured umbrellas turn into fearsome weapons. Thrown to the ground, half stunned, the Prisoner is brutally dragged through the Village to the hospital, where staff in white coats are waiting for him. One of them comes straight over to him, holding a syringe.

A few moments later, strapped down on a stretcher, the Prisoner is taken to the operating theatre. Though tranquillised, the Prisoner is conscious and his eyes follow the alarming preparations of the medical staff.

A huge audience, in which the white coats of the doctors mingle with the stripped shirts and top hats of Council Members, settle down in front of a closed-circuit television screen in the hospital common room. An attractive young blonde, Number 86 of the Social Group, appears on the screen. Wearing an austere white coat, she gives a live commentary on the 'Instant Social Conversion' operation – in other words, a lobotomy – which she herself carries out, leading an impressive medical team and at the same time directing the cameras.

*NUMBER 86: The prime concern is to locate the link point of the frontal*
*lobes ... the ultra sonic beam is now focused on the exact link point of the*
*frontal lobes. Lanolin barrier to minimise external cell break down and*
*subsequent scar tissue. Relaxant to preclude muscular reaction.*

She approaches the Prisoner as he lies motionless on the operation table, apparently in a strange state of semi-wakefulness. But after she injects his arm his eyes start rolling, and an improbably ecstatic smile briefly illuminates his face. The operation then reaches a decisive stage:

*NUMBER 86: Now to step up the voltage until the ultrasonic bombardment causes permanent dislocation.*

Later, when the Prisoner wakes up fully dressed on a hospital bed, he seems rather stupefied, but much changed: he is calmer, with the hint of a smile on his lips. The doctor sitting at his bedside tells him with the utmost professional solicitude that 'just at the most interesting moment you went to sleep'. Then seeing him raise his hand to his temple, where he has a plaster; the doctor advises him to keep it on for a couple of days and to take it easy. Finally, after congratulating him with a few vigorous friendly pats on the back, the doctor entrusts him to the care of young Number 86, now wearing a flattering little blue dress, to take him home.

Outside the hospital the Prisoner, now 'cured', is welcomed by the jubilant crowd of Villagers. Cheerful brass band music accompanies the buggy that we see climbing the little grey-cobbled lane which leads to Number 6's house, and at the top of which rises the imposing building of the Green Dome. The converted individualist's fellow citizens, now friendly towards him, line the street to applaud him as he passes.

Number 2 is there to welcome him home in person. After he has gone, the young woman installs the Prisoner in an armchair and strokes his forehead, telling him to relax while she makes him a cup of tea. But despite his peculiar mental state, his mistrust is not completely extinguished, and it does not escape his notice that his charming nurse drops a tablet into his drink. His capacity for quick reaction does not seem to have suffered too much from the operation either, and having sent her to fetch a rug from his bedroom, he pours the drugged tea into a vase.

After the young psychiatrist has gone off in the belief that he is tranquillised, he still has sufficient reserves of clear-mindedness to make Number 2 believe that he is actually drugged. For it is the acting master of the Village who now leans over him, then snaps his fingers to wake him, with the intention of taking advantage of his trance to finally obtain the answer to that question:

*NUMBER 2: Time for our talk, Number 6.*
*PRISONER: Our talk?*
*NUMBER 2: Oh yes, now that all your aggressive anxieties have been expunged, let us say forever, I'll know that you'll feel free to speak.*
*PRISONER: Feel free to speak.*
*NUMBER 2: Particularly about that little incident which has been causing you such absurd distress . . . the trivia, the trivia of your resignation. Yes, you resigned, why, why prematurely. Why did you resign?*

Number 2 insistently repeats his question, but the Prisoner continues to pretend that he is drugged, gropes for words, falters, then suddenly gets worked up and starts shouting. Number 2 then suspends his interrogation, but only temporarily:

*NUMBER 2: Lay back and rest, lay back and rest, we can have our little chat later on . . . when you've had time to collect your thoughts.*

As soon as he has gone, the Prisoner rushes to a mirror, tears off the plaster and finds a curious reddish scar on his temple. He is unaware that Number 2 and Number 86 are watching him on the control screen. He is also unaware that the operation we saw him undergo on our screen was just another masquerade, dreamt up by the Green Dome to make him think that he really has been lobotimised. Number 86's tranquilliser was intended to reinforce this illusion, by transforming his personality for a short while, the aim of the whole scheme being to weaken his defences and get him to talk.

Number 2 finds the Prisoner's behaviour suspect and judges him to be abnormally suspicious and aggressive. He sends the young woman to give him another dose of the drug, despite her warnings about the danger of repeating it so soon. She finds her patient very excited and while she makes the tea he drums his fingers incessantly on the table. She then thinks of a more natural way to calm him and get him to drink the drugged concoction she has just served him.

NUMBER 86: *D'you like my dress?*
PRISONER: *More feminine than slacks. One thing, though ... I cannot stand girls who don't know how to make a decent cup of tea. Come, a lesson ... empty pot, rinse out, warm the pot – always – rinse out ... and now, one for me, one for thee and one for the pot ... one for luck ... boiling water ... switch off, let it stand for one moment ... oh, pour the milk for me please ... cup, saucer, spoon ... good. Oh, the sugar, please, in end cupboard ... thank you. Pour, should be just about nice ...*

He obviously notices Number 2's envoy drop a tablet into his milk. But she does not realise that he swops the cups round while she is looking for the sugar in the cupboard. Number 2, watching on the control screen with the Supervisor, follows with satisfaction what he takes to be a charmingly domestic scene, equally unaware of what has happened. A few seconds later, he soon starts to sing a different tune at the sight of the drugged young psychiatrist's suddenly completely abnormal behaviour. He immediately summons her by phone to report to the Green Dome.

Left on his own, the Prisoner, obviously worried about the scar on his temple, goes out for a walk. In one of the flower-lined streets of the Village, he exchanges a few words with the lobotomised man with whom he had a conversation in the hospital about the Aversion Therapy Room. This encounter does not serve to reassure him, quite the contrary, and when he comes to his private gymnasium a strange inhibition prevents him from reaching up to the horizontal bar, still more from hitting the punchbag. Number 2's ploy seems to be working perfectly: all aggression has left the Prisoner, who now behaves as though he really has been lobotomised.

He is just as incapable of responding to the first blows landed on him by the two thugs he despatched at the beginning of the episode, who hope to take advantage of his supposed mental decline to exact cowardly revenge. But subsequent punches succeed in rousing his fighting spirit, which suddenly overcomes the psychological barrier erected in his mind by Number 2's mystification. This time his adversaries do not even get the chance to run away. A few seconds later they are both lying on the ground, out for the count.

Looking pleased with himself, the Prisoner raises his hand to his temple. Having dealt with his cowardly attackers, he now turns his own aggression against another adversary, on different ground.

On his way to the Village centre he meets young Number 86, as attractive as ever in her little blue dress, but above all just as drugged. Apparently walking on air, she tells him with an ecstatic smile that the flowers she has just picked are for Number 2. By telling her it is Number 2's order, the Prisoner has no difficulty in persuading her to look at the shiny watch he dangles before her eyes. Hypnotised, believing she is speaking to Number 2, the young woman then gives him a full report on the simulated operation on Number 6, and the doses of tranquilliser she was instructed to give him. When she has finished he gives her further instructions to carry out 'when the village clock strikes four', but we do not hear what it is he tells her to do.

Shortly afterwards, Number 2 is told of the unexpected arrival of Number 6 at the Green Dome. Once inside the huge circular office, the Prisoner

indulges in his favourite sport, that of faking a condition believed to be genuine; a sport at which he is a grand master, since the Village authorities constantly provide him with opportunities to practice.

It is with the happy and disarming smile of someone who is heavily tranquillised that he tells Number 2, who is at first surprised, then delighted, of his intention to tell all. Better still, to do so publicly, so as to set an example to Villagers who still have secrets! Moreover, he expresses the desire to take the opportunity to thank all those – the Committee, the ladies of the Appeals Sub-Committee – who have helped him in his 'Social Conversion'. Number 2's satisfaction knows no bounds, and it is his own voice that announces the marvellous news to the whole Village over the loud-speakers:

*NUMBER 2: Your attention please. Here is an exciting announcement. Following his successful social conversion, Number 6 has expressed the touching desire to address you all in person. All of you who are not otherwise occupied should come immediately to the Village Square.*

As soon as he appears on the balcony overlooking the square, standing next to Number 2, the Prisoner is wildly cheered by the crowd of Villagers in the brightly coloured costumes.

*PRISONER: Fellow citizens, you are cheering me. You are cheering me. That is a mistake . . . it is Number 2 you should applaud. Until he brought about my social conversion, and believe me it was him, and not your committee, until then, I was a rebel. An Unmutual senselessly resisting this, our fine community.*
*To borrow one of Number 2's sayings . . . the butcher with the sharpest knife has the warmest heart.*

Murmurs have now risen in the crowd, while Number 2 looks anxiously at the speaker, perhaps wondering about the success of his conversion. But what follows is more reassuring:

*PRISONER: Some of you have resisted in the past, have withheld knowledge that is important to Number 2. Now, thanks to Social Conversion, I want to tell you all something. And I trust that my example will inspire you all to tell, to tell . . .*

The Prisoner raises his eyes to the heavens, obviously playing for time, waiting . . . waiting for the four strokes from the Village bell-tower for the words shouted from the crowd by the young blonde in the blue dress, in obedience to the instructions she received whilst in a state of hypnosis.

*NUMBER 86: Number 2 is Unmutual, Unmutual . . . Social Conversion for Number 2! The Unmutual!*
*PRISONER: Number 86 has a confession, that Number 2 is Unmutual.*
*NUMBER 86: Unmutual . . .*
*PRISONER: Look at him . . . an Unmutual who desires to deceive you . . .*
*NUMBER 86: Unmutual . . .*
*PRISONER: Your welfare committee is a tool of those who wish to possess your minds . . .*
*CROWD: Unmutual, Unmutual, Unmutual . . .*
*PRISONER: You still have a choice . . .*
*NUMBER 86: Number 2 is Unmutual . . .*
*PRISONER: You can still salvage your rights as individuals. Your rights to truth and free thought. Reject this false world of Number 2. Reject it now . . .*

The hate-filled crowd which dragged the Prisoner to hospital now rises up against Number 2, who tries to run away and is chased through the Village to the Green Dome.

The only people left on the deserted streets are the Prisoner and the enigmatic butler beneath his huge black-and-white umbrella.

\*

Despite the Prisoner's victory in defeating a particularly unpleasant enemy through his art of mental warfare, this episode is one of the most pessimistic in the whole series. Never has the society of the Village seemed so oppressive. It is shown to be a society in which simply asserting one's individuality is enough to get oneself classified as anti-social, a pariah. A society in which dissidents are systematically treated as sick.

Never has it seemed so clear that the absolute power of the Village Authorities rests on the mob of right-thinking Villagers. A mob that can only respond to the Prisoner's exhortations to liberate themselves as though his were the words of a new master urging them to bring down the old.

# Episode Thirteen:
# Do Not Forsake Me, Oh My Darling

This episode does not begin with the usual opening sequence, but in a comfortable office where two men are busy looking at slides. It is soon revealed that these two men belong to the Secret Service and that they are trying without success to discover, in what look like innocent holiday snaps, a code that will help them find Professor Seltzman, a scientist who has mysteriously disappeared.

With a clap of thunder, the usual opening scenes are finally shown. But there is a second departure from the usual ritual: the music is different and the post-credit sequence has been dropped.

Professor Seltzman is also the topic of conversation in the Green Dome's circular office, where a very familiar scene appears on the control screen: that of the Prisoner pacing up and down in his villa like some wild animal in a cage. Number 2, an elderly man with grey hair, explains to his visitor, whom he addresses as 'Colonel', what his new assignment is. The newcomer, a stout middle-aged man, fairly tall, with a face which appears rather kindly but somewhat lacking in personality, is amazed to learn that the Village Authorities want him to find the missing scientist, a neurologist who has discovered a scientific method of transferring the mind of one person into the body of another.

*NUMBER 2: Colonel, you must be aware that all native powers have in their persons one or two of each other's spies.*
*COLONEL: Yes.*
*NUMBER 2: From time to time diplomatic swops take place ... imagine the power we would have if the spies we returned had the mind of our own choosing ... we could break the security of any nation.*

In fact the Village already has a Seltzman machine that can be used to make the transfer, but it cannot carry out the reverse procedure without the scientist's help. Now, Number 6 is known to be the last person to have been in contact with Seltzman.

Number 2 gives the Colonel a tour of the Village's impressive medicoscientific installations, in particular an 'Amnesia Room', where 'unhappy memories' can be erased from the minds of those who have divulged their secrets, allowing them to be put back into circultion to gather more information. Finally he shows him Seltzman's famous transfer machine. In the meantime guards in MP uniform enter Number 6's villa; a few seconds later their buggy is speeding towards the hospital.

The Prisoner emerges, his mind fixed on a single objective: to find Seltzman. And for a very good reason ...

He wakes up in his London home – we learn this when he opens his blinds, revealing the buildings opposite – apparently free of all 'unhappy memories' of the Village, but a prisoner in the body of the Colonel. Everything seems quite normal to him – today is the birthday of someone called Janet – until the moment he looks into a mirror. Under the impact of shock, random memories of his life in the Village and of the hypnosis to which he has recently been subjected then start to surface in his confused mind.

The young woman who rings the doorbell and whom he lets in barely looks at him. She is looking for someone else, someone she calls 'Darling'; this is Janet, the Prisoner's fiancée, who having seen the Lotus parked outside the house thinks he must have returned. We also learn that he disappeared a year ago and that he was working for the young woman's father. Very quickly the hapless Prisoner abandons the idea of trying to make himself recognised as himself and instead introduces himself as a friend of the former occupant of the house. But he promises that at her birthday party that same evening he will give her a message from her fiancé, so cruelly absent. She leaves and we see him smash his fist into the mirror. It shatters, causing the unbearable image of his new face to disintegrate.

Janet's father is none other than Sir Charles Portland, one of the two men we saw examining the coded slides. The young woman bitterly reproaches him for having sent her fiancé on a mission and since then concealing from her the truth about his whereabouts.

Despite the Colonel's heavier body, a little of Number 6's fire is visible when the Prisoner comes bursting into the Secret Service offices and demands to see Sir Charles. The details he is able to give his former colleagues about them and about him – his code number ZM.73 and the names under which he has worked in different European countries – fail to convince them of his true identity. But as soon as he utters Professor Seltzman's name and refers to his invention, he is ushered into the office of his former boss.

He is no more successful with Sir Charles, although he tells his prospective father-in-law things known only to him, reminding the old gentleman of the dish he ordered – jugged hare – at the lunch they had together, the day after he asked permission to marry Janet. An old Secret Service hand, Sir Charles retorts quite rightly that this information may well have been extracted from Janet's fiancé under sedation or hypnosis. By whom, and above all in whose interests? At the end of the interview Sir Charles is at least determined to do everything possible to find out who is behind these machinations, whatever they might be.

As he leaves, the Prisoner again hears in his mind the phrases imprinted on his psyche by hypnotic suggestion in the Village: *'Where is he? Where is he?'*

Night and day he is followed by one of Sir Charles' men, who has attached a homing device to his Lotus. But the British Secret Service agent is not the only one to take an interest in his movements. When he returns home, we see parked alongside the pavement a few metres from his house a strange hearse, beside which stands a sinister-looking undertaker.

Despite the appalling situation in which he finds himself, the Prisoner has lost none of his fighting spirit. At home, where he finds some cash that he left in the safe concealed behind his television set, he also has the satisfaction of establishing that his handwriting has not changed.

That evening at Janet's birthday party he finally manages to convince the young woman herself of his true identity. He gives her an initial message from her lover: before he left, the secret agent gave his fiancé a slip of paper for safekeeping, and he now asks her, on behalf of her lover, to get it 'if you want to see him again'. Disturbed by the intimate details he reveals to her as they dance, she agrees to go and fetch it. When she brings it to him in the garden, he gives her another message in a language that cannot lie: that of love. A long, passionate, familiar kiss convinces her that she has at last found the man she loves, inside a different body.

The precious slip of paper is a receipt, and the next day he collects from a photographer the slides he ordered before his abduction. Naturally, he is followed by his two 'guardians'. At home, a code based on the numeric equivalent of the letters of Seltzman's name and the numbers of the slides of ordinary tourist views reveal to him the place where the missing neurologist is living: Kandersfeld, in Austria.

At the wheel of his powerful sports car the Prisoner soon reaches Dover. On the Continent the Lotus races along the French autoroutes, but when it comes to the Austrian Alps a car picking up a short bleeping signal from it climbs the winding road behind it.

The Prisoner sits down on the terrace of a café in Kandersfeld, a café reminiscent of another.

*WAITER: Welcome to the village, sir.*

The waiter recognises Seltzman from the photo the Prisoner shows him, and readily points out the place where he can be found: a small barber shop that he runs under the name of Hallen.

Professor Seltzman is an old man with white hair, with a sensitive intelligent face; he is wearing the white coat of his new profession. At first he receives his visitor's astounding revelations with mistrust, but he finally allows himself to be convinced by what he accepts as scientifically incontestable proof. Without looking at it, the Prisoner reproduces in the same handwriting the address on the envelope of a letter he once sent the Professor.* The shaken scientist then explains to the man he now treats as a friend that the mind-transfer reversal process exists but only in theory, and that put into practice it could be very dangerous. The old man is extremely worried, however, that the Prisoner might have been used in order to lead others to him and his invention.

The first 'visitor' is the British Secret Service agent, whom the Prisoner recognises at once. He uses the Colonel's fists as effectively as his own when the man sent after him by Sir Charles discovers him hiding in the Professor's underground laboratory.

But just as he is about to finish him off, an infinitely more dangerous man comes down the steps: a sinister undertaker armed with some kind of gas pistol.

The next image, that of the blue-green roof of the Green Dome, comes as no surprise.

Number 2 extends a very friendly welcome to the two new arrivals, Professor Seltzman and the Prisoner. The Prisoner stares in amazement at the control screen on which he sees his own body, wired up to some strange equipment.

*NUMBER 2: Ah, Herr Professor... welcome to our humble village. Had a good trip? At least let me offer you some breakfast.*
*SELTZMAN: You have kidnapped me for one reason. My answer is No!*
*NUMBER 2: You are livery this morning, Professor.*
*SELTZMAN: Surely neither of us wants to prolong this interview.*
*NUMBER 2: Life is not your due sweet resignation.*
*SELTZMAN: Nor is it for many other scientists. Rutherford, for example, How he must regret having split the atom.*
*NUMBER 2: Yes... almost as bad as splitting the identity of two human beings. Unlike all the king's men, only you can put them together again.*
*SELTZMAN: Don't rely on it.*
*NUMBER 2: Why make this stand now? You must have known what you were doing when you invented the wretched process.*
*SELTZMAN: Only people like you make it wretched.*

---

* The handwriting is Patrick McGoohan's, and in the address appears for the first time the name of the village where the series was shot, which was to remain secret until the televising of the final episode: *Portmeirion* Road.

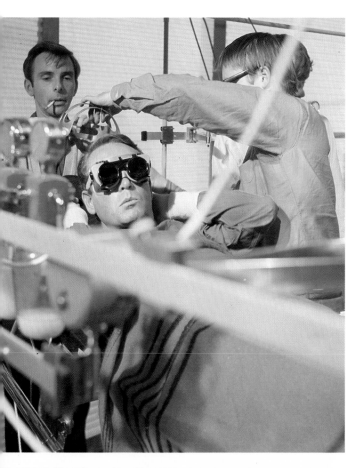

Yet, for friendship's sake, the Professor allows himself to be persuaded to free the Prisoner's mind from the body in which it has been trapped. But on one condition only: that he is left alone while he attempts the operation.

Number 2 agrees willingly, all the more so since he is relying on the Supervisor's hidden cameras to relay it to the Village scientists.

Twelve hours later (this is the length of time the Professor requires to prepare) the transfer operation begins. The Professor connects the Prisoner and the Colonel, both now put into a state of deep lethargy, to the transfer machine, to which he also connects himself, between the two patients. An army of characters in white coats follow his every movement on the screen in the Control Room.

It is an impressive spectacle. But while flashes of light seem to escape from the three men's heads, and a powerful electric current runs through their bodies, the scientist's hands and face tremble more and more violently, as though under incredible tension. Suddenly the old man collapses.

On Number 2's orders two doctors and a nurse are immediately despatched to treat him. However, the experiment seems to have succeeded perfectly. The Colonel is the first to get up. Number 2 reassures him about the health of the Professor, whom the medical team is taking care of, thanks him warmly for his 'invaluable' help, and tells him that a helicopter is waiting for him, now that his mission is over. A few seconds later the scientist regains consciousness.

*SELTZMAN: You assured me he was in good health . . . you must contact Number 1 and tell him I did my duty . . .*

These are in fact the Colonel's last words before his mind meets death in the worn-out body of the old scientist, who voluntarily subjected himself to a current far too strong for his weak constitution. As for Professor Seltzman's mind, it has just flown away from the Village in a helicopter, in the still-young body of the Colonel.

Number 2 does not immediately appreciate the full extent of the disaster. The Prisoner's mind, having just woken up in his own body, is much quicker off the mark:

*NUMBER 2: The Colonel . . . the man who is just flying out of here . . .*
*PRISONER: Is not who you thought it was . . .*
*NUMBER 2: I don't believe it . . . I watched, I saw everything . . .*
*PRISONER: The good doctor's mind now inhabits a body perhaps not to its liking, the Colonel's . . . Doctor Seltzman had progressed more than anyone of us had anticipated. He can and did change three minds at the same time. He's now free to continue his experiments in peace . . .*

For the first time someone has succeeded in escaping from the Village. But it is not the Prisoner. And the final, heartening victory is primarily that of the idealistic and cunning old scientist.

Despite the optimistic ending, which broaches the theme of the responsibility of science, the episode is a little disappointing; it seems to be simply an ordinary spy story, entertaining but no more. It is as if some Green Dome somewhere has intervened to put an end to the scandal created by the televising of a work of such explosive quality.[*] But this is just an interlude . . .

---

[*] The real explanation lies in the history of the making of the series (see the article entitled 'The Prisoner' in part 3 of this book).

# Episode Fourteen:
# Living in Harmony

It is like dreaming, or rather waking from a nightmare. The Village has disappeared and the Prisoner is free. Free to roam on horseback, dressed like a cowboy, across huge empty spaces, in the landscape reminiscent of the Wild West. But he is still his old self: in the next scene he violently throws down his sheriff's badge and gun onto the marshal's desk. After his 'resignation' he walks off, carrying his heavy saddle over his shoulder.

The loner's path soon crosses that of a sinister-looking gang of armed men who a little while later leave him lying on the ground in a little town called Harmony, which also looks like something straight out of a western, even up to the Indian guy sitting on the ground with a sombrero on his back. He watches the stranger get to his feet, pick up his hat and saddle, without making the slightest move to help him.

*INDIAN: Welcome to Harmony, stranger.*
*PRISONER: Harmony? Never heard of it.*
*INDIAN: Not many people have señor. It's sorta exclusive.*
*PRISONER: So am I. Where is this town?*
*INDIAN: You'll find out señor, it's not wise to ask too many questions. Hey hombre, you look like a man who could use a drink ... Why not try the saloon?*

In the saloon, Cathy, a dark-haired young barmaid sexily dressed in a pink and black flounced frock with a low neckline, offers him a glass on the house. The interest she shows in him does not seem purely professional. The stranger does not drink this first glass; just as the barman places it down in front of him a revolver fired from the back of the room smashes it to pieces. Violence is apparently the only language the Kid speaks – the Kid being a sinister silent young man with the physique of a tightrope-walker and a crazy look in his eye, wearing an eccentric black top hat. Having calmly drunk a second glass in a tense silence, the Prisoner, despite the gun trained on him, settles his account with the young thug with a single punch.

The Judge, an elderly grey-haired man in a black suit and frilled shirt, obviously the real boss in town, invites the Prisoner over to his table, addressing him as 'Sheriff'.

*PRISONER: I don't know you.*
*JUDGE: I know you. I know all about you. That's why you're here.*
*PRISONER: Where?*
*JUDGE: Here.*

He then suggests that the Prisoner work for him, but the ex-sheriff refuses to carry a gun any more.

*PRISONER: I'm not for hire.*
*JUDGE: You've turned in your badge.*
*PRISONER: And my gun.*

*JUDGE: What were your reasons?*
*PRISONER: My reasons?*

The stranger very quickly discovers that the town is under the thumb of the corrupt Judge and his henchmen, and that they will stick at nothing to try to make him change his mind. Most of all he learns that it is difficult to leave Harmony. It proves impossible to buy any kind of horse, and the local population takes very badly the disdain he shows towards such a good town.

*ELDER: Well stranger. Fancy living in Harmony?*
*PRISONER: It's not my kind of town.*
*ELDER: It's a good town.*
*PRISONER: Enjoy it.*
*ELDER: Why what's wrong with our town Mister?*
*PRISONER: Maybe I don't like the way it's run.*
*ELDER: Oh, if you do just as the judge says, he'll look after you.*
*PRISONER: I look after myself.*
*ELDER: It's a good town.*
*PRISONER: Keep it.*

Other inhabitants side with the Town Elder and the two men soon attract a small, menacing crowd. Suddenly the Indian rushes at the Prisoner, shouting that the stranger has insulted their town. The Prisoner grabs a stick but when he turns round he finds himself face to face with two gunmen. A little later he is behind bars in the town prison, where the Judge, to save him from the townspeople, places him in protective custody. To placate them, he offers them another victim, Cathy's brother, who, despite the young girl's pleas, is dragged out of his cell and lynched.

The barmaid has evidently fallen in love with the stranger, so different from the saloon's uncouth clientele, and that same evening she helps him escape from prison by getting his warder, the Kid, drunk. Her task is made easier by the unbalanced youth's passion for her – a passion as violent as it is unhealthy.

The Prisoner does not get far. On the road north – according to Cathy, the only way out – he is caught in a lasso by the Judge's men, who drag him unceremoniously along the ground back to the saloon, where the town's court is now in session. It is not the Prisoner who is the accused – he was only in 'protective custody' – but Cathy, who is guilty of 'aiding a criminal to escape'; as the Judge remarks, she did not know that the Prisoner was not a criminal.

The Judge seems to have a peculiar concept of justice. When the court finds the young woman guilty, he tells the stranger he will let her go when he decides to work for him. The Prisoner is a man of honour and he cannot bear to see the woman who risked everything to help him, remain in prison. But though he agrees to wear a sheriff's badge again, he still refuses to carry the guns that come with the job. The whole town of Harmony then seems to conspire against him to break his resistance.

First the Kid, who has clearly taken offence at Cathy's love for the stranger. In the saloon he starts provoking the Prisoner by sliding a gun down the counter at him. Then, faced with the stranger's total lack of reaction, he shoots at him. The first bullet grazes the Prisoner's cheek, the second wounds his hand, but he remains cool. The arrival of the Judge puts an end to this dangerous game, but he warns the new sheriff that 'it's not safe to walk around without guns'.

The men the Judge gets to persuade him to carry a gun do not succeed in bending his will either. But the fight that takes place is extremely violent, and the Prisoner, his face all bruised, only just wins.

The violence escalates. That evening in the saloon Will, a slightly tipsy customer holds Cathy a little too close for the Kid's liking; the Kid shoots him dead. But when the sheriff, still unarmed, turns up a few seconds later everyone present tells him it was Will who drew his gun first.

However, a small group of Harmony townspeople, led by a fellow called Jim, seem to have grown tired of the Kid's excesses and of the corrupt Judge's clique and ask the Prisoner to help them 'clean up the town'. But the Judge gets wind of the plot and before long the new sheriff finds Jim's body in his office. Never have we seen him so close to giving in and arming himself, but his spirit of determination quickly triumphs over this moment of weakness and he decides to stake everything on getting away from this cursed town, this time taking Cathy with him.

The first part of his plan works quite well. After nightfall he succeeds in disabling the Judge's men who are guarding the outskirts of Harmony, and in seizing two horses. But the young woman does not make it to the rendezvous. Just as she is about to leave after work, the Kid jumps on her and brutally tries to kiss her. The young barmaid, powerless to break free of his embrace, bites him hard on the lip. The enraged madman strangles her, then walks off leaving her body lying on the ground.

The town of Harmony has won. But not quite. Although the Prisoner, after burying the murdered young woman goes, armed with his revolver after the Kid, he takes care before putting on his belt to remove the sheriff's badge pinned to his jacket. And after a few seconds' dramatic confrontation, it is as a private individual that, true to the ending of a traditional western, he shoots down the murderer.

But this western is not yet over, and it is not as genuine as it looks.

The Judge, escorted by his henchmen, finds the Prisoner in the saloon, sitting at a table with a bottle in front of him.

*JUDGE: You beat him . . . and he was the fastest I've ever seen.*
*PRISONER: The fastest you ever will see. I quit.*
*JUDGE: You aren't quitting while I've got Cathy. Just get it clear you work for me, guns and all.*
*PRISONER: You haven't got Cathy any longer. She's dead.*
*JUDGE: But he was only supposed to . . .*
*PRISONER: Rough her up a little bit?*
*JUDGE: Wait. You work for me whether you like it or not. Nobody walks out on me. I'm not letting you join some other outfit. I'll kill you first. You've got five seconds to make up your mind . . .*

The spectacular gunfight that follows is worthy of the great Western tradition; the fearless, noble stranger who single-handedly takes on the villains running the town. The courageous good guy is also the fastest on the draw, and the ex-sheriff shoots down one of the shady Judge's gunslingers. But the well-oiled machinery of this archetypical western suddenly snarls up: the Judge pumps several shots into the hero, who falls, then lies sprawled on the ground, lifeless . . .

When he opens his eyes a few seconds later it is not the tradition of the western that is being respected, but that of the series. The stranger in Harmony may have escaped death, but the Prisoner has not escaped the Village. The man lying in the saloon is no longer in cowboy clothes, but wearing a dark blazer with white trim. When he gets to his feet, staring in bewilderment at the stage set around him, we see a pair of headphones fall on the floor. Then one by one he turns around the cardboard cut-outs representing the characters in the drama he has just lived through.

Meanwhile, grating chords have been gradually replacing the typical western music, but that very familiar sound of brass band music now blends to even greater sinister effect. Finally, after walking through some countryside, the Prisoner comes upon a particularly harmonious-looking baroque-style square. A few seconds later the metal double doors to the Green Dome's circular office open before him. The characters he gazes at for a moment in silence look quite real. The Judge from Harmony is wearing a badge with the Number 2 on it; the Kid wears badge number 8; and as for the dark-haired young woman with the sad face and jaunty canvas cap, leaning against a strange-looking bicycle, we discover that she is Number 22. All three have apparently just removed their headphones.

*NUMBER 8: Interesting ... that he can separate fact from fantasy so quickly.*
*NUMBER 2: I told you he was different. I knew it wouldn't work. Fill him with hallucinatory drugs, put him in a dangerous environment, talk to him through microphones.*
*NUMBER 8: It's always worked and it would have worked this time...*
*NUMBER 2: But it didn't, did it? Give him love, take it away. Isolate him. Make him kill, then face him with death. He'll crack. Break him, even in his mind, and the rest will be easy. I should never have listened to you.*
*NUMBER 8: It would have worked if you had kept your head and not created the crisis too soon.*
*NUMBER 2: How could I control it? Tell me that. You said yourself we would get involved and do what we would do in the real situation.*
*NUMBER 8: Well then, don't blame my method, just your own damned lack of self-control.*
*NUMBER 2: It's all right for you. I have to answer for this failure. It seems I'm not the only one who got involved...*

The two other participants seem to find it similarly difficult to break free of the illusion. Young Number 22, overwhelmed by the Prisoner's appearance, cannot hold back her tears, and goes running out of the circular office. Outside, she sits on the steps of a dummy saloon bar, crying for her vanished love.

Nor has Number 8 entirely kicked over the traces of the Machiavellian psychodrama conceived to break the Prisoner. Understanding the reason for the despair felt by the girl he still sees as Cathy, and prey to the morbid jealousy of the Kid, he strangles her, this time for real! The stranger to Harmony comes running when he hears her cries of terror; she dies in the arms of the man she genuinely loved in that imaginary world, while betraying him in reality. After his crime Number 8 sinks into madness. He ends up by killing himself in a fit of delirium, by jumping from the gallery above the saloon and its *trompe-l'oeil* décor, of which only the hardness of the ground is real.

There is no external element to detract from the Prisoner's victory, made bitter by the death of the young woman, in whom he saw a victim more than anything else. It is thanks only to his moral integrity that he has succeeded in preserving his spiritual integrity to emerge unscathed from the 'trip' intended to break him mentally. His enemies' weapons are once more turned against them; the hallucinogenic drugs prove to be infinitely more dangerous for those who are less at one with themselves than he is.

# Episode Fifteen:
# The Girl Who Was Death

After the usual opening sequence the pages of a book open on the picture of a village – an ordinary, reassuring, typical English village. In the foreground is a sturdy fruit tree in flower, bright green grass, a cricket match; everything seems normal. And yet . . .

The scorekeeper, who is watching the crowd through binoculars, seems particularly interested in one of the players, though he lingers a while on a lovely pair of legs belonging to a pretty blonde; she looks charming in her spring outfit: a white dress and wide-brimmed hat. But he does not see that someone in the bushes has replaced the ball with another, which explodes when the batsman hits it.

We find the Prisoner in ordinary clothes. Unless the story takes place before his resignation, he has apparently resumed his job. He reads in the newspaper about the death of the 'Colonel', a Secret Service agent killed by an exploding ball during a cricket match.

His colleague Potter, the man with the binoculars, now disguised as a shoeshine boy, tells him more:

*PRISONER: Busy, Potter?*
*POTTER: It's our form of Siberia.*
*PRISONER: What was the Colonel up to?*
*POTTER: Doctor Schnipps. Crazy scientist. For the last twenty six years he's been building a superrocket. To destroy London.*
*PRISONER: Where?*
*POTTER: Well that's just what the Colonel was trying to find out.*

At that moment Potter receives a telephone call and we see him raise to his ear a shoe brush with a concealed transceiver inside it. Having 'hung up', he conveys to the Prisoner his boss's instructions: he is to go to the local record shop, where he will be given a message. Throughout their conversation, they have failed to notice a pretty blonde, dressed in white, standing in place of a mannequin in a nearby shop window.

In a booth at the record shop the Prisoner listens to the message with which he is able to converse, recorded on a disc. The message is very clear: 'Find and destroy Professor Schnipps' rocket.' His boss being unable to provide him with any lead to go on, he is told to 'take over where the Colonel left off'.

On the cricket pitch the Prisoner, his face now disguised behind thick whiskers and an impressive moustache, narrowly escapes the booby-trap ball intended for him. He manages to catch it and throw it straight back in the direction of a small wood beside which we see the blonde girl. On the site of the explosion he finds another message, written in lipstick on a handkerchief, telling him to meet at the pub.

From now on we are swept along at a dizzying pace through a completely crazy spy story, a kind of surrealist *James Bond* made with the collaboration of the Marx Brothers. The Prisoner escapes one deadly trap set by the mysterious blonde only to find another message sending him straight into another. As he drinks beer at the pub, an alarming warning gradually appears in the bottom of his glass: YOU … HAVE … BEEN … POISONED … We do not know whether it is thanks to his experience as a secret agent that he immediately finds an effective antidote: having calmly put down his empty glass, he orders a large number of others, each one containing a different drink: whisky, vodka, brandy … which he consumes one after the other! As he rushes to the gents, he passes a bewitching blonde with an immensely long cigarette-holder. Like her dress, it is white.

The next message, written on a towel next to the basin, sends him to the Turkish baths, where he turns up in a Sherlock Holmes disguise. He almost suffocates! Then after the Turkish bath, he is forced, under the name of Mr X, into the boxing ring to confront the champion, Karmanski, called 'the Killer'. During the fight the brute with the cauliflower ears passes on a message from 'the lady', giving him his next rendezvous: the Tunnel of Love at a nearby funfair.

There, for the first time, he hears the voice of the female killer, emanating from a small tape-recorder in the back of the carriage he gets into, still dressed as the sleuth of Baker Street:

*VOICE: Hello… no, don't turn around. I have you covered. The tunnel of love is very fitting. Because I'm beginning to love you. In my way. All my life I've been looking for a worthy opponent. You have passed my first little test brilliantly…*

Just as the Prisoner throws it into the water, the tape-recorder explodes.

Having tried in vain to catch up with the white figure on the big wheel, the merry-go-round and various other fairground sideshows, the Prisoner comes upon the fatal blonde just as she is roaring off at the wheel of a superb white Jaguar. He pursues her in a powerful sports car, shedding his Sherlock Holmes costume while driving. On the car radio the Prisoner again hears the teasing voice:

*VOICE: I love you madly … and I love the way your hair curls on the back of your neck. You'll make a beautiful corpse. I am going to do you the honour of letting you die superbly…*

The breakneck chase becomes even more unreal when the driver of the Jag causes both the Prisoner's car and the road to turn by simply moving her finger. The Prisoner does not lose control of his car and arrives still in one piece in the deserted village of Witchwood. The Jaguar and the blonde have mysteriously disappeared, but that captivating voice suddenly comes over a loud-speaker:

*VOICE: I'm glad you could come. This is to be our love tryst. You may not see my face, but you may know my name… My name is Death. I'm sorry my father could not be here to greet you… but he's busy with his rocket. You are a born survivor. I am a born killer. We were made for each other. But I fear this is where it must end. Is your heart pounding? Your hands shaking? That's love, my darling! My father was a great man. But the war ended before he was recognised. But when London lies in ruins he will be a god.*

In the fantastic setting of the ghost village, the death traps succeed one another at an infernal pace, each one more ingenious, more spectacular than the last.

175

Just when the Prisoner at the very last minute has stopped a machine-gun from firing, after it is automatically set off when he passes, a trap door opens beneath his feet and he is suspended over electrified spikes, slowly rising towards him. He saves himself in the nick of time by throwing a plank of wood onto them.

Locked into the candlestick-maker's, where hundreds of candles, all lit and emitting a lethal gas, will explode if they are blown out – the voice over the loud-speaker tells him this – he manages to blow them out all at the same time and blast the door open.

Out in the street he finally comes face to face with the woman with a deadly passion for him; still in white, now wearing a pointed helmet, she has an automatic rifle trained on him. But he gets into a bulldozer and, shielded from the bullets, drives it at her.

*SONIA: All right darling you win. I've just realised something. I don't want to kill you anymore. You are the best. If I kill you, what will be left for me? Life would be a bore. Why don't you join us, my father and me? We could have a wonderful life together. You would be a constant challenge to us.*

Squealing joyfully, she nevertheless continues to attack him, first with a mortar, then with grenades. She finally destroys the bulldozer with a bazooka, hailing the explosion with a casual 'Bye bye, lover!' Then convinced that her 'lover' is dead, she touches up her femme fatale make-up and walks away from Witchwood with a spring in her step.

But the Prisoner is not dead and wastes no time in climbing out of the underground shelter beneath the bulldozer that saved him from the flames, and going after the graceful white-clothed figure to a helicopter. Without the pilot's realising, he clings on to it just as it is about to take off. After a perilous journey he finally discovers Dr Schnipps' hideout, where his daughter has come to join him: a lighthouse situated on the high cliffs of a deserted shore.

When he reaches the end of a long tunnel in the seabed he finds himself in a strange room humming with machines, the walls of which are covered with engravings of Napoleon, Josephine and war scenes from that period. But the soldier in Napoleonic uniform who suddenly appears is real enough.

Just as large as life are Napoleon and Josephine, whom we find at the top of the lighthouse – Napoleon being the crazy scientist, and Josephine the blonde killer, as ravishing as ever in her pure Empire-style white decolleté dress. Dr Schnipps, as expected, is about to issue orders to the soldiers standing to attention in front of him.

*SCHNIPPS: You're quite sure you killed him?*
*SONIA: Father . . . who taught me?*
*SCHNIPPS: You're a girl after my own heart. If only your dear mother could see you now . . . good old Josephine.*
*SONIA: Tell me again about her last cavalry charge.*
*SCHNIPPS: Not now child, we have work to do. Gentlemen . . . yes, all right. It's very good. In one hour's time London will lie entirely in ruins.*

The Emperor pours over a plan of the hated capital, imagining it reconstructed according to a 'Napoleonic' perspective, with the name of Trafalgar Square banished from living memory.

Meanwhile, the Prisoner has not been wasting his time: having overpowered a number of soldiers, one by one, and dressed himself in one of their uniforms, he blithely sabotages all the weapons and ammunition he can lay hands on. This allows him, shortly afterwards, to escape with ease the small group of soldiers sent after him. The poor Imperial troops are brought down in a single body by their own guns firing backwards!

But he does not escape his dear killer, who pulls her own weapon, in perfect working order, on him. A few moments later he is securely tied to a chair.

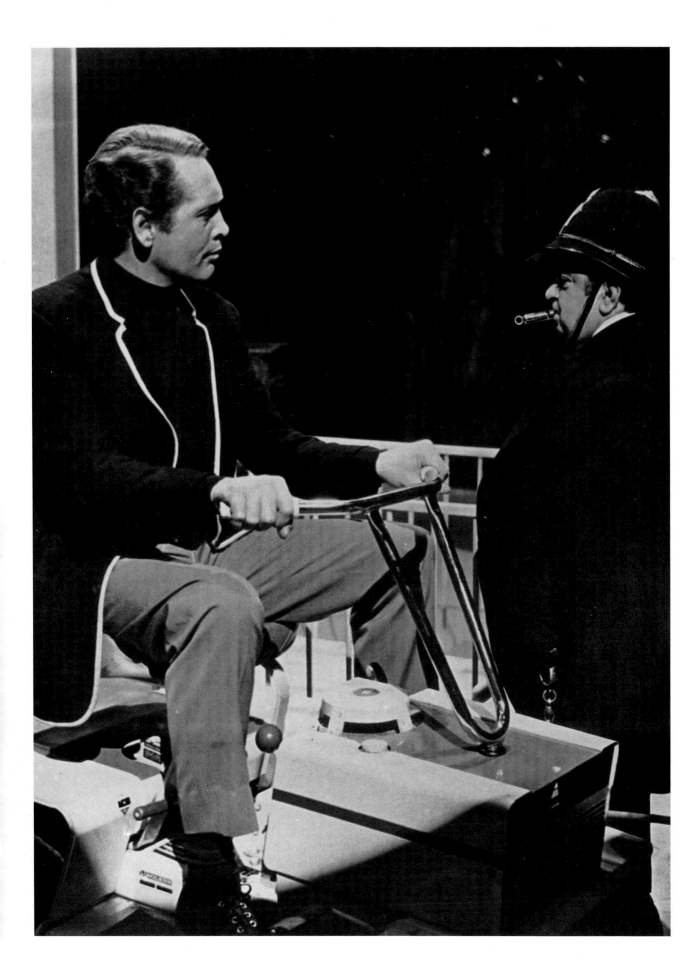

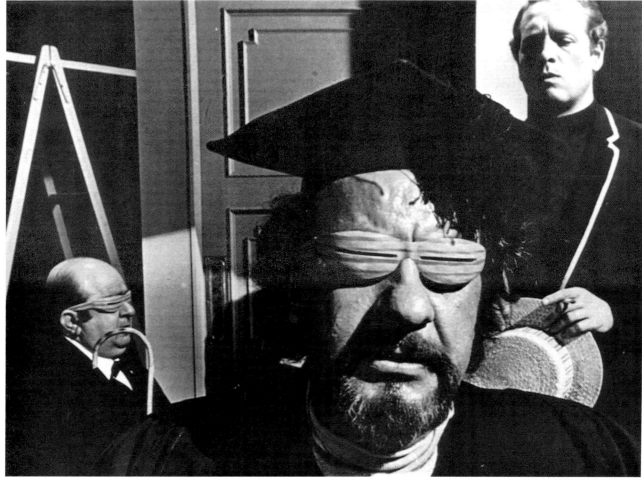

*SONIA: I'm afraid there won't be a next time for you darling. I'm going to give you the most original death in history ... you're going for a rocket ride ...*
*PRISONER: Oh the rocket, that reminds me, where is it?*
*SCHNIPPS: It is here.*
*PRISONER: Here?*
*SCHNIPPS: All around you ...*
*PRISONER: All around us.*
*SCHNIPPS: The lighthouse itself ...*
*PRISONER: Is the rocket.*
*SCHNIPPS: This is the nose cone we're in now. So you see, when the rocket reaches London, you'll be the first to know. Won't that be exciting?*

The Emperor spends a little too long packing bulky files into bags, giving the Prisoner, who has been left on his own, time to free himself; not, as is usually the case in a thriller spy story, by breaking his bonds but simply by lifting the detachable back-rest on the chair to which he is tied. He quickly climbs down a rope to a small boat, from which he watches the lovely Sonia throwing the now harmless grenades at him.

The explosive removed from them, which remains inside the rocket, puts an end to Sonia's life, as well as her father's, and his insane scheme ... and also brings to an end the wonderful story that the Prisoner has just been telling three little children in a nursery in the Village!

*PRISONER: And that is how I saved London from the mad scientist.*

In the Green Dome's circular office (the new) Number 2 (alias Schnipps, alias Napoleon) observes on his control screen, with a particularly glum look on his face, the charming spectacle afforded by the nursery where the Prisoner is now kindly tucking the children into bed.

*NUMBER 2: He might drop his guard with children ... he might give something away ...*

His assistant is all in black, apart from her white badge. Her name is not Sonia, nor even Death; she is just a number ...

*SONIA: Well it was worth a try, Number 2.*
*NUMBER 2: He told them nothing. He told them a blessed fairytale. That one wouldn't drop his guard with his own grandmother ...*

In the nursery the children are now in bed and the Prisoner turns out the light.

*PRISONER: Goodnight children ... everywhere.*

The final word is addressed with a mocking smile to Number 2. The final scene shows the Prisoner taking mischievous pleasure in placing a soft toy – a funny-faced clown – in front of the camera.

The Village Authorities do not seem to be aware of the dangers inherent in subversive stories dreamt up by the Prisoner for those destined to become Numbers – although from the Authorities' point of view it might not be a totally pointless exercise to associate love and death in their young minds.

This hilarious, entertaining episode comes as something of a relief from the thought-provoking, challenging stories presented in the rest of the series.

# Episode Sixteen:
## Once Upon A Time

In the Village a very strange week is about to begin – a decisive week for the Prisoner, for Number 2, and for the viewer. Right from the start there is a sense that the so far cyclical pattern of the series could well turn into a spiralling vortex.

It is the same Number 2 as the one who appeared in 'The Chimes of Big Ben', but he seems to have lost his plumpness and, notably, his joviality. Pre-occupied, with drawn features, he rudely orders the Butler to remove the breakfast he has hardly touched.

*NUMBER 2: Wait! Remove it ... I told you to remove it ...*

And no previous incumbent of the job has ever dared to address the real Village Authority in the tone of voice he adopts when speaking on the red phone about Rover, whose palpitating mass spills over the spherical chair it is sat in:

*NUMBER 2: And you can remove that thing too – I'm not an inmate. You can say what you like. You brought me back here. I told you the last time, you were using the wrong approach. I do it my way or you find somebody else.*

This time he is heard: the spherical chair and its disturbing occupant sink into the ground. He then presses a button.

The inside of Villa Number 6 fills the control screen. The Prisoner is having his breakfast after his fashion: all the while he is eating, he never stops pacing the room, cup in hand, like some wild animal.

*NUMBER 2: Why do you care?*

Then he picks up the yellow phone and puts the question directly to Number 6:

*NUMBER 2: Why do you care?*
*PRISONER: I know your voice.*
*NUMBER 2: I have been here before. Why do you care?*
*PRISONER: You'll never know.*

The Prisoner brings their conversation to an abrupt end by going out, clapping ironically when the door opens automatically. His gesture is under-lined by a few brief chords of mocking music.

*NUMBER 2: Wait and see.*

A moment later he is furiously rifling through the thick file on Number 6. Very familiar scenes then come up on the screen, forming a remarkable anthology of the Prisoner's fits of rage:

PRISONER: *Going to escape and come back, wipe this place off the face of the earth, obliterate it and you with it... Is this what they did to you, is this how they started to break you before you gave them what they were after... I've resigned... I will not be pushed, filed, stamped, indexed, briefed, debriefed or numbered...*

Suddenly Number 2 makes his decision. With the edited highlights of the Prisoner's rebellion still running, his subversive declarations counterpointing Number 2's own conversation, he picks up the red telephone.

NUMBER 2: *Degree Absolute... I require approval.*
PRISONER: *Unlike me, many of you have accepted the situation of your imprisonment and will die here like rotten cabbages...*
NUMBER 2: *If you think he's that important, there's certainly no other alternative. You must risk either one of us...*
PRISONER: *I intend to discover who are the prisoners and who're the warders...*
NUMBER 2: *I am a good man... I was a good man, but if you get him, he will be better... and there's no other way... I repeat no other way...*
PRISONER: *I will not make any deals with you. I've resigned.*
NUMBER 2: *Degree Absolute tonight... please.*
PRISONER: *I will not be pushed, filed, stamped, indexed, briefed, debriefed or numbered...*
NUMBER 2: *A week... that's not long enough. You don't want to damage him...*

That evening preparations for the final test to which the Prisoner will be subjected are carried out in a terribly tense atmosphere. Having been told that he has been placed 'under orders' for a period of one week, the Supervisor is instructed by Number 2 to release all subsidiary personnel. As soon as the superfluous technicians have left the Control Room in an orderly fashion, the bald-headed man, acting on Number 2's orders, proceeds to put Number 6 into a deep, electronically induced hypnotic trance. A strange lamp comes down over the face of the sleeping man.

This time it is not a man in a white coat who comes into the Prisoner's bedroom but Number 2 himself. He settles down in an armchair beside the Prisoner's bed, and reads out nursery rhymes.

When daylight comes Number 2 seems very tired, and it is a puffy face with drawn features that we see at the window overlooking the empty square of the sunlit Village.

As for the Prisoner, he has literally slept like a baby all night long, with the soothing sound of Humpty Dumpty's antics in his ears. And when Number 2 wakes him, he leaps out of bed with a smile and with the rather innocent look of a little boy on his face.

NUMBER 2: *Want to go walkies? Wash and dress quickly and I'll show you some nice things. Walkies...*

The Prisoner rushes to the bathroom in his pyjamas, radiant as a kid who just seen his first Christmas tree.

It is a surprising trio that assembles some time later in the Green Dome: the Prisoner is sitting in a wheelchair pushed by the butler. He seems to have regressed into a carefree little boy, totally absorbed in consuming the ice-cream cornet that Number 2, at his side, has brought him on the way here.

183

Having entered the Village's underground installations, and gone down countless metal corridors, they end up in an amazing play room, with a baby's playpen, a see-saw, a rocking horse, a blackboard ... While the Butler, now wearing extraordinary goggles with only a slit to see through, shakes a rattle, Number 2 closes the heavy metal door, locking them all in. Then having adjusted a pointer on the dial attached to the door, and drawn a heavy black velvet curtain across it, he declares theatrically:

*NUMBER 2: This is it ... for better or worse, who knows ... One week. One teeny weeny week my boy. Neither of us can leave. Till death do us part ... and I brought it on myself. Who knows? Come ahead son, let's see what you're made of. Find out what's in that noddle of yours ...*

*All the world's a stage*
*And all the men and women merely players*
*They have their exits and their entrances*
*And one man in his time plays many parts*
*His acts being seven ages.*

*William Shakespeare ... he summed it all up, so they say ... At first the infant, mewling and puking in the nurse's arms ... be still ... Even as a child, there is something in your brain that is a puzzlement. I intend to discover it. A, find missing link. When I have found it, I will refine it, tune it and you will play our game. B, put it together, and if I fail ... then C – BANG!*

What we now see are the different acts of a play Shakespeare might have written had he been familiar with psychoanalysis. In the course of this psychodrama Number 2 plays the various characters representing authority met by the Prisoner during the different ages from birth to his resignation, that he has already lived through.
First, his father:

*NUMBER 2: I am your father. Do I ever say anything that makes you want to hate me?*
*We're going for a walk, aren't we? Into the park, isn't it? I always speak well of your mother, don't I?*

Number 2 is obviously trying to win the child's confidence, and to take advantage of the Prisoner's regression to find out where in his brain lies the origin of his distrust of all forms of authority.

The 'father' and 'son' are seated at either end of the see-saw. As they go up and down alternately the Prisoner meekly repeats the words of the nursery rhyme that goes: 'See saw Margery Daw, Jacky shall have a new master', whilst in the background we see the mysterious butler playing on the child's swing.

Then the teacher:
In a small adjoining room, the office to which he has summoned his pupil, Number 2, dressed now in black gown and mortar board, plays the harmonium while questioning the Prisoner, who stands respectfully behind him, holding a boater. The little boy refuses to betray one of his friends:

*NUMBER 2: Who was it? This is the ninth day since the incident. You have been in my study every morning at this time and you still refuse to co-operate. Today is your last chance. It wasn't you?*
*PRISONER: No sir.*
*NUMBER 2: You know who it was?*
*PRISONER: Yes sir.*
*NUMBER 2: Who was it? This is cowardice.*
*PRISONER: That's honour, sir.*
*NUMBER 2: We don't talk about such things.*
*PRISONER: You should teach it, sir.*
*NUMBER 2: You're a fool.*
*PRISONER: Yes sir, not a rat.*
*NUMBER 2: Rat?*
*PRISONER: Rat.*
*NUMBER 2: I'm a rat?*
*PRISONER: No sir, I'm a fool, not a rat.*
*NUMBER 2: Society . . .*
*PRISONER: Yes sir.*
*NUMBER 2: Society is the place where people exist together . . . that is civilisation. The lone wolf belongs to the wilderness. You must not grow up to be a lone wolf!*
*PRISONER: No sir.*
*NUMBER 2: You must conform. It is my sworn duty to see that you do conform. You will take six . . . of the best.*

The schoolboy again protests his innocence, and the number of strokes goes up to ten. But as the dwarf approaches with the cane in his hand, the Prisoner then asks for twelve, 'so that I can remember'.

Some time has elapsed and the Prisoner is now a young man who has just passed his final exams. It is graduation day:

*NUMBER 2: Congratulations my boy. You will do well. We are proud of you. Proud that you have learnt to manage your rebellious spirit. Proud that your obedience is absolute. Why did you resign?*

Number 6's resistance then reveals itself in the mind of the model student. The more Number 2 insists, repeating his question, the more agitated the Prisoner becomes, protesting that it is a 'state secret' until he ends up shouting: 'No! No!' The meek little boy whom we saw only a little while before licking his ice-cream is now capable of physically attacking the representative of authority. It is the butler who puts an end to their violent brawl by coshing the young rebel on the back of the head. When Number 2 gets up, his clothes in a mess, it takes him a good few minutes to catch his breath.

*NUMBER 2: I'm beginning to like him.*

In the next scene – a particularly crazy one – the 'schoolmaster' tries to teach his 'pupil' to count while the Prisoner rides a rocking horse, looking up now and again at a strange lamp that baths his face in a dazzling light. Oddly, the 'child' is completely incapable of getting any further than 5 and refuses to utter the number 6!

Two fights of incredible physical and mental violence follow. Although these are ostensibly coaching sessions – one in boxing, the other in fencing – the true stakes involved remain constantly to the fore and the two adversaries seem to be engaged in a real battle to the death.

They both wear the appropriate kit for the two sports, and Number 2 of course is the coach. Amidst all the professional talk and the punches and thrusts, the eternal question keeps recurring: 'Why did you resign?' At the end of the fencing lesson, Number 2 – disarmed, with his back against a door, and having removed his mask – urges his young adversary to kill him. The Prisoner, who has also removed his mask, and whose face shows that he is under incredible stress, tries three times to stab the man he perceives with his whole being as a deadly enemy. But, despite the hypnosis, his natural reluctance to strike a defenceless man finally prevails and his sword plunges harmlessly into the door beside Number 2's face.

NUMBER 2: *You missed boy. You still can't do it.*
PRISONER: *Sorry, sorry...*
NUMBER 2: *Sorry. You're sorry for everybody. Is that why you resigned?*

The sight of the two men shaving while the butler makes coffee suddenly brings us back to real time – Village time, that is. It is not clear how many hours or days have passed since the beginning of Operation Double Absolute, but in the timescale of the psychodrama the Prisoner has now reached the stage of life when he needs to find a job:

NUMBER 2: *Yes, well I must say I'm considerably impressed. Of course naturally I shall have to discuss with my directors. But you seem admirably suited. Just to bring matters up to date. Why exactly do you want this job?*
PRISONER: *It's a job.*
NUMBER 2: *No other reason at all?*
PRISONER: *No.*
NUMBER 2: *You have no respect for tradition?*
PRISONER: *Pardon?*
NUMBER 2: *No respect for tradition for a long established firm of bankers?*
PRISONER: *I was very good at mathematics.*
NUMBER 2: *So were we all. Otherwise we wouldn't be in it would we?*
PRISONER: *I don't mean that.*
NUMBER 2: *What do you mean?*
PRISONER: *I mean I can work.*
NUMBER 2: *Tell me what hours.*
PRISONER: *I don't care.*
NUMBER 2: *Why?*
PRISONER: *Well, it's the way I'm made.*

The Prisoner has also reached the age of breaking laws. Traffic regulations, for instance. When he drives round the room in a little car, the butler, dressed as a bobby, stops him with a blast of his whistle. Number 2, in the traditional scarlet robes and wig of the English judiciary, then plays the judge before whom the motorist appears on a charge of speeding.

The absurd setting (throughout the 'trial' the butler never stops spinning the wheels of an amazing wooden contraption in front of the 'judge') yet again fails to obscure the violence of the confrontation, which surfaces with every exchange of an apparently crazy dialogue. And behind the ostensible trivial charge in the psychodrama lies another, infinitely more serious ... Finally the sentence is passed:

NUMBER 2: *... Twenty units.*
PRISONER: *I can't pay.*

*NUMBER 2: Nothing?*
*PRISONER: Units are not for me.*
*NUMBER 2: You are a member of the Village.*
*PRISONER: No.*
*NUMBER 2: You are a unit.*
*PRISONER: No.*
*NUMBER 2: Of society.*
*PRISONER: No.*
*NUMBER 2: Contempt.*
*PRISONER: No.*
*NUMBER 2: Of court.*
*PRISONER: I accept ... I accept the ruling. Thank you.*
*NUMBER 2: Six days in jail.*
*PRISONER: I was rebelling, my lord.*
*NUMBER 2: Six days!*
*PRISONER: I was rebelling against the figures, my lord.*
*NUMBER 2: Six days. Take him away.*

During these last exchanges Number 2 and the butler drag the 'convict' to the back of the room where a kind of self-contained living area has been set up (some kitchen facilities and a basin are visible) behind heavy bars. When these bars close on the person who is now a prisoner three times over, he suddenly recovers all his aggression:

*PRISONER: I shall appeal against unfair treatment.*
*NUMBER 2: You've had the same treatment as everybody else.*
*PRISONER: That's why I'm going to appeal. Let me out ... this is unfair treatment ... Why, why, why did I resign?*

He continues to shout, shaking the bars dementedly, while the camera draws back from the 'cage' to reveal the rocking horse pathetically tipping backwards and forwards in the foreground.

Later Number 2 wakes up fully clothed on the table on which he collapsed after this particularly trying session.

His face looks more and more tired, almost as drawn as that of his hypnotised 'patient', and it is with a heavy step that he walks across the toy-strewn room.

Inside the cage – which suddenly appears to be the ultimate reality behind the smiling Village – the Prisoner seems not to have slept. Standing behind the bars, which he grips with his hands locked in cuffs, he continues to ask the same question:

*PRISONER: Why?*
*NUMBER 2: Why did you resign?*
*PRISONER: For peace.*
*NUMBER 2: Peace?*
*PRISONER: Let me out.*
*NUMBER 2: You resigned for peace?*
*PRISONER: Sure. Let me out.*
*NUMBER 2: You're a fool.*
*PRISONER: For peace of mind.*
*NUMBER 2: What?*
*PRISONER: Too many people know too much.*
*NUMBER 2: Never.*
*PRISONER: I know too much.*
*NUMBER 2: Tell me.*
*PRISONER: I know too much about you.*

The violence of this symbolic – and deadly – conflict now reaches its peak. At first the fury of the two adversaries who confront each other on either side of the bars remains verbal:

*NUMBER 2: Who am I?*
*PRISONER: You are an enemy.*
*NUMBER 2: I'm on your side.*
*PRISONER: Yeah...*
*NUMBER 2: Why did you resign?*

The series' leitmotif question keeps returning to Number 2's lips, but it is now the Prisoner who leads the attack:

*PRISONER: Know who you are?*
*NUMBER 2: What?*
*PRISONER: A fool...*
*NUMBER 2: What?*
*PRISONER: Yes, an idiot.*
*NUMBER 2: No! I'll kill you.*

The Prisoner does not allow his opponent to regain the initiative. Dashing over to the kitchen, he brings back a knife, which he hands to Number 2, saying: 'Kill me!'

Having ordered the dwarf to open the door, Number 2 now holds the knife-point pressed to the Prisoner's throat. The Prisoner holds his gaze with an ironic look, but suddenly drops to the floor. Lying on his back, still hand-cuffed, he once again challenges Number 2:

*PRISONER: Kill me lying down.*
*NUMBER 2: Get up you fool.*
*PRISONER: You can't...*
*NUMBER 2: In the war, you killed...*
*PRISONER: Yes.*
*NUMBER 2: You killed for fun.*
*PRISONER: For peace.*
*NUMBER 2: Do as I say...*
*PRISONER: I did what I was told...*

It is war. A tape-recording of the sound of violent explosions fills the room, while the butler works a machine that produces thick smoke. The mental combat that pits the Prisoner against the representative of the Village Authorities now takes place within the context of the Second World War. Number 2 and the Prisoner – who is of course under his orders – are bombing enemy territory. Both wearing flying suits and oxygen masks. Suddenly their plane is hit, and they have to bail out – they jump down from the plank on which they are perched. The Prisoner immediately finds himself in the position of being a POW, being interrogated in German by Number 2. The Prisoner tells him: 'I do not wish to kill.'

But suddenly his behaviour becomes oddly exuberent, his speech increasingly incoherent. And when Number 2, resuming his interrogation in English, asks him why he resigned, the Prisoner replies mockingly: 'Six!' Then in a completely normal voice, he declares that he is hungry and asks for supper. As we have suspected for some time already, the Prisoner is no longer under the influence of hypnosis, and has become himself again – a state of being that Number 2 has perhaps never known.

With Number 2 now lying on the table and the Prisoner leaning over him, it is the Prisoner who now conducts the interrogation, questioning him about Degree Absolute:

*PRISONER: You chose this method because you knew that the only way to beat me was to gain my respect?*
*NUMBER 2: That is correct.*

PRISONER: *And then I would confide.*
NUMBER 2: *I hoped that you would come to trust me.*
PRISONER: *This is a recognised method?*
NUMBER 2: *Used in psychoanalysis. The patient must come to trust his doctor totally.*
PRISONER: *Sometimes they change places.*
NUMBER 2: *It is essential in extreme cases.*
PRISONER: *Also a risk.*
NUMBER 2: *A grave risk.*
PRISONER: *If the doctor has his own problems.*
NUMBER 2: *I have.*
PRISONER: *That is why the system is known as Degree Absolute?*
NUMBER 2: *It's one or the other of us.*
PRISONER: *Why don't you resign?*
NUMBER 2: *Very good. You're very good at it... Play something cheerful.*

The butler, apparently a Jack-of-all-trades, attacks a jolly tune. Number 2 seems to have recovered some of his former joviality and leads the Prisoner into the kitchen, where he uncorks a bottle. Then, after they have toasted each other, he gives his 'guest' a guided tour of the premises.

NUMBER 2: *Let me show you around. This delightful residence is known as the Embryo Room... In it you can relive from the cradle to the grave, seven ages of man. William Shakespeare.*

Number 2 explains that there is no way out before the time set aside for the experiment has elapsed. And to convince him of this, he shows him the metal door, hermetically sealed for one week. On the dial he is amazed to discover that they have only five minutes left before they embark on what he calls 'a new phase in our relationship'. We have reached the last act.

Number 2 again leads the Prisoner over to the cage.

NUMBER 2: *Also self-contained. Kitchen, bathroom, air-conditioning. Food supplies for six months. You could go anywhere in it. It even has a waste disposal unit.*
PRISONER: *It moves.*
NUMBER 2: *It's detachable.*
PRISONER: *What's behind it?*
NUMBER 2: *Steel... steel.*

The sound of the bars slamming shut is very like that which marks the end of each episode – but this time they close on Number 2. And they have all the solidity of the real. The Prisoner hands the key to the cage to the butler, who gives him a formal bow.

NUMBER 2: *He thinks you're the boss now.*
PRISONER: *I am.*
NUMBER 2: *I'm Number 2. I'm the boss. Open the door.*
PRISONER: *Number 1 is the boss.*
NUMBER 2: *No.*
PRISONER: *Three minutes. You're scared.*
NUMBER 2: *No.*
PRISONER: *You can't take it.*
NUMBER 2: *Fool...*
PRISONER: *Yes, a fool. Not a rat.*

The Prisoner has won! What we now witness is an extraordinary count-down, in the course of which Number 2 loses confidence, face, all his dignity, and finally his life.

*NUMBER 2: I'm Number 2.*
*PRISONER: You are number nothing.*
*NUMBER 2: I'm Number 2.*
*PRISONER: One minute thirty-five seconds.*
*NUMBER 2: Why did you resign?*
*PRISONER: I didn't accept. Why did you accept?*
*NUMBER 2: You resigned.*
*PRISONER: I rejected.*
*NUMBER 2: You accepted before you resigned.*
*PRISONER: I rejected.*
*NUMBER 2: Who?*
*PRISONER: You.*
*PRISONER: Why me?*
*PRISONER: You're big.*
*NUMBER 2: Not tall.*
*PRISONER: Not tall . . . big.*

Terrified, Number 2 suddenly realises he has only one minute to go. While the Prisoner mercilessly counts off the seconds, he throws himself on the floor, crawls on his knees, then starts to grovel at his conqueror's feet, followed wherever he moves by a spotlight.

*PRISONER: You snivel and grovel . . .*
*NUMBER 2: I ask.*
*PRISONER: You crawl.*
*NUMBER 2: Yes, crawl.*
*PRISONER: To ask? Why?*
*NUMBER 2: To know!*
*PRISONER: Ask on! Ask yourself!*

Back inside the cage, Number 2 is now in the grip of panic. Distraught, hardly able to stand, he continues to make abject pleas; between each phrase he swallows a mouthful of alcohol from the glass he never puts down. In a strangled voice he counts off the very last seconds of his life, his subjugator punctuating each figure with the same single word: 'Death!' When he comes to the end of this dramatic litany with the figure zero, the Village boss falls to the ground, defeated once and for all.

With a little smile the Prisoner checks that his enemy is dead, and at that moment the heavy metal doors open to let in the Supervisor.

*SUPERVISOR: Congratulations. We shall need the body for evidence. What do you desire?*
*PRISONER: Number 1.*
*SUPERVISOR: I'll take you.*

Free to leave the scene of his rebirth, the Prisoner has not only waged a successful battle. He has won the war.

As he walks off down the Village's futuristic corridors, followed by the enigmatic butler and the bald-headed Supervisor, the quest of this strange knight of our times seems suddenly akin to that of all those who have preceded him.

But whilst he will at last know the *truth*, will he not confuse it with *freedom*?

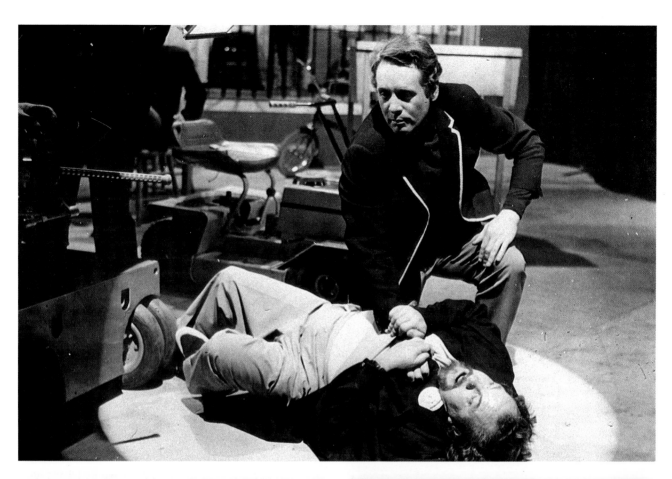

# Episode Seventeen: Fall Out

The opening shots in this episode tell us that this is a continuation of the previous episode, of which a gripping summary is provided, followed by an equally surprising prologue: a series of aerial views – almost touristic views – of the Village.* The theme music that accompanies this opening sequence is also different.

From the blue-green roof of the Green Dome the camera takes us without any transition into the Village's underground corridors, where we find the Prisoner, the Supervisor and the butler in search of the mysterious Number 1.

Their first stop is a strange cloakroom where, standing next to rows of empty coat racks, is a mannequin in the Prisoner's image, dressed in his 'civilian' dark suit – the Prisoner as we knew him in 'Arrival', before his release from hospital, the first time he appears in the clothes worn by 'Number 6'. An impersonal voice suddenly rings out:

*VOICE: We thought you'd feel happier as yourself…*

We may be rather disconcerted by the opening sequence, but nothing – not even all the disconcerting episodes that have come before – prepares us for the shock of hearing the famous Beatles song 'All You Need Is Love' suddenly blasting out. Not to mention the sight of the three men walking along a corridor carved out of the rock past an amazing line-up of juke-boxes.

They eventually come to a medieval-looking door, bearing the inscription WELL COME in enormous letters. The dwarf turns a key in the lock and we hear a thundering of boots, and at the same time an astonishing cave is revealed. At that moment we would be hard put to say what is most surprising: the troop of soldiers in what looks like MP uniform, marching along in step? The striking group of characters in white hoods, all wearing the same mask, half black, half white, distinguishable from each other only by the plaques identifying them as 'Activists', 'Reactionaries', 'Pacifists', 'Defectors' etc.? The operating table with men in green coats bustling round it? The strange metal cylinder that looks like a space rocket with a luminous eye that has an enormous figure 1 over it? The empty dais with a superb blue carpet and a richly decorated throne-like chair in the centre that seems to be awaiting some eminent occupant? Or the magistrate in scarlet robes and the wig traditionally worn by English judges?

The Supervisor, having donned one of the hooded robes and covered his face with one of the enigmatic masks, joins the group of men in white, taking his place behind the plaque marked 'Identification'. The President of what seems like a Court of Justice then opens the proceedings.

---

* In the original version the opening credits include a first-time revelation: the name of the place where the series was shot – the Hotel Portmeirion in Wales. They also mention the name of the architect: Sir Clough Williams-Ellis

*PRESIDENT: We are gathered here to resolve the question of revolt. We desire that these proceedings be conducted in a civilised manner but remind ourselves that humanity is not humanised without force and that errant children must sometimes be brought to boot with a smack on their backsides.*

*We draw your attention to the regrettable bullet. The community is at stake and we have the means to protect it. The assembly is now in security...*

*I understand he survived the ultimate test. Then he must no longer be referred to as Number 6 or a number of any kind. He has gloriously vindicated the right of the individual to be individual and this assembly rises to you, sir.*

*Sir. We crave your indulgence for a short while. The transfer of ultimate power requires some tedious ceremony and perhaps you would care to observe the preliminaries from the chair of honour.*

The Prisoner climbs the steps of the dais and with a little smile of satisfaction takes his seat on the 'throne', to a sudden burst of solemn, slightly sinister music in pure Village style. 'His' servant, the butler, now comes and stands beside him.

This strange Court of Justice, surrounded by armed men, now procedes to examine the case of two characters who pose a particular threat to democracy. But in order to answer the case against him, one of the accused must first be brought back to life. This character in question is Number 2, who fell dead, defeated by the Prisoner, at the end of the experiment known as Degree Absolute.

As the peculiar cage in which his body lies descends into the huge assembly room, smoke escapes from the rocket bearing the number 1. Then its eye begins to flash, and there is an insistent bleeping sound. The President of the Tribunal stares at it for a while, seeming to communicate in some unknown manner with the mysterious occupant of the machine, then he suddenly cries, 'Resuscitate!'

On a giant screen we see the deceased Number 2 leap up, holding his glass, turning towards us again the frantic face we saw in the final moment of his life. In the underground chamber men in surgical coats carry his body on a stretcher to the operating table. A moment later they cover his face with a thick layer of shaving lather, then pull down over his head a hood rather like a hair-drier. This is the start of another 'medical' routine, this time a totally crazy one.

The President of the Tribunal tells the jury that he is going to consider three instances of Revolt. Then he calls Number 48.

Number 48 is a young hippy, casually and untidily dressed, wearing a black braided jacket and a ruffled shirt unbuttoned to reveal his chest. He has a red flower stuck into the top hat that he wears on his dishevelled blond curly hair. Attached to an extraordinary metal mechanism, he rises from the ground in clouds of smoke, to the puffing sound of a steam engine.

*NUMBER 48: Thanks for the trip, Dad.*
*PRESIDENT: Be grateful for the opportunity of pleading your case before the assembly.*

The young rebel then sings a Negro spiritual, 'Dry Bones'. The President's angry calls for order fail to stop him. He continues to sing, then when the soldiers have released him, to dance and race round the chamber like a madman, causing indescribable chaos. The scene turns to outright lunacy when the men in white hoods, and the President himself, start clapping their hands and singing in chorus the words of the famous spiritual.

Suddenly, inexplicably, order is restored and the young hippy is declared guilty by the President. This 'democratic' community seems to have a curious concept of Justice, for the charge is read out *after* this declaration. It is the masked character whose plaque bears the word 'Anarchist' who gets up to read it.

*ANARCHIST: The prisoner has been charged with the most serious breach of social etiquette – total defiance of the elementary laws which sustain our community, questioning the decisions of those who voted to govern us, unhealthy aspects of speech and dress not in accordance with general practice, and the refusal to observe, wear or respond to his number.*

Young Number 48's sole response is to give the bell that hangs on the chain round his neck an ironic tinkle. The President then gives the order for him to be held in the Place of Sentence until after the Prisoner's 'inauguration'.

A moment later the young 'convict' sinks into the ground in a cloud of smoke, still singing the spiritual that tells of the miracle described in the Book of the Prophet Ezekiel.

Now it is the turn of the resuscitated Number 2 to face judgement. But the man who opens his eyes on the operating table, then slowly walks over to the Court, is a very different person from the jovial bearded Number 2 who appears simultaneously on the screen, shaken with a colossal laugh. His hair is cut short and, most striking of all, his face is now completely beardless. He is left with just a small moustache!

Standing in front of the President, with a wave of his hand he silences the hilarity that has seized the whole assembly, the armed soldiers included.

*NUMBER 2: I feel a new man. My dear chap, how have you been keeping? The throne at last eh . . . I knew it. It had to be . . .*

*And you my little friend. Ever faithful. Come on, come on, come on. New Allegianoes. Such is the price of fame and fortune. Dear me. How sad.*

*My Lords, ladies and gentlemen, a most extraordinary thing happened to me on my way here. It has been my lot, in the past, to wield a not inconsiderable power. Nay, I have had the ear of a statesman, kings and the princes of many a land. Governments have been swayed, policies defined and revolutions nipped in the bud at a word from me in the right place and at the propitious time.*

*Not surprising, therefore, that this community should find a use for me. Not altogether by accident that one day I should be abducted and wake up here amongst you.*

*What is deplorable is that I resisted for so short a time – a fine tribute to your methods.*

*I wish to thank you for a recognition of my talents which placed me in a position of authority second only to ONE. This authority gave me the right to make decisions. My last decision concerned this gentleman here ... which could be resolved only in the death of either one or the other of us. He emerged victorious, I apparently dead...*

Again he appears on the screen, his face drawn, a glass in his hand, as the last seconds of his life are counted off.

*NUMBER 2: Was it the drink? You couldn't even let me rest in peace. How was it done?*
*PRESIDENT: There have to be some security secrets that are kept from a late Number 2.*
*PRISONER: Did you ever meet him?*
*NUMBER 2: What's that?*
*PRISONER: Did you ever meet Number 1?*
*NUMBER 2: Face to face?*
*PRISONER: Yes.*

Number 2 roars with laughter, and walks over to the mysterious rocket whose observation 'eye' opens and closes as he approaches the real Master of the Village. His face now bathed in a violent green light, the deposed chief is evidently hesitant to look him in the face.

*PRESIDENT: You transgress.*
*PRISONER: Hold him.*
*PRESIDENT: In the Place of Sentence?*
*PRISONER: Until my inauguration.*
*PRESIDENT: Secure him.*
*NUMBER 2: Be seeing you.*

During these final words he again approaches the mysterious contraption, from which increasingly thick smoke emanates. Suddenly we see him spit at the menacing eye.

After this incredible sacrilege the guards seize him. Never has his laughter been so enormous as when we see him sink into the ground, and he is still laughing when he signs off with an energetic 'Be seeing you!' before disappearing.

The solemn moment has arrived. The Court is about to rule on the case of the ultimate rebel.

*PRESIDENT: We have just witnessed the two forms of revolt. The first, uncoordinated youth rebelling against nothing it can define. The second, an established, successful, secure member of the Establishment turning upon and biting the hand that feeds him. Well, these attitudes are dangerous, they contribute nothing to our culture and they must be stamped out.*
*At the other end of the scale we are honoured to have with us a revolutionary of a different calibre. He has revolted. Resisted. Fought. Held fast. Maintained. Destroyed resistance. Overcome coercion. The right to be Person, Someone or Individual. We applaud his private war and con-*

*cede that despite materialistic efforts he has survived intact and secure. All that remains is, recognition of a man. A man of steel... A man magnificently equipped to lead us, lead us or go... In this connection we have a prize. You will see that your home is being made ready. Above and beyond this we have the means for you to desert us and go anywhere. Key to your house. Traveller's cheques – a million. Passport. Valid for anywhere. And, er, petty cash. You are free to go.*

*PRISONER: Free to go?*
*PRESIDENT: Anywhere.*
*PRISONER: Why?*
*PRESIDENT: You have been such an example to us.*
*PRISONER: Why?*
*PRESIDENT: You have convinced us of our mistakes.*
*PRISONER: Why?*
*PRESIDENT: You are pure. You know the way. Show us.*
*PRISONER: Why?*
*PRESIDENT: Your revolt is good and honest. You are the only individual, we need you.*
*PRISONER: I see.*
*PRESIDENT: You do. You see all.*
*PRISONER: I'm an individual?*
*PRESIDENT: You are on your own.*
*PRISONER: I fail to see.*
*PRESIDENT: All about you is yours. We concede. We offer. We plead for you to lead us.*
*PRISONER: Or go.*
*PRESIDENT: Go if you wish.*
*PRISONER: But I ... I don't know.*
*PRESIDENT: Take the stand. Address us.*
*PRISONER: Should I?*
*PRESIDENT: You must. You are the greatest. Make a statement. A true statement which could only be yours. But for us. Remember us. Don't forget us. Keep us in mind. Sir, we are all yours.*

The Prisoner seems to have made his decision. He slowly descends the steps of the ceremonial dais, and with a satisfied look pockets the key, the cheque book and passport, then turns to address the assembly, casually tossing up and catching the purse full of 'petty cash'.

We hear only the first word of his speech: 'I'. Everytime he opens his mouth the members of the assembly shout back in chorus 'Aye, aye, aye', and the rest of his statement, which he insists on delivering, in tones of increasing rage, is lost in an indescribable cacophony of shouts and applause.

Suddenly the President, who has so far remained strangely impassive, effectively calls for silence simply by raising his finger. His face drawn, his hair dishevelled, the Prisoner has just been made aware that he is still in the Village.

*PRESIDENT: Sir, on behalf of us all, we thank you. And now I take it that you are prepared to meet Number 1. Follow me if you would be so kind sir.*

The following scenes already belong to history – the history of the series, unfolding at an incredibly rapid pace.

The Village's futuristic subterranean installations are an awe-inspiring spectacle. The Prisoner first descends deeper underground, standing on a metal platform, then at the end of a corridor guarded by armed men, he enters a circular room where technicians in white hoods are busying themselves with their work. We then realise that he is inside the rocket. Inside two transparent capsules, bearing the inscriptions 'ORBIT 2' and 'ORBIT 48' respectively, he finds the two rebels who have been found guilty. Number 2 is still shaken with gales of laughter, while the young man continues unflaggingly to sing 'Dry Bones'.

The Prisoner is joined by his inseparable servant, who bows formally, then points the way: a spiral metal staircase. At the top the door opens on to a small circular room. In the foreground, on a table, we see globes of all sizes. On the far side of the room, with his back to us, facing a screen, is a white-hooded figure. On the screen appears that quasi-mythical scene in which the Prisoner declares, right at the beginning of the story: 'I will not be pushed, filed, indexed, stamped, briefed, debriefed or numbered. My life is my own.' As these last words are spoken the figure in white slowly turns round and offers the Prisoner a crystal ball. His future seems to be merging with his past! He can see in it the symbolic bars from the end of each episode slamming three times in his face.

The images succeed each other even faster. The masked figure in the white hood, now completely turned towards the Prisoner, stands with his arms outstretched, revealing the enormous number on his robe. At last the identity of Number 1 is going to be revealed.

The Prisoner angrily throws down the crystal ball, which smashes on the ground, and tears off the black-and-white mask. Underneath is the grinning face of a monkey! In just a few seconds more the Prisoner will have learned a terrible secret . . . Beneath the simian mask appears an even more terrifying face: his own, his features twisted by a malevolent grin. The real Master of the Village then cackles dementedly.

The next scene, in which we see the Prisoner chasing his diabolical white-robed alter ego round the table covered with globes, is nightmarish, unreal. Finally Number 1 disappears at the top of a staircase leading to the nose of the rocket. His sneering face taunts the Prisoner one last time, and the latter, mad with rage, closes a trap door on this damnable part of himself. At that very moment in the assembly chamber, the President sees the rocket's eye close.

Delivered from evil, the Prisoner can at last escape the Village. But he will first of all destroy it. He picks up a fire extinguisher and cautiously descends the staircase, at the bottom which stands his faithful servant. The strange little silent man then expresses himself for the first time, simply by glancing conspiratorially towards the white-hooded technicians poring over their instruments. With the aid of the extinguisher and his fists, the Prisoner quickly renders them harmless. The armed men in the corridor meet with a similar fate.

The Prisoner then quickly remounts the staircase to the rocket's control room, and with a few quick and precise moves he programmes the launching, starting the countdown. On the screen appears the grave face of the President of the Court, standing in the huge chamber before the cylinder, which is now releasing thick smoke. At that moment organ music starts to play, resounding as though in a cathedral. Having tried in vain to contact those in control of the rocket, he quickly realises the significance of the spacecraft's ignition, and in a complete panic, incapable of preventing the imminent disaster, he orders the evacuation of the Village.

Meanwhile, the Prisoner and his accomplice have freed the young hippy and the former Number 2, and a few seconds later, disguised in the white hooded robes, they burst into the chamber, submachine guns in their hands. Then they blithely start firing at everything that moves, shooting down masked figures and military personnel indiscriminately. Suddenly the

Beatles' song blasts out again, the words 'All you need is love, love, love . . .' bizzarely punctuated with the sound of automatic fire.

Panic reigns. The President in his scarlet robes and white wig goes frantically running down a corridor, followed by a terrified crowd of hooded figures, soldiers, technicians, and even men in wet suits on motorcycles.

Above ground, it is also the end of the world, or rather of a world, that of the Village. Evacuation orders over the loud-speakers mingle with the noise of dozens of helicopters rising above the pretty baroque houses. Villagers in the grip of panic are streaming in every direction, in the flower-lined streets, on the square, on the beach.

In the underground chamber the victorious rebels get inside the fully equipped cage. At this point we notice that it is on the back of a lorry. The lorry moves off, driven by the butler, and takes an underground passage.

In the Village the evacuation is coming to an end. To the drone of helicopters is added the screech of the beach buggies' sirens as they hurtle down the streets, driven by soldiers. Suddenly, just by the Green Dome, the space rocket, programmed by the Prisoner to take off, rises into the sky slowly and powerfully, amid a deafening roar. For the last time an enormous white ball rises to the surface of the water, but instantly shrivels up in the flames escaping from the rocket's exhaust. This is the end . . . We get aerial shots of the abandoned Village.

At the precise moment when the rocket leaves the ground, the fugitives' lorry rams through a metal gate at the end of the tunnel, and drives along a country lane, before coming onto a motorway.

The serious bowler-hatted figure at the wheel of an impressive black limousine that comes up alongside for a moment before overtaking, cannot believe his eyes. The three rebels are dancing about, laughing like lunatics, to the music of the spiritual 'Dry Bones' playing on his car radio.

In the course of this episode this timeless series has rediscovered its own era, and this short scene tells us a great deal about it than any history book ever will. The singing of the escapees from the Village seems to resound like an echo of the tremendous explosion of liberating joy that shook the sixties.

The lorry is now on the A20, twenty-seven miles outside London. The young hippy is the first to be dropped off. We see him hitching a lift, first on one side of the road, then on the other. Which direction he goes in seems to be of little importance to him; only the journey matters.

The second to go is the former Number 2, who gets out in London, and disappears through the gateway of that imposing edifice, the Houses of Parliament. A policeman salutes him as he passes.

When a bobby takes too close an interest in their strange vehicle the Prisoner and his small companion run to catch a double-decker bus. We next see them outside the Prisoner's house. The butler gestures to his master to take a seat in the gleaming Lotus 7 parked alongside the pavement. But just as he settles into it, a kind of black hearse drives slowly past. The door of the house opens *automatically* in front of the little butler, then closes behind him. The Lotus is now driving in the London traffic. A clap of thunder breaks overhead, the same as at the start of the series. Out of the horizon a car hurtles towards us on an empty road. It is the Prisoner's Lotus. And a close-up of his determined face fills the screen, exactly as at the beginning of the whole story.

It is as if the whole series has just closed upon itself and upon the bewildered viewer.

Having discovered that his mysterious oppressor was none other than himself, the Prisoner has succeeded in destroying the nightmarish prison in which that evil part of himself was holding him captive.

But the way the door to his London house opens, symbolically, in the same way as that of his villa in the Village, tells us that he carries within himself other Villages and that the private war to remain oneself and to free oneself has to be constantly fought again.

The real response to the enigma posed by the series was in fact given during the previous episode; it is a response as old as the world. *QUESTION YOURSELF!*

*'It turns out that the answer is given on a different level from that on which the question was formulated.'*

Martin Buber *(The Path of Man)*

# Behind and Beyond *The Prisoner*

# Danger Man

## JACQUES BAUDOU

Before he came to incarnate – rather than merely to portray – the Prisoner, Patrick McGoohan had achieved international celebrity in another television spy series, *Danger Man*, in which he played the part of a secret agent by the name of John Drake.

While *Danger Man* does not possess the allegorical and metaphysical dimension of *The Prisoner*, it remains none the less one of the best spy series ever produced, perhaps the best of those in the realist vein (which must exclude *Mission Impossible, The Avengers* and *The Man from U.N.C.L.E.*).

But it not only constitutes an important stage in Patrick McGoohan's career, it also in many respects anticipates *The Prisoner*, the concept of which was born of this long association with John Drake (for many English critics[*], the identity of Number 6 is in no doubt whatsoever), and with the disturbing, Kafkaesque and paranoid world of intelligence that it depicts. For this reason it certainly deserves to have a small space devoted to it in this book.

Behind *Danger Man* lies the determination of two men: Lew Grade and Ralph Smart. Grade was, in 1960, one of the directors of the Birmingham-based ATV, one of the constituent companies of ITV, the British commercial television company.[†]

He developed a policy of producing programmes suitable for export to the vast American market. As early as 1955/6 his efforts were crowned with success, with *The Adventures of Robin Hood*[‡] showing for three years on the CBS network. In subsequent years this original success was followed by sales to the American networks of *The Buccaneers* (with Robert Shaw) and *The Adventure of Sir Lancelot.* But he was less fortunate when he tried to do the same with *The Adventures of William Tell* and *The New Adventures of Charlie Chan*. However, success returned with *The Invisible Man* in 1958.

Then came *Danger Man*, fitting in with this deliberate policy of opening up to the USA; the decision to make NATO John Drake's employer was symptomatic of this determination.

The second man, Ralph Smart, an Australian born in London, turned to television adventure series, having worked as a film director and scriptwriter.

He had worked as scriptwriter and director on *The Adventures of William Tell, The Adventures of Robin Hood* and *The Adventures of Sir Lancelot*, before winning his spurs as producer of *The Buccaneers* and more importantly *The Invisible Man*. (It was his idea to keep secret the identity of the actor who played the part of Peter Brady, the scientist who becomes a victim of one of his own experiments on invisibility.)

Called upon to come up with a new idea for a series, he became the creator of John Drake and *Danger Man*, on which he was to put his personal mark, not only by producing the series but also by writing many episodes and directing several.

When Ralph Smart created *Danger Man* in 1960 the other spy series were still in limbo (*The Avengers* did not appear until 1961; *Man from U.N.C.L.E.* in 1964; and *I Spy* in 1965) and James Bond had not yet had his screen incarnation (*Dr No* was not released until 1961). The spy novel, however, was finding favour with the public, with Ian Fleming and his agent 007 getting an enthusiastic reception. At the beginning of the sixties the spy was incontestably the number one hero, the dominant figure in popular literature; McGoohan, Sean Connery, Michael Caine and a few other subsequently made the spy a nearmythical creature. Ralph Smart must take credit for having been the first to anticipate the impact this type of character could have on the screen, and to have undertaken the first television version. In fact it seems – and we will come back to this later – that originally John Drake's image was to have been closer to that of the James Bond type of secret agent, than the image he had in the version that was eventually filmed.

[*] Such as Richard Meyers, for instance. See *TV Detectives*, p. 111.
[†] ITV is currently composed of a cartel of 15 private companies serving the regions, 70 per cent of productions being assured by the five largest: Thames, London Weekend, Granada (Manchester), Central and Yorkshire TV.
[‡] With Richard Greene in the title role and Donald Pleasance as Prince John.

A second idea governed the creation of *Danger Man*: 'It is our intention to use picturesque and interesting settings as well as to produce an exciting action-packed series. Today television can bring images from all over the world into the home of every television viewer. The popularity of travel documentaries proves that there is a lot of interest in faraway countries. In *Danger Man* we intend to go all over the world for the settings of our plots,' declared Ralph Smart.[*]

There remained the task of finding that rare pearl – the actor capable of embodying John Drake, of giving him a face. Ralph Smart had imagined his hero without thinking of any particular actor, but when he saw Patrick McGoohan on stage in *Brand* and on television in *The Big Knife*, his choice fell on this already renowned television actor (in 1959 McGoohan had been named Best Television Actor of the year).

If Lew Grade is to be believed, it was his way of moving that secured him the part: 'He moves like a panther, with a firm and decided step.' But his rather strange physique and his intense steely look were equally persuading.

Though capable of using his fists, or some other weapon if necessary, John Drake relies more often on his ability to respond to adversity or to the unexpected, on his ingenuity, his talent for assuming different roles in order to carry out his missions.

Although he has said, 'I do not like violence and you can see for yourself that Drake always tries to avoid it', Patrick McGoohan, aware that in order to compete with American adventure series the action scenes had to be very good – and it was intended there should be at least one brawl or engagement per episode – was insistent that these should be the object of very special attention and that they should be designed to have the maximum punch.

'In *Danger Man* there is action, a lot of action, but never any gratuitous violence. If a man dies it is not just another cherry falling off the tree. When Drake fights, it is a clean fight. He has a horror of bloodbaths and though he carries a revolver he only uses it in cases of absolute necessity. He does not shoot to kill...'[*]

In departing from the clichés of the spy novel, the char-

In any case Patrick McGoohan took the role of John Drake seriously, to the extent of having significant changes made. 'The very first script that came into my hands contained a sequence that had me with a charming young lady in a hotel bedroom. I thought this was going too far and I said so to the executive producer. We reworked the script and this scene was dropped. And all other scenes of the same kind planned for later were also left out.'[†]

Tom Soter, who interviewed Patrick McGoohan for the magazine *Top Secret* (vol. 1, no. 2, December 1985) reports that the producers wanted an agent in the James Bond mould, as quick at repartée as he was in drawing his gun, and getting a new girl into his bed every week, but that McGoohan had a completely different view of the character.

'I tried as much as possible to make him an enigmatic character, in the hope that you would never be sure what he was really going to do in the next sequence. His main weapon against his adversaries is his intelligence.'[†]

acter, redefined according to Patrick McGoohan's wishes, gained in credibility and in substance. And Drake could become the hero of a series that – unlike most of the series that were to follow – could try to give a realistic view of the world of espionage. Complicated though the plots sometimes were, they were always totally plausible and set in a political context that was extremely close to the real political context of the period. The missions Drake was given required the appointment of a particularly gifted and qualified agent, but there was nothing 'superhuman' about Drake himself. Judge for yourself: Drake investigated a number of suspicious deaths or the disappearance of a cipher agent; tried to establish the sincerity of a young woman who had asked for political asylum; recovered diplomatic documents stolen by Sicilian bandits; was entrusted with the protection of political or diplomatic personalities; saved an American consul and his family from the clutches of a terrorist group; infiltrated an IRA commando unit; hunted down a master spy who was thought to have disappeared, or took on the identity of a Czech engineer in order to destroy an East-West channel for traffic of a rather villainous nature.

[*] Quoted by Dave Rogers: 'Daring to be dangerous', *Top Secret*, vol. 1, no. 1, August 1985.
[†] Quoted in *Primetime*, No. 9.

[*] Quoted by Dave Rogers, *Top Secret*, vol. 1, no. 1, August 1985.

Each mission was conducted at a spirited pace, with no dead time, as the format of the programme dictated; since each episode of this first series lasted only thirty minutes the emphasis had to be on action and suspense.

Drake's missions took him across the entire globe, from the Caribbean to Kashmir, from Vienna to Paris, from the Arab states to the Balkans, from Hong Kong to Central Africa. Whilst most of the filming took place in the MGM studios at Elstree, a second team directed by John Schlesinger went off to film location shots to add 'veracity' and local colour.

Finally, to cite one last notable characteristic, John Drake was the first secret agent to use sophisticated gadgets devised by a special department (a rival of the one run by Q in the James Bond stories). In the episode 'Time to Kill', for instance, Drake extracts from various parts of his car apparently inoffensive components of what, when pieced together, turns out to be a rifle equipped with sights, totally undetectable in its dismantled and dispersed state.

On 11 September 1960 the first episode of *Danger Man* was broadcast on ITV. In a pre-credit sequence a

stopped, since it had not fulfilled the expectations of its makers.

However, although *Danger Man* did not meet with the anticipated success in the States, a very large number of foreign television companies around the world bought it and it soon became a 'hit'.

So the decision was taken to revive the programme, and in October 1964 the first episode of the second series of *Danger Man* was shown on British television. But the series had undergone some changes. In the first place, there was a change of format. The length of each episode was now sixty minutes instead of thirty, which had repercussions on the structure of the new scripts. A change in the definition of character too: John Drake was no longer a NATO agent; he now belonged to Her Majesty's Secret Service, worked for a department called MI9 and was answerable to a boss named Hobbs, played by Peter Madden. In Ralph Smart's mind, this new series would allow Drake to be 'humanised'. 'Drake is now less cold. less perfect, less infallible and he behaves in a much more human way. He can make mistakes and he is more likeable.'

figure appears superimposed on a Washington federal building, and lights a cigarette to reveal his features. The man then walks to a white sports car, puts his raincoat on the back seat and drives off. Meanwhile, a voice says: 'Each government has its secret service. The United States has the CIA, France the Deuxième Bureau, England MI5. NATO too has its secret service. A dirty job to be done? That's usually when they call on me. Or someone like me. By the way, my name is Drake, John Drake.' This presentational gimmick, which set the right tone, was to be repeated thirty-eight times, from September 1960 until January 1962, announcing yet another adventure of this efficient and enigmatic globe-trotting operative, whose relations with his unknown superiors remained extremely vague.

In the summer of 1961, the series was shown on the American CBS network, replacing the Western series *In the Name of the Law* starring Steve McQueen. But whilst it proved a great success in England, in the States *Danger Man* passed practically unnoticed. Consequently, production of the series was immediately

And Patrick McGoohan puts it even more strongly: 'Drake now finds himself emotionally involved in his relations with other characters. Maturity has given him a greater sense of understanding of others.

'He sometimes rebels against the missions he is given. He now looks at women with much more interest, for one of them could be the lucky girl who will persuade him to leave the job and find some other less dangerous way of making a living.'

And the producers add: 'The broader conception of the character is accompanied by a greater depth in the approach to his job. The scripts tackle the professional aspects of espionage, as well as its political character. They take their bearings from developments that have taken place in a world that has changed radically since the first series was produced. One thing has not changed: the action. Tension and suspense are the key words of scripts that do justice to the title: the accent is on *danger.'*

* Quoted in the ITC production company's press file.

In reality the character of John Drake had not been very noticeably affected by this announced change. His missions retained their characteristic plausibility and realism. And the exoticism of the places to which they took him remained an essential ingredient.

The most important change, in my view, was the increased complexity of the plots, which the change of format automatically allowed. It now became possible to devise less linear plots, to think up more elaborate narrative developments, more subtle too, and more intriguing, to treat the suspense in a less concentrated, less condensed way.

This gave John Drake a wide variety of roles to play (and allowed Patrick McGoohan to portray a host of colourful characters) since he was obliged to assume a cover identity on many of his missions. The most striking example was perhaps his transformation into a bespectacled professor who displays 'advanced' artistic tastes in order to win the friendship of naval officer Denis Rawson in 'A Delicate Pursuit'.

Finally, the last important development: the greater emphasis placed on the use of gadgets – a pipe that fires a

It is impossible to see *Danger Man* now without being tempted to detect seeds of the future *Prisoner*. It is well known that some of the team that made the new series had already worked on *Danger Man*. David Tomblin, for instance, who had been first assistant throughout the entire filming of *Danger Man* and became producer of *The Prisoner*. Or George Markstein, one of the great English espionage writers of the years 1970–80 (whose contribution Patrick McGoohan clearly underestimates), who was script editor for the fourth season of *Danger Man* and took up the torch again for *The Prisoner*, putting his name to the script of the first episode.

It is less well known that Portmeirion, that extraordinary village-hotel that serves as the setting for *The Prisoner*, had already been used in several episodes of *Danger Man*, and notably in the first, 'View from the Villa'.

In fact three episodes seem to me to foreshadow in a striking way certain aspects of *The Prisoner* – 'Not So Jolly Roger', in its remarkable use of an extremely unusual setting: an abandoned Second World War surveillance station, stuck in the middle of the North Sea, 'The Ubi-

dart which sends out a radio signal, a toilet case that turns into a short-wave radio and so on – a use that is never gratuitous and does not share the flashiness of the Bond-type gadgetry.

The second series of *Danger Man* extended over two seasons, broadcast between 13 October 1964 and 26 November 1965 (32 episodes in black and white), then from 13 December 1965 until 7 April 1966 (13 episodes in black and white). It was shown in the USA in 1965–6 under the title *Secret Agent*, and this time it enjoyed a notable success.

A fourth season was envisaged with the changeover to colour, but only two episodes were filmed. These were shown in June 1968.*

Some months after this fourth season had been abandoned, Patrick McGoohan came to Lew Grade with an idea for a new spy series: *The Prisoner* – but that is another story . . .

* In the USA these two episodes, with an additional linking sequence, were broadcast as a full-length television film under the title *Koroshi*.

quitous Mr Lovelace', in its disturbing dream-like quality and the nonsensical character of some of the dialogue and 'Colony Three' almost all of which takes place somewhere in Eastern Europe in a fake English village by the name of Handen; the plot explores notions of power and identity.

And to conclude, I would like to underline the fact that many of the producers who took part in the *Danger Man* venture counted among the most notable English film directors: Charles Crichton (*The Lavender Hill Mob, A Fish Called Wanda*); Clive Donner (*What's New Pussycat?*); Don Chaffey (*Jason and the Argonauts, One Million Years BC*), Robert Day (*She*), Seth Holt (*The Nanny*), Charles Frend (*The Cruel Sea*).

Since then, some of the script writers have also made great careers for themselves: Brian Clemens, for example, became script writer, then producer of *The Avengers*, and later created *The Professionals*.

It was this combination of talent that made *Danger Man* a great TV series.

# the Prisoner

While *The Prisoner* was in the process of being made the decision was taken to distinguish it from other television series. More than twenty years have passed since then, and whilst any biographical details remain uncertain, there are nevertheless enough known facts to afford us a fairly complete picture of this enterprise.

By the 1960s solid foundations for television production had already been laid, and although the rules have changed over the years it is on these foundations that a great many new series are devised every year. Some will remain at the concept stage; others will not get much further than the pilot programme; a great majority, lacking flavour and originality, will quickly fall into oblivion. There is no magic recipe: in this area, as in others, only talent, whether in the script writing, the direction, or the concept, distinguishes a success from a failure. Everyone starts out from exactly the same position. The aim is to tell a story in fifty minutes, with reversals, tension, suspense; to stir emotions by using regular characters in a situation well established from the outset, so as to win viewer loyalty. An arrangement to meet every week at a particular time is then established between the hero and his public. To come up with a series of stories like this is the equivalent of producing a film every week without the luxury of time and money that the cinema enjoys, while at the same time preserving cinema technique.

*The English television star in front of the cameras, and behind them, for a new series...*

The English company ITC, a subsidiary of ATV, a network of independent channels in Great Britain, made a name for itself by its ability to successfully devise and produce these famous stories for sale throughout the world, and most importantly, in the United States, which remains the most profitable market for this type of production. Of course a company takes financial risks in investing in some 13 to 30 episodes of a series, but in the 1960s, ITC was nevertheless doing extremely well. No doubt the shrewdness of its director Lew Grade had a great deal to do with this international success. He was not averse to backing new ideas: he adapted *The Saint*, took on puppet series, made a frog the host of a show, brought together Roger Moore and Tony Curtis, favoured space-age special effects and made spy stories before they became fashionable – including *Danger Man*, the series that propelled actor Patrick McGoohan to television stardom.

*The Prisoner* benefited from this affluent period when ITC was preparing series such as *Man in a Suitcase*, continuing to produce *The Saint*, and filming the first colour episodes of *Danger Man*. The basic idea for *The Prisoner* came from George Markstein, who had the job of overseeing the scripts of *Danger Man*. A novelist renowned for his knowledge of the secret services (there was a good reason for this, since he actually worked for them), Markstein claimed to know of the existence of 'rest homes' where retired spies could happily live out their days without the risk of former enemies making attempts on their lives – or of revealing their secrets one evening after a few drinks too many, or in a moment of premature senility. This idea had to be expanded into a more 'adventurous' concept: what if a spy was imprisoned, against his will, in one of these secret places? The workings of the pilot could revolve round this prisoner's attempts to escape and his resistance to the pressures put on him. Out of this was born the idea of a real village under close surveillance, endowed with the latest electronic devices. The locality of the village would be unknown; it was a concept of great visual possibilities.

Markstein suggested this scheme to Patrick McGoohan, who agreed to back the project, seeing in it not only a potential series for Everyman Films Ltd, a production company which he had set up in 1960, but a means of getting personally involved in the production and direction; above all it was an opportunity to express his ideas on freedom, progress and individualism. This was the grain of sand that put a stop to the brilliant commercial enterprise that *Danger Man* represented: suddenly, only two episodes into the new season ('Koroshi' and 'Shinda Shima', both of which were set in Japan), the star of the series did not want to go on playing the secret agent John Drake. For a while Lew Grade hoped to persuade the recalcitrant star to go back to the studios to continue with the prolific production of this successful series; but this was not the whim of a star wanting to renegotiate his contract (which, as it happened, was coming to an end), and whom a cheque would have appeased. McGoohan

minimum of thirty episodes. A new action spy series was born, and no one yet realized how different it would be from any other.

However, there was one noticeable difference right from the start. The budget allocated to the series came to £75,000 per episode, exceptionally high for the time. There were two reasons why such a large sum was allocated to this series rather than *The Saint* or *Man in a Suitcase*. In the first place McGoohan's reputation as a superstar of the small screen represented an important selling point and so guaranteed the series' profitability. Agreements for transmission and foreign sales were indeed concluded solely on the strength of McGoohan's celebrity and that of his previous role as secret agent; and also on the strength of the occasion that this new production represented. For not only was McGoohan acting, he was producing and devising the series, which seemed a triple guarantee of success. So, a big budget for a big,

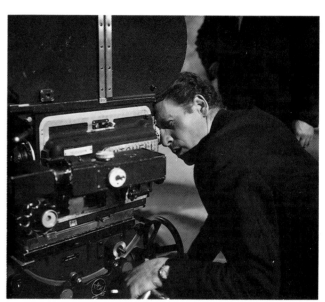

After Danger Man, *Patrick McGoohan became the soul and supervisor of a series in which he is much more than an ordinary actor.*

was tired of his part, convinced that *Danger Man* no longer had a great deal to offer, and fired with enthusiasm for a completely new project in which he had already immersed himself.

Lew Grade was keen to continue with *Danger Man* but even more so to keep McGoohan as house star. At one of the traditional early-morning meetings at ITC, at which Lew Grade would discuss his future productions, McGoohan, who had brought with him a treatment, script outlines, photos of a possible film location and a provisional budget, put forward Markstein's idea. Lew Grade admitted to not really understanding the story, but trusting his famous businessman's intuition he agreed to finance the series. The first two colour episodes of *Danger Man* were therefore also the last and so as not to waste their investment, ITC re-edited them to make a full-length film. Everyman Films was contracted initially to produce thirteen episodes of the new series. In accordance with ITC practice, if things went well, further episodes would be filmed after this first batch to form a

and seemingly risk-free project.

Secondly, the unusual aspect of the making of the series had to be taken into account: it would require extensive shooting on location, always much more expensive than filming in a studio, and a great many new props – cars, costumes etc – to be acquired. In short, a whole world had to be created, entailing considerably more funding than the usual filming on standard sets (generally already in stock) of other ITC series, and impossible to achieve with location shots filmed only on the streets of London. They came up against the problem that faces all science fiction productions. A plain old orbital station corridor is actually very rare in reality, and the merest pair of space boots can make the life of the ideas man hell. It was for these same reasons, among others, that it was easier to film *Kojak* in the streets of Manhattan than *Star Trek*, for which life in the twenty-third century had to be imagined and realised. In the case of *The Prisoner* the investment had to be higher than that allocated to an ordinary spy series, even though it was thought to be nothing more nor less than the sequel to *Danger Man*.

*The Prisoner* came so close on the heels of *Danger Man* that some members of the technical and artistic team continued to work on the new project, while others fell back on *Man in a Suitcase*. Production of the only two colour episodes of *Danger Man* ended in April 1966, while pre-production on *The Prisoner* had already started in March. McGoohan had managed to get Everyman Films Ltd appointed producers of the series, which meant that, together with David Tomblin, who was co-producer, he had total control: control over development of the project and the scripts, and over selecting the scriptwriters; control over the appointment of directors, musicians, technicians; control over the level of distribution ... In short, the smallest contributor to the series was on the payroll of Everyman Films Ltd, and not of ITC, who merely footed the bill, which explains how McGoo-

Doom ... But he was also involved in *Superman, Gandhi, Never Say Never Again* and Terry Gilliam's recent *Adventures of Baron Munchhausen*, of which he was production manager.

The first step was to establish the basic team that was to work on *The Prisoner*. Naturally, Markstein was story editor; his role, as it had been on *Danger Man*, being to maintain coherence between the different stories, to find writers and explain to them what kind of script was expected of them – no easy task given the ambiguity of the series. Most of those who were old hands at writing for series did not actually grasp that, over and above the action, the brawls and the suspense, the idea was to tell the story of a man's quest for individuality in the face of a society that tried to crush it. So McGoohan himself wrote the second episode, 'Free for All', under a pseudonym, while Anthony Skene, a well-known writer, became sufficiently impregnated with the concept of the series to

han gradually established himself in the position of supervising everything, a position in which he proved to be a kind of meglomanic meddler, and which was to lead to the final scrapping of the series. It was to be admitted, however, that it was this same attitude, commercially suicidal, that made *The Prisoner* an artistic masterpiece.

David Tomblin, who had been assistant producer and second string producer of countless British productions (including *The Invisible Man* and *Danger Man*) was McGoohan's technical partner in Everyman. His experience was of enormous help in defining the series. He was producer, production manager and occasionally director and scriptwriter. It was he who locked himself away with Markstein in order to write 'Arrival'. Since that time his name has appeared on the credits of the most extraordinary cinematographic productions of the past fifteen years, since he was part of George Lucas's team for *The Empire Strikes Back*, then for practically all the other films made by Lucasfilms: *Raiders of the Lost Ark, Return of the Jedi, Indiana Jones and the Temple of*

deliver 'Dance of the Dead', by far the most obscure and symbolic story of all. Gerald Kelsey, a regular contributor to ITC series, wrote 'Checkmate' which plays with the idea that all the Villagers are pawns, and exploits the theme of constant surveillance. Vincent Tilsey wrote a more traditional story of an abortive escape in 'The Chimes of Big Ben'. And subsequently authors were approached and given ideas for themes on which their episode had to be based.

Jack Shampan, who had done several set sketches as part of McGoohan's presentation of the series to Lew Grade, was appointed artistic director. He had already held this position on films such as *Modesty Blaise*, and was one of the regular team working on *Danger Man*. He created the sets for the Control Room and also all the props, such as the cordless phones, the buggies, the signboards, the spherical chairs (a model called Eero Aarnio), and so on. And most importantly, Shampan worked on the design of the Village guardian, Rover, a contraption that was supposedly controlled from a dis-

*The equipment designed for 'A, B and C' by the set designer Jack Shampan.*

tance by the Village Masters. Originally, it was to have been constructed with a motorized chassis and a hemisphere with a spotlight on top; it had to be automotive but also able to travel on water, like a hovercraft. It was even envisaged that this diabolical contraption should be able to climb walls!

Brendan J. Stafford was not unknown either: he had been director of photography for all the *Danger Man* episodes, and practically all the ITC series. His contribution was considerable and he was often pushed beyond his limits when he tried to put into practice

McGoohan's avant-garde ideas for camera shots. Meanwhile a composer by the name of Robert Farnon was working on the theme music.

At this stage of pre-production all those involved agree that decisions were always taken as a group, even though McGoohan's avant-garde ideas for camera shots. Meanactively supervising at every stage, McGoohan being particularly keen to give the series a 'look' that would create that feeling of indefinable strangeness that was to characterise the Village. It was, for example, clear to him that in order to make the place totally unindentifiable, no temporal reference to style or fashion should pollute this enclosed universe. In fact, rather as was the case with *The Avengers* or *Thunderbirds*, it was partly this detachment from reality that explains why, twenty years on, *The Prisoner* has not aged one iota, the fact being that no mini-skirt, no peculiar haircut, no outdated model of car is constantly cropping up to remind us how old the production is. In this respect Portmeirion was his masterstroke. The Village-Hotel, built in Wales by Clough Williams-Ellis, was *the* Village, and no other place in the world could have been a better location for the series. The mixture of architectural styles, resulting largely from the mixture of various elements gathered from around the world by Ellis over the years, its perfect integration into the site, its varied landscape (sea, forest, hills) and its peaceful atmosphere made it the only possible choice as the setting for *The Prisoner*. As it happened, some astute assistant producers had already found Portmeirion and used it as a location for films and serials that were supposed to take place in Italy, or other foreign countries. *Danger Man* was of course one such series, so McGoohan had already become interested in this extraordinary locality. Very soon the most typical aspects of Portmeirion were included in the scripts: the green dome, which had been part of a fire station, became Number 2's house, a cottage overlooking the square was chosen as Number 6's house, etc. McGoohan also developed other key elements of the series 'look': the villagers' costumes, the big symbolic penny-farthing. basing all this on the completed script of 'Arrival'.

In view of the closeness of the defunct *Danger Man* to all this it might have seemed obvious to name the hero of *The Prisoner* John Drake, allowing us to follow the secret agent in a new story ... albeit quite different from his previous adventures. But McGoohan wanted to put *Danger Man* behind him, rather than let himself get trapped in this one part; he also wanted to feel free to interpret the role of Number 6 without being influenced by Drake's personality, which he had helped to develop over succeeding episodes. Moreover, it was legally impossible to use the name John Drake without first getting the agreement of Ralph Smart, producer of *Danger Man* and creator of the character – an expensive business, and one that would not have been very fair: remember that poor Ralph had just seen his series shelved, with its leading actor entirely to blame. McGoohan and his friends turned the situation to their advantage: the man's name would never be mentioned, no matter what situation he found himself in. He would be Number 6, 'he' or 'old chap'. This decision called for a lot of juggling in

*Don Chaffey, the director who did most of the filming at Portmeirion.*

*Don Chaffey and McGoohan, during filming, with Freddy Piper and Rosalie Crutchley.*

the dialogue, particularly in episodes like 'A, B and C', 'Many Happy Returns' or, worse still, 'Do Not Forsake Me, Oh My Darling', in which Number 6's past career as a secret agent becomes part of the plot. Not even his fiancée ever calls him by his first name!

Then it came to choosing directors. Patrick McGoohan had been greatly impressed by the talent and personality of Don Chaffey. They had worked together on a film for Disney and on a great many episodes of *Danger Man*. One of Chaffey's successes for the big screen had been *Jason and the Argonauts*, a mythological adventure in which the stress was laid on special effects by the master Ray Harryhausen, who in fact readily admits that *Jason* was without doubt the best film he has been associated with; the rhythm and style of Don Chaffey's direction was not outclassed by the special effects, which is unfortunately the case with Harryhausen's other films, even the most recent. Don Chaffey had also directed some of the most famous episodes of *The Avengers*. His creativity, his talent, his dynamic energetic personality, as well as his familiarity with all things 'different' certainly counted for a lot in McGoohan's choice. Rather than offer him the direction of one episode among others, the actor-producer wanted to entrust Don Chaffey with the direction of the first episode so that it should be he who established the visual foundations of the series. As for Chaffey himself, he liked to work over long periods rather than the six to ten days' shooting of a single episode in a series. This was what he had already done with *Danger Man*, doing several episodes at once and filming for months at a time. It was therefore decided that he would take part in all the pre-production phases, that he would establish the style of the series and would make four or five episodes, as well as the opening credit sequence, and many of the more general scenes that could be included in future episodes and which constituted a real film library of available shots. This choice – in itself a wise one – was also motivated by the idea that in this way the location shooting at Portmeirion could be done with a single director, and not with a succession of directors, each of whom would be unfamilar with the team and the location – costly considerations that would have slowed down production.

Meetings followed one another and the main contributors to the series now had a clear and precise vision of the first episodes, thanks in particular to the intensive preparation of Don Chaffey. However, the team was seized with a moment's panic when Shampan's Rover failed lamentably. In fact the prototype that had been constructed could run along the ground quite well but sank the first time it went out on the water. Don Chaffey then suggested replacing this expensive and now unusable contraption, which in any case he did not like, with something more mysterious and less complicated: a simple white balloon of very large size. The idea for this came to him when he had dealings with the British Civil Service; the stupid and dutiful bureaucrat with whom he was confronted made him think of a white balloon. So Rover was born, and with it one of the most striking and fantastic features of the series; a very large majority of viewers remember *The Prisoner* as 'the series with the big white ball' and there have been a countless number of interpretations of the symbolism of this guardian. Filled with air or helium, the balloon was launched either underwater or in the open, connected to wires by which it could be pulled to make it bounce along the streets of the Village. These scenes were later edited in reverse to give the impression that Rover was prowling the streets, which explains why the inhabitants of the Village freeze as it passes. This version of Rover's origins is certainly the most likely, but it also claimed that the incident which

*Rover in front of the camera. The symbol of the series comes to life!*

destroyed Shampan's machine occurred after two weeks of shooting, during the early nautical scenes of 'Free for All'. Unprepared for the sinking of the mechanical Rover, McGoohan and Tomblin supposedly raised their eyes heavenwards and saw a pilot balloon. Yet it seems doubtful that a contraption like Rover would not have been tested before the film crew set off for Portmeirion and that they would have waited until shooting started on 'Free for All' to check whether it really worked on water. Moreover, none of the hundreds of photographs taken each day by the set photographer at Portmeirion shows the first version of Rover. Some of the extras remember the arrival of a load of pilot balloons on the first day of shooting, but no one remembers the 'igloo with the gyro-searchlight'. Don Chaffey himself insists on his involvement in the creation of this mysterious monster shortly before the cameras started rolling.

This took place in Norfolk, on the Lotus test track, where in fact the first shots of the opening credit sequence were filmed, the later ones being done in London. A great many shots of McGoohan at the wheel of his car were filmed, and lots of these were included, rather ineptly as a matter of fact, in 'Do Not Forsake Me, Oh My Darling', and more subtly in 'Many Happy Returns'.

Filming, properly speaking, actually started on 5 September 1966, in Sir Clough Williams-Ellis's village, Portmeirion. Patrick McGoohan arrived with his whole team and took over Portmeirion and its environs. Equipment was stored in the village houses, the garages were full of minimokes and Rovers and the production offices were set up in the Town Hall. Then work started, in particularly mild weather with no rain until the last day's shooting.

Angelo Muscat, the Butler, was the only actor present throughout the filming; together with Patrick McGoohan

he was the only regular star of the series. It cost so much to bring an actor so far from London and pay his expenses that many of the cast, principally those who played the part of Number 2, never came to Portmeirion – most of the time doubles were used. Someone from the area was given the job of recruiting extras from among the local population, and on the morning of 5 September some ninety-five people, who were to be paid £2 10s a day, turned up and were kitted out with the Villagers' costumes. Of course not only was this crowd often difficult to control but in addition actors and crew turned the rest home for men of letters and senior officials into a

September 1966. Sir Clough Williams-Ellis's village is invaded.

rubbish tip and the streets of Portmeirion were strewn with their cigarette-ends. All this provoked the anger of Clough Williams-Ellis, who realised a little late in the day what the agreement made with Patrick McGoohan to allow the filming of the series in his village, actually meant. Very soon instructions were appearing in the daily schedules urging the team to respect Portmeirion. Very soon too, tourists were getting mixed up in it: before, they had only come to visit Portmeirion, or to enjoy the peace and quiet of the place; now they were coming to watch the filming of this new series, for McGoohan was a real star.

Filming was unusually intensive from eight in the morning until six in the evening, every day, weekends included, with only two days' break, on 24 and 25 September, when shooting was practically over. There were of course two film crews, and multiple cameras, the second crew taking care of the general footage, mostly filmed with doubles: shots over a character's shoulder, walks through the village, scenes that were to be projected on the monitors in the Control Room or Number 2's house. Evenings were cut short by the screening of the rushes at the local cinema. It should be made clear that this frantic use of time was basically motivated by financial considerations, despite a generous budget.

In any event one thing is certain: from the first days of shooting no one could really understand what it was all about. However, McGoohan's confidence and the preparatory work done by Chaffey and Tomblin did the job. They at least seemed to know how this multicoloured crowd, these balloons, these taxis and this helicopter would all turn out ... and to know the meaning of what was happening. McGoohan in fact always said that at the time he had the final episode and the answers to all the questions already in his head.

The filming was completed without mishap, with no delays and no major catastrophe, apart from McGoo-

han's injury when running along the beach at low tide for the post-credits sequence. The 'family' atmosphere that McGoohan had wanted to create with Don Chaffey as permanent director bore fruit.

'Arrival' was filmed first of all, with only the first Number 2; then, as early as Saturday 10 September, they began shooting 'Free for All'. This episode needed a bigger crowd of extras, particularly for the election meetings at which Number 6 harangues the Villagers.

Officially it was Patrick McGoohan himself who directed this episode, but it is hard to imagine Don Chaffey remaining idle and not helping his friend. Besides, it

*Patrick McGoohan sets up the shot, revises his lines, then goes in front of the cameras. Note that two cameras are needed to film the shot and reverse shot between McGoohan and Virginia Maskell.*

was also often the case that McGoohan was listed as director on the top of the daily schedules for episodes made by Don Chaffey. Agreement between the two men was so great that it seems certain that a harmonious working relationship was established. On Wednesday 14th, the helicopter made its first appearance for the sea chase in 'Free for All'. Work on the chase continued the next day, together with filming of Rover and of the credits

*The helicopter arrives in the Village.*

*The Rook and Number 6 take direction from Don Chaffey.*

sequence on the beach. Shooting for the first episode, this time of all the scenes in which the helicopter appeared, plus aerial views of the village, resumed on Friday 16th.

Work on the third episode, 'The Queen's Pawn', started the following day. Only two shots required the presence of Number 2 and these were postponed until they could be done in the studio. On 20 and 21 September came the famous scenes on the giant chessboard with the Villagers, Number 6 included, as pawns as well as the final scenes with the SS *Polotska*, concluding the filming of this legendary episode. The fourth episode, 'Dance of the Dead', was shot on the 23, 26 and 27. And the last three days of shooting were spent getting footage for 'The Chimes of Big Ben'. In fact this episode required very few shots of the Village. More general shots of McGoohan walking through the Village were also taken to complete the film library. Finally the grand parade in 'Arrival' was reshot with some sixty extras. On the Saturday evening there was a farewell party and the whole team left on Sunday 2 October.

On Monday 3rd filming in the studio began. During the month that the others had been working in Portmeirion, Jack Shampan had taken over the MGM studios at

*On the giant chessboard in 'Checkmate'.*

Borehamwood, where he had built the permanent sets: Number 6's house, which also served as his London home, the one in the Village being a replica of the earlier version. Then the inside of Number 2's residence, with its entrance hall, the giant screen on which the images could be back projected (a less expensive procedure than doing it as a post-production special effect) and the electronically controlled chairs, tables and armchairs that could be made to rise from a chamber under the floor. Finally, the Control Room with its giant screen, its surveillance stations, the mechanical eye in the ceiling and the seesaw in the centre was completed.

It was here that Peter Swanwick the actor who played the Supervisor who appears in almost every episode presided. Portmeirion, or at least some of it, was created in another studio in order to complete a large number of sequences. It may seem stupid and pointlessly expensive to do it this way, but it is actually much simpler to film certain scenes, dialogue scenes in particular, in a controlled environment (for light, weather, camera angles), than to send a whole crew out on location for an ordinary close-up, a scene with only three characters, or a single reverse shot. The whole art consists of matching the shot taken on location so that the difference is undetectable. Yet a discerning eye will notice the huge photographic enlargements of the Village that serve as a backdrop to the set, the ground which is a little too even to be true, and sounds like floorboards, and above all that artificial beach on which McGoohan and Leo McKern chat to each other while Nadia tries to escape, in 'The Chimes of Big Ben': even the wave machine fails to make it look genuine.

Afterwards other sets were constructed for only a few scenes in one episode, sometimes even for a single shot.

*Filming 'Dance of the Dead' with Mary Morris at the head of a large female cast.*

The room in which the filing cabinets seem to stretch away into infinity (an effect created with a painting) and in which a mechanical arm drops the Prisoner's file into place was constructed specially for the credit titles sequence.

Once again two crews worked simultaneously with multiple cameras and the secrecy surrounding the production was maintained. There were few visitors, and in any case those who came were hard put to understand what was going on.

The first four episodes filmed at Portmeirion were the first to be completed. Each episode taking two weeks' shooting, 'Arrival' was followed in mid October by 'Free for All'. Peter Wyngade became the Number 2 for 'Checkmate' at the beginning of November, and the month ended with filming of the interiors for 'Dance of the Dead', which, being by far the most obscure and most symbolic episode, was considered too disconcerting and for this reason was rejected as a possibility for the second episode in the order of transmission. Although certain references indicating that this episode takes place very shortly after 'Arrival' were left in, it was a wise decision to move it back, even though, with the ending having been cut short, the final version gives the impression that the mysterious Number 1 is none other than the teleprinter in the closing scene. Furthermore, as the first four episodes were the only ones to have been largely filmed at Portmeirion, it was thought that it would be better to spread them out amongst those that had been entirely produced in the studio, with an artificial Village, or with shots taken from the film files.

'The Chimes of Big Ben', filmed at the end of November, uses a great many Village sets recreated in the studio: the outside of Number 6's house, the famous beach on two levels, and so on. Also an outside location available to the MGM studios was used in this episode for the first time: an imposing house looking onto a square with an old tree in the centre and houses all around. This had nothing to do with the architectural style of Portmeirion, but it answered the purpose and became the Exhibition Hall. Subsequently, this same famous set recurred in other episodes: it became, for instance, the entrance to the sports centre where the two Number 6's in 'The Schizoid Man' fight it out.

As soon as 'The Chimes of Big Ben' was finished, Leo McKern was used again at McGoohan's request – McGoohan had been very impressed by this actor, who quickly became his friend. McGoohan then wrote 'Degree Absolute' in thirty-six hours; it was filmed entirely in Number 2's room, in the Control Room, and above all in the Embryo Room, a totally black set in which Number 6 was to undergo the final treatment. This episode contains sequences in which McGoohan and McKern play out such an exceptional duel that McKern collapsed, psychologically drained by the tension. So there were a few day's delay in finishing this episode, the last of the first season of *The Prisoner* as McGoohan had envisaged it.

By the end of 1966 'Arrival' was practically finished, edited and mixed, and copies had been made. But the first change had already been made: the music that Farnon had come up with and recorded on 19 December

*The Control Room constructed in the MGM studios.*

*The semi-hysterical filming of 'Degree Absolute' on the unique set of the Embryo Room.*

was not at all suited to the images. Wilfred Josephs composed a new theme and at the same time recorded some pieces of incidental music.

It was at this point, however, that tensions began to make themselves felt. Psychological exhaustion certainly had a lot to do with it, for Patrick McGoohan was getting increasingly involved in a production on which not only had he staked his career, his future, his money, but into which he felt an increasing desire to introduce his own ideas.

A perfectionist, he began to get mixed up in everything, and it was not long before he was encroaching on the jobs of those whom he was paying. After all, he was the boss. He knew what he was doing, and above all he was one of the few who understood what it all meant. So no protests were made when McGoohan started to rewrite future scripts and send back scenes with which he was not entirely satisfied. He sacked some people, including a poor Italian director who only worked for one morning, and hired others such as Leo McKern, Kenneth Griffith and Alexis Kanner. But he was entitled to do so after all; probably his only mistake was exercising this right too often, delegating less and less, taking on the most minor tasks and making himself even more tired, something he could have done without. Slowly the series ran into problems. The style of the later episodes is noticeably different and more bizarre from that of the earlier ones. The production began to suffer: the director of one episode, for instance, was taken on only two days before shooting started.

ITC meanwhile were preparing for the sale of the series. A press book for the series was put together: it contained a few photographs of Portmeirion and some of the MGM sets, a vague description of the plot, stressing the unusual and provocative aspect of the enterprise and its intellectual depth. There was also some mention of action, adventure, suspense, but it was made clear that the series was for family viewing: no murders or sex. McGoohan was in fact known for his excessive prudishness and the romance with Nadia in 'The Chimes of Big Ben', which was reduced to a lock of hair being nonchalantly stroked, is a good example of this.

Of course the press book concentrated entirely on bringing Patrick McGoohan to the fore, crediting him with total authorship of the work. This was part of ITC's commercial strategy and no one, not even George Markstein, took offence. Even today it is the stars that 'carry' a programme, rarely a director and still less a scriptwriter.

However, the press book did not reveal the existence of Portmeirion, for all its appeal. By common consent and on Sir Clough Williams-Ellis's insistence, it was decided that the Village should remain secret; this only reinforced the mystery already surrounding the series.

During this time the editing was done, but that too underwent numerous changes. Ahead of his time, McGoohan wanted to make the action ever faster. So at the editing desk, in order to make the production pacy, he asked his chief editor to keep each shot to the absolute minimum, at the risk of being close to losing the continuity. Whereas in a normal piece of editing, for instance, the character enters from the right, moves across the pic-

ture to leave it on the left-hand side then into another shot, the Prisoner sees the bell tower, climbs it, surveys the Village, hears the bell, descends, crosses the square, arrives at the restaurant – all in the space of some fifteen seconds! This is not so far removed from the clip-like images of the 80s, and one only has to examine the credit titles sequence to see that this is so: the whole basis of the series – the Prisoner's resignation followed by his abduction – is encapsulated in less than a minute, with a pace and effectiveness rarely achieved.

But after at least two episodes had been completely finished, McGoohan and his team realised again that the music simply did not work for the series. Wilfred Josephs had composed a particularly avant garde theme, based on percussion and brass, but whilst this music, with its bizarre and discordant timbre, seemed to go well with some episodes, it was not at all right for the credit titles sequence. McGoohan gave the matter some thought, tried out a few ideas on the piano, whistled others, and discussed the problem with Ron Grainer, a highly renowned English composer who had scored many very

*ITC's marketing department gets hold of* The Prisoner.

effective theme tunes and who had become famous particularly for the music he had composed for *Doctor Who*, a science fiction series that over the past twenty-five years has become a real institution in Great Britain. Grainer composed a first version that was soft and mysterious, then eventually some music based on electric guitar – violent, very syncopated, particularly striking – which was kept for the credit titles sequence. With it, the sequence took on another dimension. But it was not until February 1967 that Grainer had completed the orchestration. Finally, Albert Elms was also asked to write some incidental music – pieces ranging from the most langorous type of music to the most disturbing – Grainer being too busy to compose them himself. Thus, Elms wrote the music that accompanies the pursuit and action scenes, for instance. In addition there were brass band tunes, pieces by Vivaldi and Bizet (In 'Hammer into Anvil'), as well as, later in the series, pop songs and even the bizarre and discordant timbre, seemed to go well with some episodes, it was not at all right for the credit titles sequence. McGoohan gave the matter some thought, tried out a few ideas on the piano, whistled others, and discussed the problem with Ron Grainer, a highly renowned English composer who had scored many very effective theme tunes and who had become famous particularly for the music he had composed for *Doctor Who*, a science fiction series that over the past twenty-five years has become a real institution in Great Britain. Grainer composed a first version that was soft and mysterious, then eventually some music based on electric guitar – violent, very syncopated, particularly striking – which was kept for the credit titles sequence; with it, the sequence took on another dimension. But it was not until February 1967 that Grainer had completed the orchestration. Finally, Albert Elms was also asked to write some incidental music – pieces ranging from the most langorous type of music to the most disturbing – Grainer being too busy to compose them himself. Thus, Elms wrote the music that accompanies the pursuit and action scenes,

By March, the first episodes had reached the final form in which we know them today, but a few copies dating from before these changes must have inadvertently become mixed up with the right ones. This is why a meticulous search has recently turned up the original soundtrack of 'Arrival' and an entire copy of the first version of 'The Chimes of Big Ben'. To this day, it is not thought that any other episodes were edited and copied before the change of music.

We now come to the episodes for which the scripts arrived rather belatedly on George Markstein's desk. It is noticeable in fact that with time running short continuity errors slipped here and there into following episodes: for instance, in 'A, B and C' a drug is necessary to put Number 6 to sleep, whereas a luminous device worked from the Control Room takes care of this problem in 'The Schizoid Man'.

It was in fact with 'The Schizoid Man' that filming in the studio resumed during the last week of December, continuing after the end-of-year holidays into a second week, in January 1967. Pat Jackson, who was the director of this

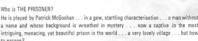

Who is THE PRISONER?

He is played by Patrick McGoohan . . . in a new, startling characterisation . . . a man without a name and whose background is wreathed in mystery . . . now a captive in the most intriguing, menacing, yet beautiful prison in the world . . . a very lovely village . . . but how to escape?

THE PRISONER is the most challenging and unusual series ever filmed for television, devised by Patrick McGoohan himself. It is a series with depth: stories that will make viewers think, and, at the same time, will keep them on the edge of their seats in excitement as the Prisoner resists every physical and mental effort to break him. There is mounting suspense as each new dramatic story is unfolded . . . stories of one man's tremendous, unflinching battle for survival as an individual in a macabre world in which every move is watched by electronic eyes and in which all his neighbours are suspect.

Where is the village? Who are his captors? Who are his fellow prisoners? What country is he in? Viewing appeal which is simultaneously electrifying, controversial and gripping.

A series of one-hour dramas filmed in colour, for ITC WORLD-WIDE DISTRIBUTION.

*Promotional material for the series.*

for instance. In addition there were brass band tunes, pieces by Vivaldi and Bizet (In 'Hammer into Anvil'), as well as, later in the series, pop songs and even the Beatles' 'All You Need Is Love'. So the already completed episodes were re-edited with the new music, but retained here and there as much as possible of Josephs'. McGoohan took advantage of the opportunity to make further changes – on the soundtrack, for instance, such as the jingle on the Village radio, or the characteristic sound of Rover – and to tidy up some particular instances of the editing. The most important change he made at this stage was the replacement of the original ending of the credit titles sequence (in which the penny-farthing turns into the Earth, from which the word POP emerges) with a shot of Rover bursting out of the water. Perhaps it was thought that this attempt to explain the symbol of the Village was far too esoteric and that it was better not to explain anything.

episode and a veteran of ITC, admits to having been particularly enthusiastic on reading the script. And it has to be said that this story of a reverse double, written with great intelligence by Terence Feely, author of a totally surrealist play, was a radical change from the 'Barons's' usual episode. McGoohan himself was so enthusiastic about the script that for a while he thought of getting Feely to join Everyman Films Ltd. With McGoohan constantly face to face with himself, this episode was particularly complicated in film. It was his stand-in, Frank Maher, who substituted for him in the scenes in which, having played the first role, McGoohan then had to play the other once the film had been wound back in the camera. But when one of the two characters is seen from behind, it is Frank Maher playing. Similarly, he was invaluable during the filming of the fights in which Number 6, facing the camera, confronts his double who is seen from behind), for he was also a stuntman. For the ending

*A scene from 'Arrival' dropped at the editing stage.*

*Pat Jackson face to face with Angelo Muscat.*

the script of 'The General', which he started to shoot forty-eight hours later. There was probably some incident, otherwise Scott would not have landed on the set with so little preparation. As for Colin Gordon, he made such a good impression that the end of Lewis Greifer's script was changed so that Number 2 was not electrocuted in the explosion of the famous computer known as the General. Meanwhile, Shampan was designing the Village's underground corridors and coming up with a new style of guard, so like American MPs that it would be hard to tell the difference.

In March 1967 another unit was sent to Portmeirion to film the episodes that were to follow those shot in September, but this time someone else stood in for the absent Patrick McGoohan. His work in the Borehamwood studios was taking up all his time, and it was David Tomblin who acted as director for this second filming which consisted mostly of comings and goings, chases on foot or in buggies, and some brawls. Also shot at this stage were the scenes needed for 'It's Your Funeral' (the final procession) and for '1, 2 and 3' (the new title of 'Play in Three Acts'). For 'The General', the villagers were filmed chasing a stand-in for the Professor. Very few extras were needed this time, which also made it possible to get one or two shots that McGoohan wanted to add to the earlier episodes. It is however, extremely probable that McGoohan made a quick trip to Portmeirion, just for a day, to do a little filming for 'Hammer into Anvil' and 'Many Happy Returns'.

Filming in the studio resumed on 18 March with 'Hammer into Anvil', the third episode directed by Pat Jackson, and the last episode of the series of thirteen was 'Many Happy Returns'. Georgina Cookson, who had already made a brief appearance in '1, 2 and 3', now played the part of Mrs Butterworth, the delightful occupant of Number 6's London house, who in the end turns out to be Number 2. This time, Number 2's face was not of course shown, as it usually was, in the credit titles sequence. 'Many Happy Returns' required a weeks' shooting on location, followed by a week in the studio. It was Michael Truman who was to have directed this epi-

*During the shooting of 'Schizoid Man' Frank Maher stands in for Number 12 and then for Number 6...*

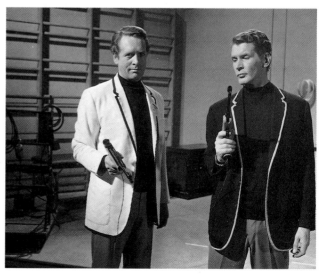

sode but there was a serious difference of opinion
between him and McGoohan. So once again, 'the boss'
took over the running of things, and in desperation acted
as director himself. This is why his pseudonym, Joseph
Serf, appears on the credits.

The ITC management soon became aware of situations
of this kind, for rumours about McGoohan's erratic attitude were beginning to circulate. Moreover, expenses
were running high. It was already the end of April and
most of the episodes were still being edited, re-edited,
disassembled or having new shots inserted. The editing
of the music went on until May 1967. '1, 2 and 3' finally
became 'A, B and C', and 'Degree Absolute' turned into
'Once Upon A Time'. More than a year after production of
the series started, only thirteen episodes were near
completion. *Man in a Suitcase*, on which production
had started at approximately the same time, was up to its
thirtieth episode. It was becoming obvious that *The Prisoner* was no longer the spy series, albeit a little bizarre,
that had been imagined, and that there were rather
unusual ideas underlying each script.

The thirteenth episode had just been completed and
as the series was about to be broadcast it was time to
assess operations. Taking much longer to produce than
anticipated, *The Prisoner* turned out to be very expensive and it was clear that Patrick McGoohan had subtly
and gradually diverted it from its original conception.
Feeling himself to be less and less useful and being of the
opinion that they were getting further and further away
from the balance he had hoped for between an adventure
series and the story of a man's fight for his individuality,
George Markstein decided to leave the series, whatever
the outcome. This parting was in no way amicable, and
McGoohan and Markstein, each of them claiming to be
entirely responsible for the series, have since torn each
other to pieces in the press.

It was all too much for ITC, who decided to put a stop
to the 'experiment'. So there was no question of
embarking on another thirteen episodes. The series
would end prematurely, but no doubt for reasons of
advance sales another four episodes had to be made. It is

*Filming 'A Change of Mind'. Pat Jackson, who was to direct the next epi-
sode, clearly provided director McGoohan with back-up in this one.*

*Action shot in 'A, B and C'.*

*Peter Graham-Scott with McGoohan and Betty McDowell.*

a matter of some speculation whether this news came as a disappointment or a relief to McGoohan and Tomblin, who had both been taken over, twenty-four hours a day for over a year, by this consuming series. As for the members of the film crew, most of them decided to find work quickly with the thirty new episodes of *The Saint* about to be made, or with other ITC series, rather than remain with *The Prisoner* for just four episodes.

Meanwhile, Patrick McGoohan had finally agreed to take part in a full-length feature film: *Ice Station Zebra*, a story of espionage and the Cold War, with Rock Hudson and Ernest Borgnine. This superproduction, nearly two and a quarter hours long, was to be filmed for the big screen by John Sturges. So McGoohan left for Hollywood and Tomblin found himself alone. With transmission of the series approaching, it was out of the question to await McGoohan's return to film the episodes ITC had asked for. This is why Vincent Tilsey invented a story in which Number 6's mind is transferred into the body of another man. This ingenious gimmick made it possible to do without McGoohan for nearly a whole episode. There was no question either of returning to Portmeirion, with or without the star of the series, for these were now days of budgetary restrictions. There were still some shots of McGoohan's stand-in being carried off by the Village guards; these would have to serve. So Tilsey wrote 'Face Unknown', in which Number 6, in a body not his own, is sent back to London – he alone being capable, according to the Masters of the Village, of finding the scientist who has developed a technique for transferring minds and who is the only person with the ability to reverse the process. This is pure science fiction, indeed pure fantasy. This story also contains other elements: a secret code and Number 6's fiancée. All of this was so obscure, straining the bounds of the credible, that an extra scene was inserted before the usual credit titles. Filming took place both in London and in the studio. Number 6 returns once again to the offices of the heads of the secret services, but

it is no longer Markstein that he sees – with good reason! For the first time too the viewer is given a clue as to the place were the series was filmed: an envelope shown in the episode bears the address 'Portmeirion Road'.

Pat Jackson directed this episode, his fourth, in August 1967, and when McGoohan returned from filming *Ice Station Zebra* all he had to do was lie down on a futuristic operating table, then play the final scene in which he gets up. However, he was very unhappy with the episode, of which he re-edited a great deal. It was envisaged that this stopgap episode should be shown in the middle of the other thirteen, so as to tone down its different character. But delays were building up and it was impossible to meet the date set, 24 November. So 'Checkmate' was shown in its place. At the end of October they were still working on this episode and it was not until 22 December that 'Do Not Forsake Me, Oh My Darling', the new title of 'Face Unknown', was shown.

David Tomblin then directed, wrote and produced an episode that answered McGoohan's desire to play a Western. 'Living in Harmony', filmed on a set of the old American West on the same MGM location, turned out to be a typical Western, a first for England. It tells of a new attempt to make Number 6 crack, this time by setting him in this hallucinatory environment. 'Living in Harmony' was filmed in September and completed in five weeks. McGoohan sent all obstacles flying and went on filming. He was fascinated by one of the actors in this episode, Alexis Kanner, and asked him to appear again in the series. Both men practised drawing a gun so as to play the shooting scenes as authentically as possible.

The series finally began showing on English television at 7.30 on Sunday evening. 'Arrival' was shown in London on 30 September, like a feature film in a black-and-white copy, although the series had been made in 35mm colour. But colour transmissions were still very rare at the time. In the rest of the country the programme was shown within a few days of that Sunday, either or after, depending on the regional channels broadcasting ITV programmes. Some English viewers were able to watch *The Prisoner* on Friday evenings, others on Sunday, while yet others had to wait a whole month before the series started in their region. In the order of showing, after 'Arrival' came 'The Chimes of Big Ben', 'A, B and C', 'Free for All', 'Schizoid Man', 'The General', 'Many Happy Returns', 'Dance of the Dead', 'Checkmate' (the new title of 'The Queen's Pawn'), 'Hammer into Anvil', 'It's Your Funeral', with 'A Change of Mind' to end the year. Once again attempts to include the 'stopgap' episodes in among the others had failed, since none of these were ready in time.

Reactions to this long-awaited series were mixed to say the least. A great many television viewers were initially disappointed not to find in it a spy story of the kind that John Drake offered them, others, unable to make much sense of it, even reacted aggressively. But the visual impact and mystery surrounding the series worked wonders. People hoped the Prisoner would escape, they watched out for the white balloon, they tried to work out what it all meant...

Reaching the end of his troubles, Tomblin then

*The frantic filming of 'Fall Out'.*

directed 'The Girl Who was Death, a parody of the spy film: an incredible pursuit story that turns out to be a story told to children in the Village – children that no previous episode had ever shown. The urgency of the situation and the expediency of the idea took precedence over strict fidelity to the concept of the series, and the episode was filmed in four weeks. Alex Kanner made a brief appearance and Christopher Benjamin again played the part of Potter, an informer already encountered not in *The Prisoner* but in one of the colour episodes of *Danger Man*. Some sets were constructed, such as the underground chamber and the mad scientist's rocket, which were all elements that were to be used again a few weeks later.

The first twelve episodes had just been shown, followed by 'Do Not Forsake Me, Oh My Darling' and 'Living in Harmony'. ATV then offered the production team some respite: in the first two weeks of January the two colour episodes of *Danger Man*, 'Koroshi' and 'Shinda Shima' would be shown in the slot allocated to *The Prisoner*. The series would then resume as normal. It was obvious that the theme of *The Prisoner* had changed again and that the stories were becoming more anecdotal.

Patrick McGoohan then decided to end the series by transforming the thirteenth episode, retitled 'Once Upon A Time', into the penultimate one. It was to become the first part of an ending in two acts. They simply had to reshoot the present ending, with Peter Swanwick to lead us into the next episode, and show Number 6 emerging victorious from the final confrontation and being invited to meet Number 1, when all would be revealed. McGoohan then shut himself in his dressing room for a whole weekend and wrote 'Fall Out' by himself. He came out on Monday morning, exhausted, to a team awaiting his instructions. Shampan had suggested that the Village subterranean depths should be presented as the place where everything was decided, so the series was to end in what was supposedly an underground setting. Shooting started right away in this unique place where reason was to give way to symbolism and improvisation (Kenneth Griffith wrote his own part, so incomplete was McGoohan's script) to the real allegory concealed behind the story.

At the same time a depleted crew went off at the end of December 1967 to shoot the final pictures of London. Despite the recent strain of his previous involvement, Leo McKern agreed to take on the part of Number 2 again, a Number 2 restored to life and in rebellion against Number 1. However, in the interval between the shooting of 'Degree Absolute' and 'Fall Out', McKern had shaved off his beard and he refused to wear a fake one all the way throughout the filming of this episode. McGoohan then thought up a scene in which Number 2 undergoes a face change, which got round the problem. Alexis Kanner was back again and Angelo Muscat at last became a star. Shooting took place on the same sets as were used for 'The Girl Who Was Death'. An almost indescribable chaos reigned. To add to all the lunacy, McGoohan even promised a £5 bonus to the extra dressed as an MP who managed to catch the recalcitrant hippie Kanner. For the scenes showing the evacuation of the Village, images shot for other episodes or taken from the film library were used. As for the scene with the rocket, it was faked with shots of Portmeirion. 'Fall Out' was completed two weeks before transmission, in early February 1968. McGoohan feverishly oversaw the editing, adding a considerable amount of music and songs to what had been planned.

The televising of the final episode provoked a tidal wave of calls to the ITV switchboard. Offended viewers, feeling cheated of a neat and tidy explanation, and of the revelation they had been expecting of Number 1's identity as a 'baddy' in the James Bond mould, poured abuse on McGoohan. ITC published an explanatory note in an attempt to appease minds, but it was no good, and Patrick McGoohan had to flee from Britain until the fuss had died down. Eventually *The Prisoner* sank into oblivion.

In June 1968, a few months after the scandal, the series was shown in the United States. It was the CBS network that televised it on Saturday evenings, from 7.30 to 8.30. All the episodes were shown, except 'Living in Harmony'; the determination of Number 6 not to carry weapons, as expressed in this episode, was actually at odds with the channel's policy, as well as with the mood of the times, bearing in mind that the Vietnam War was then at its height. In France 'The General' became *Le Cerveau* ('The Brain') for General De Gaulle's reign did not allow coincidence of this kind.

Several years had to pass before a repeat showing in England attracted fans at last capable of understanding the other level on which the series operates. The Six of One, a fan club of *The Prisoner*, was founded; as the years went by, retransmissions around the world confirmed its status as a 'cult series'. In 1977 the American public channel PBS showed *The Prisoner* in its entirety, strengthening its claim to being a series apart. This status has since become only more certain. Channel Four in England showed the series in colour and, for the first time in its country of origin, without cuts and on a national network.

However, *The Prisoner* remains a bitter commercial failure. The limited number of episodes in the series – too few to be regularly repeated – and the lack of success with the public no doubt explain this. Patrick McGoohan's career certainly suffered and his company, Everyman Films Ltd, did not produce anything more after *The Prisoner*. After filing for bankruptcy it was wound up in 1974, with debts of more than £63,000.

A. C.

*Free, or nearly ... Final shooting in London.*

# Patrick McGoohan

*'What comes into the world and disturbs nothing
deserves neither consideration nor patience.'*
René Char

Patrick McGoohan was born on Long Island, in the district of Astoria, New York State, where his parents, who were Irish farmers, settled eight years previously.

He was born on 19 March 1928; the time of his birth is the same as that of the Prisoner.

Young Patrick Joseph's parents left the United States shortly afterwards and so he spent the first seven years of his childhood on their Irish farm, receiving a strict Catholic education.

The McGoohans then moved to Sheffield, in England. It was there, at the age of ten, that he felt the stirrings of his first vocation: to become a priest. But the following year war broke out, and he had to go to Loughborough. During his first two years at school there he showed a greater interest in sports, particularly boxing, than in studying, although a liking for maths made his final school years less problematic. He left the college at the age of sixteen and started work, becoming involved with a local amateur dramatics society with which he made his first modest stage appearances.

At seventeen, he got a job in a bank but continued to be involved with various dramatic societies. Two years later he resigned his job preferring to go and work on a farm, but soon had to give up farm work when an allergy to feathers brought on a recurrence of the asthma from which he had suffered seriously as a child.

In 1947 he landed himself a job with the Sheffield Theatre Company that was to determine the direction of his life. A year later he was taken on by the Company as a dramatic arts student; he also became responsible for the internal organisation of shows and began to play a few roles in them, standing in at the last minute for actors taken ill. It was at the age of twenty-two that he finally became a wage-earning actor.

In 1951 he married Joan Drummond, a young actress, and in 1952, after his first daughter, Catherine, was born, he went to London in search of bigger, better-paid parts. So it was that he played Starbuck in Orson Welles' *Moby Dick*, in which Welles himself played Ahab.

In 1955 Rank signed him up and he made four films while under contract to them. After a few television appearances he was noticed by Lew Grade, who offered him the part of John Drake in *Danger Man*. Having become an international star (in 1959 he was voted best television actor of the year), he was offered the role of James Bond in *Dr No*, which he turned down. From 1960 to 1966 he made 86 episodes of *Danger Man*, without abandoning screen or stage. Then came *The Prisoner*.

The reactions to the screening of the final episode of *The Prisoner* on British television encouraged him to leave the country, together with his family, by now consisting of his wife and three daughters, in search of peace

and quiet in Switzerland. He later decided to settle in California. As his filmography shows, he has since played major parts in television series as well as the cinema. Now aged sixty-one, he still takes on some parts he is offered, but prefers to work at home, writing poetry – proof, were any needed, that he has not changed.

## His career

After his theatre début referred to above, he was noticed by the film world for his role in Orsen Welles' West End adaptation of *Moby Dick*. He then played supporting roles in *Passage Home* (1954), *The Dam Busters* (1954), *I Am a Camera* (1955), *The Dark Avenger* (1955), *Zarak* (1956).

His screen career really began when he signed a contract with Rank, which brought him leading roles in *High Tide at Noon* (1956), *Hell Drivers* (1957), *The Gentleman and the Gypsy* (1957), *Nor the Moon by Night* (1958).

Leaving Rank at this point, he returned to the theatre, playing in *Danton's Death* and Ibsen's *Brand* amongst others. For his performance in *Brand* he won the Best British Actor Theatre Award in 1959. A televised adaptation of *Brand* drew attention to him, and he landed the part of John Drake in *Danger Man* (86 episodes, 1960–6).

He did not, however, abandon the cinema: *Two Living One Dead* (1961), *All Night Long* (1961), *The Quare Fellow* (1962), *No Life for Ruth* (1962), *Dr Syn* (1963), *The Three Lives of Thomasina* (1963).

In 1967 came *The Prisoner* (17 episodes, for television).

Then his film career continued: *Ice Station Zebra* (1967), *The Moonshine War* (1970), *Mary Queen of Scots* (1971), *The Genius* (1973).

He produced two episodes in the series *Colombo*, with Peter Falk, in which he also appeared: 'By Dawn's Early Light' (1974), in which he played the murderous officer, and 'Identity Crisis' (1975), which he packed with allusions to *The Prisoner*. Since then, he has made screen appearances in: *Silver Streak* (1976), Alexis Kanner's *Kings & Desperate Men* (1978), *Brass Target* (1978), *Escape from Alcatraz* (1979), *Scanners* (1981), *Trespasses* (1983), *Baby – Secret of the Lost Legend* (1984). For television, he played in: *The Man in the Iron Mask* (Telefilm, 1976), *A Man Called Rafferty* (13 episodes, 1977), *Jamaica Inn* (Telefilm, 1982), *Three Sovereigns for Sarah* (Telefilm, 1985), *Of Pure Blood* (Telefilm, 1986), and finally, he appeared in one episode of *Murder She Wrote* (1987).

*(Information supplied by Jean-Marc Lofficer)*

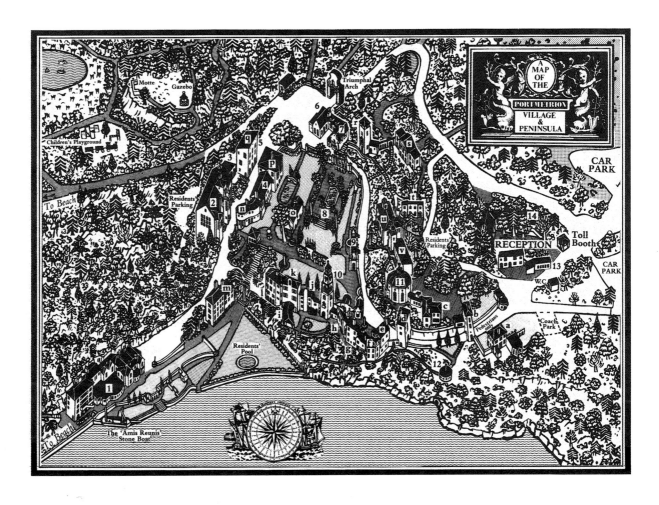

A MAP OF THE
PORTMEIRION
VILLAGE
&
PENINSULA

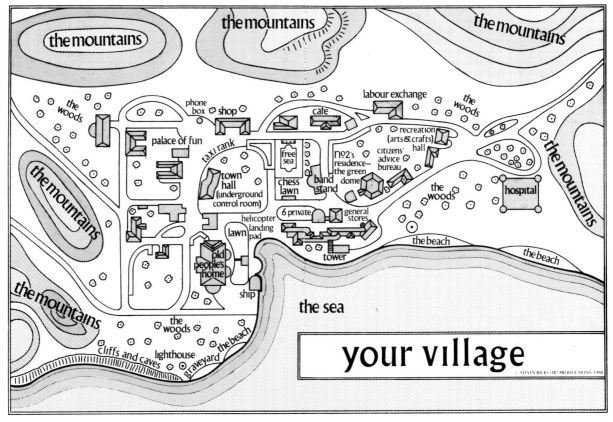

your village

# The Real Village: Portmeirion

In North Wales, in the north-east corner of Tremadoc Bay, Portmeirion Village Hotel receives more than one hundred thousand visitors each year.

This magical architectural grouping, which in itself is a work of art, was the work on an inspired architect, Sir Clough Williams-Ellis, who was neither a real eccentric, nor a real businessman, but was certainly first and foremost a poet.

His career as an architect, which began in 1904, had earned him a considerable fortune which allowed him to realise his dream of building an 'ideal village', through which he would prove that with elements taken from the most diverse arts and styles of architecture it was possible to create a completely harmonious whole. Appalled by the saddening sterility of modern architecture, which was already beginning to disfigure the landscape, he also hoped to dispute the trend, by raising a monument capable of showing that 'one could develop even a very beautiful site without defiling it and indeed ... even enhance what nature has provided for your background.'

Legend has it that, in the course of many trips around the world that enabled him to gather the most heterogenous material, Sir Clough Williams-Ellis spent a long time searching for a place in which to build his ideal village, and that he finally found it less than two hours walk from his home: a vast estate which the previous owner had allowed to transform itself into something of a jungle,

but with a view that represented for him a paradise far beyond his hopes.

Portmeirion as it is today – and as it appears in *The Prisoner* – was built over two periods: from 1925 to 1939, and then from 1954 to 1972. But its doors were first opened at Easter 1926, to a curious public, one that continued to show interest as the pieces of the puzzle came together. Sir William-Ellis very quickly realised that he would have to make Portmeirion a profitable enterprise so that the Village might live and develop as it wanted to. So it was that a hotel was built, and a toll charged for entry to the Village, the proceeds being immediately reinvested.

Until his death in 1978 – he was ninety-five years old – Sir Clough Williams-Ellis continued to enrich his village, without ever going to excess.

The strange beauty of this exotic and colourful architectural mosaic, benefitting from a micro-climate that explains the profusion of sumptuous flowers and its trees and shrubs of startling verdancy, made it a haven for artists and writers including Aldous Huxley, George Bernard Shaw, Ernest Hemingway.

Just as it is impossible to imagine that Portmeirion could have been created anywhere else, how can one envisage for a single moment any other setting for Patrick McGoohan's brilliant and visionary work? Portmeirion is therefore the only imaginary place endowed with real existence.

# Three Great Characters

Angelo Muscat masterfully portrayed the Butler, who was the only character in the series to be almost as permanent a feature as Number 6. He is apparently in the service of authority, whether that embodied by the various Number 2s, or the impersonal authority of Number 1; but in 'Fall Out' we find him siding with Number 6. His role was so important that the ITC press handout even went so far as to suggest that he might be the mysterious Number 1.

Born in Malta, he moved to Great Britain after the death of his parents. His small stature won him parts in television series such as *Doctor Who*, as well as in the theatre. McGoohan was so deeply impressed by him that he altered the script of 'Arrival', which had the butler as a tall fellow, so that Angelo could be given the part. *The Prisoner* was for him an extraordinary experience. He died, forgotten, in October 1977.

Although Peter Swanwick did not take part in every episode; the role of Supervisor for various reasons, either of availability, or plot requirements was played by other actors, he is none the less one of the key faces of the series, with his unforgettable way of pronouncing 'Orange Alert'. He had already appeared in *Danger Man* when a surgical operation in 1959 left him with a limited life expectancy. He then started to work like a man possessed, appearing in numerous television series until his death in November 1968.

Alexis Kanner turns up in three episodes in the series. He makes a brief appearance in 'The Girl Who Was Death', and plays the Kid in 'Living in Harmony', but is most impressive as Number 48, the rebel in 'Fall Out'. He had previously acted in a number of series produced by ITC, such as *UFO*. During the making of *The Prisoner* he and Patrick McGoohan became friends, to the point that McGoohan agreed to appear in a Canadian film produced by Kanner, which has never been on general release.

# The Number 2s

Every Number 2 is as much a pawn as all the rest of the Village's inhabitants. Admittedly, in the absence of Number 1 they run the Village, but they obey him, and are at his mercy: for all that they try to make us believe they have been democratically elected and that, being senior civil servants in their own country, they can seek retirement, they can be recalled at his will. They are shown taking the initiative and hatching plans. One of them even goes so far as to rebel against his Master. All the same, the Number 2s are forever replaced.

In the course of the seventeen episodes, seventeen actors shared the role of Number 2. This does not, however, mean that there was a different actor for each episode, since some of them appear as Number 2 in several episodes, and some episodes feature several Number 2s.

Guy Doleman played the first Number 2, who welcomed the Prisoner in 'Arrival', and did him the honours of the Village.

It was the less courteous Number 2 George Baker who first called the Prisoner 'Number 6', with that enigmatic phrase: 'Six of one, half a dozen of another.' Amongst other films in which the actor appeared was *On Her Majesty's Secret Service*, which many fans consider to be the best of the James Bond films.

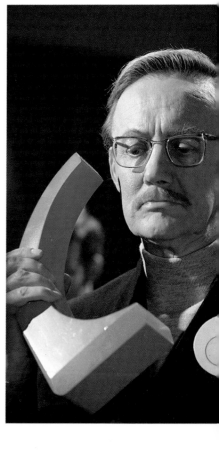

But the most popular of all Number 2s was Leo McKern, who, after 'The Chimes of Big Ben', played the role again in two later episodes. That booming and sarcastic laugh of his is unforgettable. His most recent big screen part was in the excellent *Lady Hawke*, made by Richard Donner, in which he appeared with Michelle Pfeiffer and Rutger Hauer.

Colin Gordon too appeared more than once as Number 2. He was also in *Casino Royale* and *The Pink Panther*.

Eric Portman, who died in 1969, was one of the few actors who played Number 2 to go and film in Portmeirion – for 'Free for All'. Already very ill, he had great difficulties in learning his lines and very often had to read them from placards placed near the cameras during filming.

As for Rachel Herbert, it was only at the end of 'Free for All' that she is identified as Number 2, wearing the appropriate badge. It was also only at this point that she uttered her first intelligible words.

Nor does Georgina Cookson reveal herself to be Number 2 until the end of 'Many Happy Returns', having previously appeared in the guise of the attractive Mrs Butterworth.

Anton Rodgers was the suave and charming Number 2 of 'Schizoid Man'.

Mary Morris, who died recently, took on the part in 'Dance of the Dead' originally intended for Trevor Howard. She portrays one of the most sinister and disquieting Number 2s in the whole series.

Clifford Evans played the Number 2 barely in evidence in 'Do Not Forsake Me, Oh My Darling'.

Darren Nesbit, a very familiar face in British television series, and Andre Van Gyseghem play, respectively, the new Number 2 and the outgoing Number 2 in 'It's Your Funeral'.

Peter Wyngarde, the Number 2 in 'Checkmate', is no doubt the most well known actor in this list. It was he who, with a moustache, played the part of Jason King in *Department S*, as well as in the sequel *Jason King*. He was also seen (as it were) wearing a mask in one of the leading roles in *Flash Gordon*.

David Bauer, having played the Judge all the way through 'Living in Harmony' was finally revealed to be the Number 2.

John Sharp was the overweight Number 2 in 'A Change of Mind'.

Patrick Cargill played a remarkable paranoid and sadistic Number 2 in 'Hammer into Anvil'.

Finally, Kenneth Griffith was the Number 2 who appeared as Schnipps in the story told to the Village children in 'The Girl Who Was Death', before playing the President in 'Fall Out', the last episode of the series.

# The Press Conference

In September 1967, as part of the pre-launch publicity for the programme, ITC organised a press conference intended to save its creators, and Patrick McGoohan in particular, from having to give interviews to each journalist.

The guests were first taken to the studios at Borehamwood, where they were shown the first episode, 'Arrival'. When they left the screening room, they were directed to a room specially prepared for them: behind the bars from 'Once Upon A Time', Patrick McGoohan was waiting for them, dressed in the red tunic he wears for the Kosho game, with a fur hat on his head and with Angelo Muscat at his side. And it was through the bars that he addressed the journalists. But his replies to their numerous questions were more than evasive; it is said that he asked even more than they did...

Then he came out of his prison and invited them to a buffet served by waitresses dressed like the maids in the Village, and laid out on the circular desk from Number 2's office, with his spherical chair in pride of place at the centre. An exhibition of Shampan's sketches for the sets and various props from the series – including a mini-moke – completed the whole thing. There was even a large penny-farthing in one corner, and Alexis Kanner was able to demonstrate how to ride it.

Finally, McGoohan, who had slipped out for a while, reappeared dressed as a cowboy, ready to start shooting 'Living in Harmony'.

And so, fairly baffled but above all frustrated, the journalists were taken back to London.

# The seventeen episodes: programme credits

THE PRISONER

With Patrick McGoohan, Angelo Muscat

Script editor: George Markstein
Director of photography: Brendan J. Stafford BSC
Artistic director: Jack Shampan
Theme music by Ron Grainer
Produced by David Tomblin
Executive producer: Patrick McGoohan
(ITC Productions/Everyman Films Ltd)

1. ARRIVAL
Written by George Markstein and David Tomblin
Directed by Don Chaffey

Guest stars:
Virginia Maskell: the Woman
Guy Doleman: Number 2
Paul Eddington: Cobb
George Baker: the new Number 2

With Peter Swanwick

And Barbara Yu Ling, Stephanie Randall, Jack Allen, Fabia Drake, Denis Shaw, Oliver Mac-Greevy, Frederick Piper, Patsy Smart, Christopher Benjamin, David Garfield, Peter Brace, Keith Peacock.

2. THE CHIMES OF BIG BEN
Written by Vincent Tilsley
Directed by Don Chaffey

Guest stars:
Leo McKern: Number 2
Nadia Gray: Nadia
Finlay Currie: the General
Richard Watts: Fotheringay

With Peter Swanwick

And Kevin Stoney, Christopher Benjamin, David Arlen, Hilda Barry, Jack Le-White, John Maxim, Lucy Griffiths.

3. A, B, & C
Written by Anthony Skene
Directed by Pat Jackson

Guest stars:
Katherine Kath: Engadine
Sheila Allen: Number 14
Colin Gordon: Number 2
Peter Bowles: A

And Georgina Cookson, Annette Carrell, Lucille Soong, Bettine Le Beau, Terry Yorke, Peter Brayham, Bill Cummings.

4. FREE FOR ALL
Written and directed by Patrick McGoohan (alias Paddy Fitz)

Guest star:
Eric Portman: Number 2

With Peter Swanwick (only in shots from 'Arrival')

And Rachel Herbert, George Benson, Harold Berens, John Cazabon, Dene Cooper, Kenneth Benda, Holly Doone, Peter Brace, Alf Joint.

5. THE SCHIZOID MAN
Written by Terence Feely
Directed by Pat Jackson

Guest stars:
Jane Merrow: Alison
Anton Rodgers: Number 2

And Earl Cameron, Gay Cameron, David Nettheim, Pat Keen, Gerry Crampton, Dinney Powell.

6. THE GENERAL
Written by Lewis Greifer (under the pseudonym Joshua Adams)
Directed by Peter Graham Scott

Guest stars:
Colin Gordon: Number 2
John Castle: Number 12
Peter Howell: the Professor

With Peter Swanwick

And Al Mancini, Betty McDowall, Conrad Phillips, Michael Miller, Keith Pyott, Ian Fleming, Norman Mitchell, Peter Bourne, George Leech, Jackie Cooper.

7. MANY HAPPY RETURNS
Written by Anthony Skene
Directed by Patrick McGoohan (alias Joseph Serf)

Guest stars:
Donald Sinden: the Colonel
Patrick Cargill: Thorpe
Georgina Cookson: Mrs Butterworth

And Brian Worth, Richard Caldicot, Dennis Chinnery, Jon Laurimore, Nike Arrighi, Grace Arnold, Larry Taylor, George Markstein.

8. DANCE OF THE DEAD
Written by Anthony Skene
Directed by Don Chaffey

Guest stars:
Mary Morris: Number 2
Duncan MacRay: the Doctor
Norma West: the Young Girl

And Aubrey Morris, Bee Duffell, Camilla Hasse, Alan White, Michael Nightingale, Patsy Smart, Denise Buckley, George Merritt, John Frawley, Lucy Griffiths, William Lyon Brown.

9. CHECKMATE
Written by Gerald Kelsey
Directed by Don Chaffey

Guest star:
Ronald Radd: the Rook
Patricia Jessel: the Psychiatrist
Peter Wyngarde: Number 2
Rosalie Crutchley: the Queen
George Coulouris: the Man with the Stick

And Bee Duffell, Basil Dignam, Danvers Walker, Denis Shaw, Victoria Platt, Shivaun O'Casey, Geoffrey Reed, Terence Donovan, Joe Dunne, Romo Gorrara.

10. HAMMER INTO ANVIL
Written by Roger Woodis
Directed by Pat Jackson

Guest star:
Patrick Cargill: Number 2

With Peter Swanwick
And Victor Madden, Basil Hoskins, Norman Scace, Derek Aylward, Hilary Dwyer, Arthur Gross, Victor Woolf, Michael Segal, Margo Andrew, Susan Sheers, Jackie Cooper, Fred Haggerty, Eddie Powell, George Leach.

11. IT'S YOUR FUNERAL
Written by Michael Cramoy
Directed by Robert Asher

Guest stars:
Darren Nesbit: the new Number 2
Annette Andre: the Watchmaker's Daughter
Mark Eden: Number 100

With Peter Swanwick

And Andre Van Gyseghem, Marin Miller, Wanda Ventham, Mark Burns, Charles Lloyd Pack, Grace Arnold, Arthur White, Michael Bilton, Gerry Crampton.

12. A CHANGE OF MIND
Written by Roger Parkes
Directed by Patrick McGoohan (alias Joseph Serf)

Guest stars:
Angela Browne: Number 66
John Sharp: Number 2

With Peter Swanwick

And George Pravda, Kathleen Breck, Thomas Heathcote, Bartlett Mullins, Michael Miller, Joseph Cuby, Michael Chow, June Ellis, John Hamblin, Michael Billington.

13. DO NOT FORSAKE ME, OH MY DARLING
Written by Vincent Tilsley
Directed by Pat Jackson
(No script editor)

Guest stars:
Zena Walker: Janet
Clifford Evans: Number 2
Nigel Stock: the Colonel

And Hugo Schuster, John Wentworth, James Bree, Lloyd Lamble, Patrick Jordan, Lockwood West, Frederic Abbott, Gertan Klauber, Henry Longhurst, Danvers Walker, John Nolan.

14. LIVING IN HARMONY
Written and directed by David Tomblin
(No script editor)

Guest stars:
Alexis Kanner: the Kid
David Bauer: the Judge
Valerie French: Cathy

And Gordon Tanner, Gordon Sterne, Michael Balfour, Larry Taylor, Monti De Lyle, Douglas Jone, Bill Nick, Les Crawford, Frank Maher, Max Faulkner, Bill Cummings, Eddie Eddon.

15. THE GIRL WHO WAS DEATH
Written by Terence Feely
Directed by David Tomblin
(No script editor)

Guest stars:
Kenneth Griffith: Schnipps
Justine Lord: Sonia

And Michael Brennan, Harold Berens, Sheena Marsh, Max Faulkner, John Rees, Joe Gladwin, John Drake, Gaynor Steward, Graham Steward, Stephen How, Alexis Kanner.

16. ONCE UPON A TIME
Written and directed by Patrick McGoohan

Guest star:
Leo McKern: Number 2

With Peter Swanwick

And John Cazabon.

17. FALL OUT
Written and directed by Patrick McGoohan
(No script editor)

Guest stars:
Leo McKern: Number 2
Kenneth Griffith: the President
Alexis Kanner: Number 48

With Peter Swanwick

And Michael Miller.

# Six of One

## JEAN-MICHEL PHILIBERT

To define *The Prisoner*, an outstanding and now legendary series, is perhaps to define the art of cultivating the paradoxical. And one of these paradoxes – which Patrick McGoohan could certainly not have anticipated – lies in the fact that a series of this kind should have given rise to an active and organised fan following.

For the idea of a fan club based on such a fervent apologia for the individual is indeed paradoxical; that a story as self-enclosed as this one should sustain such unbounded reverence is contradictory.

'We are not numbers,' we, like the Prisoner, proclaim. And yet we collect these numbers, we stick them on our badges, we inquire into their significance, we translate them into concepts or ideas. And we have even gone so far as to choose, as the symbolic title of the club that unites us, those numbers that in the context of the series are most pregnant with meaning: Six of One.

'Six of one ... half a dozen of the other.' This glib catchphrase is given in the series as the explanation for choosing to call the Prisoner Number 6. And McGoohan himself reiterated it.

The phrase has therefore been taken up in homage to this great actor and in order to underline the omnipresence of numbers within the series.

In December 1976, when 'Fall Out' was screened on British television, a fan by the name of Dave Barrie decided to put the question, through the intermediary of television: 'Am I the only person who adores this series?' Two weeks later he had received more than five hundred replies.

Consequently, in January 1977 – the 6th, of course – the club was founded, and Patrick McGoohan agreed to become its honorary president.

A handful of volunteers then laid the foundations of an efficient organisation: Roger Goodman, Julie Adamson, Marney Allen, Vivien Birch, Max Hora, Karen Pearce (who has since become Karen Langley) and Roger Langley, currently president of Six of One. They were later joined by Jill Mills, Arabella McIntyre-Brown, Kes Smith and Larry Hall.

The club very quickly proved to be very active, publishing several magazines: *Alert,* then *Escape,* as well as *Spokes,* the *Tally Ho* and the *Village Observer. Number 6,* the main publication at the present time, first appeared in autumn 1984 and has continued to prosper.

Within twelve years Six of One has created and made available a great deal of merchandise, which immediately became collector's items: badges, cards, posters, photographs, maps of the Village, key-rings, stickers, headed notepaper, pens, etc.

The club's tenth anniversary, in January 1987, was marked by the issue of a recording of a variation on the title music composed by Ron Grainer.

There have also been a great many publications throughout the club's existence: an episode guide, and three introductory guides by Max Hora; a book giving a scene-by-scene breakdown of the screenplay and a documentary work on the filming of the series by Roger Langley, who is also responsible for two novels inspired by *The Prisoner.*

Having made its own film, *By Public Demand,* Six of One took part in a TV documentary, *Six into One: The Prisoner File.* The club has also issued an LP record, which is still available, devoted to the series' main theme tunes.

Finally, 1988 saw the creation by a few fans of a delightful pastiche available on video cassette: *P. Nuts – The Movie – Paddy in Wonderland,* and three issues of the magazine *Danger Man,* now out of print and much sought after by collectors.

Better structured now, the team today is keen to develop the club and its international following. Those involved are: Howard Foy, Angie and Bill Faupel, Karen and Roger Langley, Dave Jones, Julie Benson, Arabella McIntyre-Brown, Catherine and Martin Goldthorpe, Jane Rawson and Max Hora.

As for Bruce Clark, the American representative of the club in the United States, he has done much to increase the membership and it was he who, in 1986, further enhanced the myth by finding an 'alternative' version of 'The Chimes of Big Ben' containing a few new scenes, in particular that in which a Number 6 with expertise in astronomy builds the 'Triquetrum', an instrument intended to determine the position of the Village, and which has since become famous ... in the Village. This version also contains different music and credit titles. It is available in the USA on video cassette.

Six of One currently has a membership of over 3,000 and despite the language barrier the French section is the third largest, after Great Britain and North America. It is the only club officially recognised by ITC, owners of the rights in the series, as a licensed partner.

The French branch of the club was founded in 1986, and I have been running it since it started. It organises an annual meeting (the last took place in April 1989 in Roanne, as part of the International Science Fiction Festival held there), and publishes *Le Rôdeur (Rover)*, Six of One's first fanzine in French. It strives constantly to promote the series and to provide a forum for discussion.

Six of One operates as a non-profit-making organisation. As it is keen to preserve intact the idea of the club, its products are available only to club members, with the sole exception of The Prisoner's Shop in Portmeirion, located in Number 6's own cottage, and run by Max Hora, where anybody can buy them.

Open to all those interested in the series, Six of One sends out to each of its members, four times a year, a great deal of information and a variety of gadgets, as well as the magazine *Number 6*.

Furthermore, the club organises an annual convention at Portmeirion, over a long weekend at the beginning of September. For three days the Village Hotel is reserved exclusively for members of Six of One. Reconstructions of some of the great moments in the series (the game of chess, the burial, the election parade, etc.) are organised, and also conferences and debates. Episodes are shown on the big screen at the cinema in Porthmadog, where

the rushes were viewed during filming; the whole thing takes place in a very colourful atmosphere. In 1988 this convention attracted more than eight hundred people from all over the world.

In 1983 a discussion took place between the various founders and organisers of Six of One: should the club become a commercial enterprise or should it retain its non-profit-making status? Happily, the latter proposal won by a large majority.

For while the club continues to exist and develop according to the wishes of its members, its *raison d'être* and real interest have always been maintained:

– To air and explain the series, as it was created, in all its visual beauty, with its symbols, costumes, technology, props, its numerous inventions, which constitute the key to a timeless world;

– To encourage and report the reflection the series calls for on the underlying issues it addresses, such as education, individual freedom, the responsibilties of science and authority, the blind and aggressive exploitation of technology.

✳

In addition to the various publications and magazines already referred to above, Six of One distributes the following books and pamphlets:

*Think Tank*, a novel by Roger Langley, inspired by *The Prisoner* (Escape Publications, 1984).
*When in Rome*, a novel by Roger Langley, inspired by *The Prisoner* (Escape Publications, 1986).
*The Making of The Prisoner*, a study about the filming of *The Prisoner*, by Roger Langley (Escape Publications, 1985).
*Escape Book of the Prisoner*, an episode guide, by Roger Langley (Escape Publications, 1986).
*Portmeirion Prisoner Production*, by Max Hora (Six of One, 1987).
*Village World*, by Max Hora (Six of One, 1987).
*The Prisoner of Portmeirion*, by Max Hora (Number Six, 1989).
*The Prisoner Episode Guide*, by Larry Hall (Six of One).
*The Prisoner*, cartoon book by Jean-Michel Philibert (storyline) and Philippe Cottare (drawings) (Six of One, 1988).

*The Prisoner* has given rise to a further three novels:

*The Prisoner*, by Thomas M. Disch (Ace Books, 1989, translated into French by Jacqueline Huet and published by Presses de la Renaissance, 1977, and reissued by Presses Pocket, 1979).
*The Prisoner: Number Two*, by David McDaniel (Ace Books, 1969)
*The Prisoner: A Day in the Life*, by Hank Stine (Ace Books, 1970).

In addition, *The Official Prisoner Companion*, by Matthew White and Jaffer Ali, written in collaboration with Six of One,

The Official Prisoner Appreciation Society, was published by Warner Books in the US in 1988, then in England by Sidgwick & Jackson.

*Video*: the series is available in nine cassettes produced by Channel 5.

*Recordings*: the series' main theme tunes are available on a compact disc entitled *The Prisoner*, produced by Control.

The addresses:

Six of One
 – in England: PO Box 60, Harrogate HG1 2TP.
 – in USA: Bruce Clark, 871 Clover Drive, North Wales, PA 19454.

*Portmeirion Village Hotel*, Portmeirion, Gwynedd LL48 6ER, Wales.

*The Prisoner's Shop*, Portmeirion Village Hotel, Penrhyndeudraeth, Gwynedd LL48 6ER, Wales. (Sells direct and by mail order everything relating to *The Prisoner*. Manager: Max Hora.)

# Table of Illustrations

Key to picture sections and full-page photographs relating to particular episodes